Values, Philosophies, and Beliefs in TESOL:
Making a Statement

CAMBRIDGE LANGUAGE TEACHING LIBRARY

A series covering central issues in language teaching and learning, by authors who have expert knowledge in their field.

In this series:

Values, Philosophies, and Beliefs in TESOL

Making a Statement

Graham V. Crookes

University of Hawai'i

CAMBRIDGE
UNIVERSITY PRESS

CAMBRIDGE UNIVERSITY PRESS
Cambridge, New York, Melbourne, Madrid, Cape Town, Singapore, São Paulo, Delhi

Cambridge University Press
32 Avenue of the Americas, New York, NY 10013-2473, USA

www.cambridge.org
Information on this title: www.cambridge.org/9780521741279

First published 2009

Printed in the United States of America

A catalog record for this publication is available from the British Library

Library of Congress Cataloging-in-Publication Data

Crookes, Graham.
Values, Philosophies, and Beliefs in TESOL : making a statement / Graham V. Crookes.
  p. cm. – (Cambridge language teaching library)
Includes bibliographical references and index.
ISBN 978-0-521-51748-5 (alk. paper) – ISBN 978-0-521-74127-9 (pbk. : alk. paper)
1. English language – Study and teaching – Foreign speakers.   2. Test of English as a Foreign
Language – Evaluation.   3. English language – Ability testing.   I. Title.   II. Series.
PE1128.A2C76   2009
428.2′4–dc22   2008045943

ISBN   978-0-521-51748-5 hardback
ISBN   978-0-521-74127-9 paperback

To my son Ikaika C.V.A.

Contents

Contents

Contents

Acknowledgments

I would like to thank the four previous classes of SLS 730 (Philosophy of Teaching) for allowing me to try out on them many of the ideas contained within these pages, as well as the co-instructor of the course on its first offering, Dr. John Norris. I am very grateful to my wife, Hildre, who read and commented on much of an early version of this work and encouraged me to complete it. I would also like to thank Jack Richards, whose support was crucial for this book, and Mike Long, for early encouragement concerning some of the more radical material included here.

1 Beginning to make a statement (of beliefs, values, or philosophy) in TESOL

Introduction

Material in the field of language teaching that is intended to contribute to language teacher development now often begins with teachers' own practices (as opposed to theories of language or of language learning). Works of this kind are very much part of the mainstream literature in the field of Teaching English to Speakers of Other Languages (TESOL) and often involve a continuing emphasis on what has come to be called "reflective" teaching in the area of English as a Second or Foreign Language (ES/FL). What is to be developed as a result of such reflection? A theory of practice, a theory of teaching, or a "philosophy of teaching," are some of the common answers to such a question.[1] Along with this, the idea of a teaching portfolio, which contains a statement of one's philosophy of teaching, is also very widely accepted and called for in real contexts (employment interviews, contract renewals, etc.). But what should be the bases for Second and/or Foreign Language (S/FL) teachers' personal theories or philosophies? What material would assist a teacher who wanted to construct a statement in this area – to write a personal philosophy of teaching statement? What are the ideas that have supported such conceptual schemes, over time and across cultures? What new or renewed ideas of this kind might be of use to the developing ES/FL professional? The present material will address such questions and thus be a resource for developing teachers, teacher educators, and researchers of S/FL teaching.

Inquiry into the conceptual underpinnings of areas of study or practice is one of the commonly accepted duties of the field of philosophy.[2] In addition, used loosely, the term "philosophy of teaching" relates to the values and principles that reflective teachers hold. Indeed, philosophy is a tradition that generates, or repeatedly resurfaces, ideas and issues that are recognized as important in the world of ideas. So in trying to understand and develop the values and beliefs on which to base their practices, reflective and conscientious S/FL teachers might well turn to philosophy, and particularly philosophical discussions that relate to teaching, for at least some of the understandings they need. Other formal sources exist, of course, which can support the development of such understandings: for example, systems of religion or politics, as well as scientific theories;

1

many of these have philosophical versions or components. In this work I[3] will draw on the philosophy of education as having particular potential for a language teacher who may be attempting to develop a philosophy of teaching. As a domain of study, the philosophy of education mediates the larger systems of meaning that humanity has developed and the specific concerns of teachers trying to make sense of their positions and practices.

This area, its developments, and its sources are not generally part of the core academic training of ES/FL professionals. So adventurous teachers and student-teachers (and their professors or teacher educators) in search of material with which to develop personal theories of S/FL teaching have had to make use of coursework and texts designed for the general reader, the philosophy buff, or the teacher in mainstream education courses (though one or two somewhat relevant titles within our field of Second Language Studies or Applied Linguistics have appeared recently[4]).

The present material outlines widely accepted philosophical foundations for teaching, along with their historical contexts, and brings them together with those developments in S/FL teaching that either derive from philosophical movements or have philosophical underpinnings. The overall intent is to provide, relatively concisely, major domains of philosophical thought concerning curriculum and practice which might be most appropriate for S/FL teachers to draw on in developing their views of practice and their vocations. Since philosophies of teaching are not entirely subject-specific, there will be a repeated need to present general and historical aspects of topics first, before narrowing the focus to matters of special concern to the ELT practitioner. An implicit concern throughout will be the matter of what might go into a philosophy of language teaching statement.

A simple preliminary conception and a rationale for a philosophy of teaching

It is generally recognized that the word "philosophy" may indicate "one's general view of life, of [people], of ideals, and of values" (Henderson, 1947: 16). "General guidance about the conduct of life is what is colloquially meant by the word 'philosophy'" (Quinton, 1995: 703). And thus, if we add the words "... of teaching" to that initial term, we may reach the sense of the phrase "philosophy of teaching" that often shows up at important points in a teacher's career, such as a job interview or a promotion application – a question about this is now commonplace in employment interviews (cf. Pike, Bradley, & Mansfield, 1997). For example, a recent work entitled *The academic job search handbook* (Heiberger & Vick, 1996) actually includes a section on the "Statement of Teaching Philosophy" which it takes for granted as potentially part of "additional application materials" (see also Stamm & Wactler, 1997). Similarly, Heiberger and Vick (1996) are giving us good advice when they suggest job applicants include a philosophy of teaching statement in their application; and a philosophy of teaching statement often now appears within a portfolio developed by prospective teachers, or is indeed required. This is the case, for example, in Wright State University Ohio's graduate TESL program (MacDonald, 1997).

Such statements are often quite brief. MacDonald specifies a one-page length, and Heiberger and Vick say:

> While the word "philosophy" is often used as part of the name for this document, it is perhaps better thought of as a brief essay that will give a hiring committee an idea of what you actually do in the classroom. You will need to make some general statements, but make sure to include examples that illustrate what you mean by them. If at all possible, describe things that you have already done, or at least seen in practice...
>
> (Heiberger & Vick, 1996: 95)

The circumstances for use of statements of this kind are a necessary constraint on their size and extent. Some circumstances allow something more substantial to be called for when we use the term "philosophy of teaching," in which case a statement of preferred methodology does not do justice to the potential of this term or topic. These more relaxed or extended circumstances include teacher preparation courses in which a teaching philosophy paper is sometimes called for (e.g., Kasten et al., 1996). Under those conditions, ideally a broad, deep, and seriously considered statement would seem to aid a teacher's development. The present work is intended to support this.

"Methods," language teaching traditions, and philosophical issues: A preview

There are a number of short publications in our literature which label themselves with the phrase "philosophy of teaching." However, on closer inspection it becomes obvious that they are an account of the one "Method," or in some cases, the set of techniques, that the author thinks best or advocates (e.g., Black, 1993[5]; Peyton, 1995; Xu, 1993); and given that a Method[6] is a fixed package of ideas, syllabus types, and pedagogical practices that would apply to all contexts, this would seem not to be equivalent to a personal philosophy of teaching. In addition, the term has come in for some criticism. Richards, for example, after following other specialists in using the term as a descriptive tool for imposing some structure on diverse approaches and conceptions of pedagogy, subsequently drew attention to the implication of power structures in the promotion or success of Methods (Richards, 1984; Richards & Rodgers, 1982). Many specialists have mentioned the difficulty of finding pure Methods in actual classroom practice (leading to a provocative phrase occasionally heard: "Methods do not exist"); Prabhu (1990) was one of many who pointed to the impossibility of any one best Method, and Kumaravadivelu (e.g., 1994) has persistently emphasized the desirability of principles but the inutility of Method as a concept in what he calls the "post-Method era." It has been suggested to me that, despite the limitations of the concept, one way for language professionals seeking to develop a philosophy of teaching, if they themselves may be inclined to use the Method term, is to probe into the philosophical adherences that certain Methods have had or still do have; while at the same time recognizing the nonempirical nature of the concept. For that matter, any quick probing of accounts of language teaching traditions (possibly concretized using the term Method) can alert the inquiring reader to some of the many philosophical issues that are implicated in these traditions. (Going back to Anthony's seminal (1963) analysis of Methods, his superordinate term "approach" refers to "a set of beliefs" or "a philosophy" concerning "the nature of learning and the nature of language.") Let me take a quick look here, while emphasizing that the following brief accounts are highly simplified (and the matters involved will come up in more detail and subtlety in succeeding chapters).

Referring to some of the standard Methods textbooks of our field, we find a review of about eight to twelve or so entities, typically a chapter on each (e.g., Larsen-Freeman, 1986; Richards & Rodgers, 1986). In the following paragraphs, I will in a preliminary fashion note how these language-teaching traditions can be linked up with philosophical concepts and issues (thus breaking ground on the content of this work overall).

Grammar–Translation Method

Many expounders of Methods identify the Grammar–Translation Method as their historically first entity, often presenting it as a German codification of general procedures used to teach Latin in Europe in the 19th century. Larsen-Freeman (1986) has little to say about the history and simply describes an imaginary classroom in which a key principle is to be able to read the literature of a foreign language in that language so that students can "grow intellectually" (p. 4). Unfortunately, the term "Grammar–Translation" is used very loosely these days to refer to classroom practices which indeed emphasize the translation of language material, mainly by reference to points of grammar. In most cases, the "literature" that is being translated is the relatively neutral sentences and short texts of beginners' textbooks. And the reason why many teachers use the techniques of Grammar–Translation is that they are convenient, expected by students, and consistent with the teacher's own training. Thus, while it is the case that a true Grammar–Translation advocate in the present time might be a teacher who believes that certain values, possibly timeless or representing the best of a culture, can be transmitted through a thorough understanding of the literature of that culture, in practice most language teachers who use Grammar–Translation techniques are probably not thinking of the values implied by the originators of this Method. Stereotypically, the relationship between teacher and student(s) in this approach might be thought to be authoritarian or "traditional." That is not necessarily the case, but it does raise the question of what the relationship between teacher and students should be.

Direct and/or Natural Methods

The "reform movement" in language teaching of the late 19th century is where Richards and Rodgers take up their second Method. The reform movement was a reaction to the limitations of Grammar–Translation and was the progenitor of some of the communicative methods of the present day. Substantial parts of its insistence on active use of the language by the learner, accurate and extensive modeling of the oral form of the language by the teacher, and inductive rather than deductive learning appear to have derived from the observation of children learning their first language. This 19th-century interest in, indeed promotion of, a "natural" aspect of learning in the behavior of the child stems from the ideas of Rousseau and his various followers, prevalent just after the French Revolution. They promoted a philosophy of the individual, particularly the child, as inherently good and naturally predisposed to learn. For Rousseau, this also involved a sense of society as potentially corrupting. Thus, it is the development of the individual (not society) that is placed foremost in this approach. And it is notable that it was within the burgeoning nonformal sector of private language schools that it particularly flourished. With its emphasis on the native speaker, this movement allows the teacher to focus just on the internal relationship between teacher and (small) class, floating rather apart from the culture or country in which the teacher is often a sojourner.

A couple of issues that emerge from a quick consideration of this language-teaching tradition are: "What is one's conception of the human being, in general?" and "What is the language teacher's central understanding of the nature of human learning?" The second question is really pointing at part of the philosophy of psychology, namely the philosophy of learning. The first question is something that most philosophical systems have a position on, usually as part of their ontology. It is also something directly tackled by the subfield of anthropological philosophy, increasingly prominent following the movement in philosophy known as existentialism.

The Audiolingual Method

Pure audiolingual teaching derives its theory of learning from behaviorism, which in turn sees the learner as a mechanistic, noncognitive system. Again, conceptions of human nature and capabilities are philosophical issues raised by any suggestion that this language-teaching tradition should be in use. A major philosopher following Rousseau was Kant, whose work, among other things, fully established the idea of human autonomy as a defining feature of humanness. I doubt if a teacher who was fully committed to the concept of human (or learner) autonomy would be comfortable working with the Audiolingual Method on any sustained basis. The philosopher Descartes thought that humans were analogous to machines, so perhaps a Cartesian might find some aspects of this Method acceptable! On the other hand, since Descartes is also responsible for the idea that inherent cognitive entities are present in our minds from birth, perhaps we should turn to the philosopher Locke, who is the modern originator of the "blank slate" view of the human mind. Whichever position is taken, I hope that alluding to these philosophers, who long precede the establishment of psychology (let alone linguistics) as a science, might suggest that the so-called Methods are not so much based on science as on philosophy. Or at least, it is primarily philosophy, and only secondarily science, that has set them on their way.

Alternative approaches?

A small set of Methods that have never really established themselves widely, or in mass education, are also canvassed in Methods surveys. Some of these are grouped under the heading "humanistic" by some specialists (e.g., Moskowitz, 1978; Stevick, 1980). To the extent that they have anything in common, it is their allegiance to or derivation from some aspects of humanistic psychology, a version of psychology that worked against the dominant school (behaviorism) before the main alternative to behaviorism (cognitive psychology) had really established itself. This again was in the 1940s and 1950s (for humanistic psychology), with its effects becoming visible in language-teaching traditions in the 1960s in opposition to the Audiolingual Method and before communicative approaches had really established themselves.

This is most obvious in Community Language Learning and in Confluent Education; it is also somewhat to be found in Suggestopedia (which is usually part of this group). As Moskowitz (1978) noted at the time, self-actualization was a central concern in these perspectives. True human learning is both cognitive and affective. Insights here into the nature of humans to some extent follow from ideas about the subconscious, but in any case constitute a critique of mainstream, deterministic ideas about humans in society that were prevalent in the scientistic 1950s but were being repelled in all quarters of society when "alternative" conceptions of culture, politics, and the individual became widely articulated during the 1960s.

Communicative Language Teaching

Most specialists would probably see this perspective and its developments as one of the three or four most important Methods. It has often been presented in our literature as merely the upshot of a coincidence between a shift in the theories of language that were favored and a general swing of the pendulum toward the functional end of language teaching. However, its inheritances are to be found much more clearly in the prominent alternative education tradition of the 20th century, namely progressivism, itself an inheritor of an earlier hundred or more years of attempts to ground teaching in a fundamentally romanticist view of the learner.

Let us quickly examine a few features of this language-teaching tradition. As most readers of this work will be aware, communicative approaches prioritize the needs of the learner via the now well-established idea of syllabus design reflecting needs assessment or analysis. Within what perspectives, one might immediately ask, are the learners' needs being considered? There are two main possibilities, particularly if one takes into account the times when this approach really got off the ground. First, there is the individual. Existentialism was the philosophical approach that (in the 20th century) really emphasized the individual as acting and choosing freely in society, capable of doing his or her own thing, and intending to do so regardless of conventional morality. And thus his/her needs and wishes should be determined and addressed in educational systems. (Historically speaking, this was a remarkable U-turn from the view of the individual that had preceded it, in the statist or totalitarian regimes associated with World Wars I and II.) At the same time, people were moving across borders in much greater numbers, often in connection with seeking work, needing the functional command of a second language that had initially been promised by the Berlitzian language schools. Thus, through these perspectives, it is clear that the language teacher had a particular responsibility to the individual (that s/he perhaps did not have before) to determine needs and arrange courses accordingly; the language teacher or syllabus designer also stood in a particular relationship to the individual in society, in a society in flux, becoming more multicultural and indeed international. These approaches to some extent changed the role of the (advanced, professional) language teacher. Extended to the present, they raise the question: "What is the role of the language teacher in a globalized, multi-ethnic world?" To answer it, a consideration of sociopolitical philosophy and other philosophical developments attendant upon conditions sometimes referred to as "postmodernity" is required.

Also implicated in communicative approaches, with their activity orientation, is a somewhat new understanding of the nature of knowledge and how knowledge of language comes about. This is clearer in the language-teaching tradition(s) that are now superseding them, all of which involve some use of the word "task-based." Understandings of "knowledge" are the domain of the philosophical field of epistemology, and it is the pragmatic perspective on epistemology that is to be found, somewhat buried, in the intellectual inheritances of communicative language teaching.

Other terms related to "philosophy of teaching"

Quite a wide range of labels is used to describe things one might want to refer to, or at least partially incorporate in, a philosophy of teaching. A range of related terms (and areas of research) can be offered that appear to relate to the object of our study, many of which overlap or operate perhaps just below the more abstract levels implied by "philosophy." Here is a preliminary and partial grouping.

My first set of terms are "teacher lore" (Schubert, 1991; Schubert & Ayers, 1992) and "teacher narratives" (e.g., Ritchie & Wilson, 2000). These terms seem to go together in referring to informal remarks, statements, or stories, that encapsulate what one has gained from a life of teaching. A fully worked out statement might be autobiographical, such as Ashton-Warner's (1963) famous work. There are just a handful of extended treatments of a personal nature in our field that could almost be included in this category – Stevick's (1980) very personal account of his experiences with humanistic approaches to language teaching might be one.

Another small set of terms seem to imply something like a collection of statements, not necessarily integrated temporally or personally. Here

8

the two main entries are "maxims" (e.g., Richards, 1996; Tsang, 2004) and "pedagogic principles" (Breen et al., 2001; cf. Breen, 1991). (Some parts of this work will be touched on in Chapter 11.)

A large group of terms reflects an active area of work with a psychological orientation. One can trace back certain aspects of this set through older literature that addresses the psychological aspects of teaching. These began to be studied once the cognitive revolution of the 1960s in psychology allowed (Anglo-American) psychologists to readmit the mental into their work.[7] Originally this came under headings that included "teacher planning" and "teacher decision-making," as well as "teacher thought processes" and "teacher cognition." And though a central part of the focus of this research was on teacher thinking and decision making in the immediate classroom context (e.g., Leinhardt & Greeno, 1986), other aspects of it came under the heading of teacher planning; and others again naturally realized that teacher decisions reflected teacher values and attitudes. Borko, and colleagues, already looking back on a developing area, remarked that

> several studies conducted over the past twelve years suggest that teachers' beliefs affect their instructional decisions. Sontag [1968] found that teachers' beliefs fall into one of three groups: traditional, progressive, and mixed... Other studies have reported that teachers' educational beliefs are related to their views about desirable teacher behavior and teacher personality traits. Still other studies have found that teachers' beliefs about important educational goals are related to their reports of their own teaching styles.
>
> (Borko et al., 1979: 141–2)

Within the field of TESOL, this has been a growth area recently, as Borg's (2003) summary and analysis make clear. Borg notes a considerable upsurge in studies since 1996 (47 works of his corpus of 64 are that recent). Approaching the area with primarily a psychological slant, in due course, he also focuses on teacher curricular knowledge. The two areas he finds most work to have been done in, in our field, are grammar teaching and literacy.

Another set of terms uses the word "knowledge." This occurs in a range of variants such as "pedagogical knowledge" (Shulman, 1987), "personal practical knowledge" (Golombek, 1998), "pedagogical content knowledge" and "specific pedagogical knowledge" (Spada & Massey, 1992). A prominent major study in the TESOL area that uses a broader but related term is Woods's (1996) review of ELT professionals' "beliefs, attitudes, and knowledge"; finding these hard to separate one from another, Woods unifies them with the acronym BAK.

Beliefs is certainly an important term in this area, but clearly a very broad one.

Many of the terms mentioned so far seem to refer to cognitive entities, which in turn are generally assumed to be in the mind. If something is in the mind, we can refer to it as part of our consciousness; thus the "consciousness of teachers" is a label that would presumably apply, or be relevant, to the development of a teacher's philosophy of teaching. Putting it this way allows us to note another relevant disciplinary area. Consciousness has been of interest in the sociology of education at least since the 1970s. The important educational sociologists Young and Whitty wrote that the term

> has led its more enthusiastic advocates... to locate hopes for educational change with teachers reflecting upon the assumptions which underlie their everyday practices and thus recognizing the possibility of changing them. There is something of a parallel here within the field of curriculum studies, where the realization that teachers have the power to resist innovations in the classic Research, Development and Dissemination mode has led to a celebration of the self-critical researching teacher as a primary agent of change (see Stenhouse, 1975). Whitty [1975]... argues that the recognition that definitions of knowledge, ability, etc., are potentially changeable must now be linked to an understanding of why and how particular definitions do in fact prevail in the current context of schooling.
>
> (Young & Whitty, 1977: 18)

Implied here is the idea that a teacher's consciousness would to some extent be a reflection of the times, but that certain crucial terms within it might be manifestations of power or a particular perspective and should thus be subject to critique and investigation. (Implications of this will be reflected in Chapter 9.)

My final set of terms uses or contains the term "theory." Thus we have "personal theories," "practical theories" (e.g., Marland, 1995), "subjective theories" (e.g., Grotjahn, 1991), "theories for practice" (Burns, 1996), and so on. Theory was itself originally something philosophical. One can of course have "folk theory," in which case the entity is presumably subject to anthropological and cultural study, though in modern parlance, theory is probably most recognized as a product of the natural and social sciences.

All of these sets of terms are obviously close and overlapping, but let us focus for a moment particularly on the connection between theory and knowledge. In some of the uses I have just mentioned from the literature on teaching, theory is being presented as something that teachers possess. If this position is accepted, a connection can be made between that theory and the theoretical knowledge produced by applied linguistics research. Certainly, while some parts of (S/FL) teachers' knowledge come directly from teachers' own experience, and some can come from teacher research, we cannot ignore that part generated through one socially approved means of obtaining formal knowledge: "science." What the connection (if any) actually is, how it is made, and whether the connection is unidirectional or bidirectional, are rather uncertain matters, however; one might say that the relationship between these two domains of theory has been fraught (cf. Crookes, 1997, 1998). Golombek remarks that:

> L2 teachers' knowledge is, in part, experiential and constructed by teachers themselves as they respond to the contexts of their classrooms. However, research in teacher education has largely focused on developing an empirically grounded knowledge-base to be given to teachers rather than on examining what teachers' experiential knowledge is and how they use that knowledge (Carter, 1990). Imposing a codified knowledge on teachers and separating them from their experiential knowledge "may lead to closed worlds of meaning rather than opening windows on possibilities" (Harrington, 1994: 190).
>
> (Golombek, 1998: 447)

As a result of her research on second language teachers, Golombek comes to agree with Woods (1996) in taking the position that it is extremely difficult to separate teachers' knowledge and what might be seen as more abstract matters of belief or value. (An emphasis on knowledge as experiential will appear again in the present work in Chapter 6, and typifies a pragmatic epistemology.) It is notable that in her work (one of still relatively few studies of second language teachers' knowledge), Golombek prefers not to separate cognitive knowledge from teachers' "moral and affective ways of knowing" (and indeed prefers to talk about "knowing" as well as "knowledge"):

> What these teachers knew was clearly woven together so that they used this knowledge in a holistic way.... The way L2 teachers understand and respond to their classrooms is mediated by their experiences as teachers, learners, and persons outside the classroom: personal and interpersonal factors and values, as well as their professional knowledge.
>
> (Golombek, 1998: 400)[8]

These items just listed, then, are all sources for the development of a philosophy of teaching.

Teacher education courses are at fault, in Golombek's view, for failing to "acknowledge teachers' personal practical knowledge." She would like to see "participants' personal practical knowledge" integrated with the "empirically grounded knowledge" that is indeed the common core of graduate coursework in our area. We should note, however, that the process by which teachers integrate or digest research-based theory has not been subjected to much investigation. A recent prominent review asserts that, "As yet, however, researchers still only minimally understand teachers' processes of interpreting and personalizing theory and integrating it into conceptual frameworks that guide their actions in practice" (Beijaard, Verloop, & Vermunt, 2000: 749).

Besides science, the other obvious form of theory that would be relevant in the development of teachers' personal practical knowledge, an "external" source for such knowledge, is philosophy.[9] This is a specifically nonempirically grounded form of knowledge, one that comes from "rational" rather than "empirical" analyses. If most teacher education programs, whether related to S/FL teaching or any other domain, do not do an adequate job of allowing scientific knowledge to be absorbed or digested by teachers, this is also likely to be true of philosophical knowledge. Obviously, I hope that a work of the present kind will head off that problem.

Sources and processes for developing a philosophy of teaching

Sources

We should try to establish what range of sources exists for the material from which to develop a philosophy of teaching. Naturally, one's personal life experiences are influential, and we could consider here experiences as a student (for many adults this is counted in decades of years), as well as any previous experience as a teacher, with other teachers, and under the influence of various educational institutions. Also, a philosophy of teaching, or "your" philosophy of teaching, is clearly a personal matter. Thus, the words of teachers themselves must be important. Teachers' personal narratives and life histories are important, though hard to summarize or even present in a short space.[10] Toward the end of this work, I will, however, refer to some studies in our field that draw upon teachers' personal accounts of practice and values.

In referring to one major relevant distinction, Feinberg (1995) notes that, on the one hand, there is "philosophical discourse about education," but on the other hand, the field of philosophy of education particularly concerns itself with philosophical discourse about *schools* in regard to their educating functions. Feinberg comments that "Philosophy of Education is institutional philosophy. It is a reflection on the aims of actual organizations and the practices of established institutions that are involved in some official or semiofficial way in educating people" (p. 27).

One other obvious source is *histories* of education, which naturally contain a wide range of ideas and perspectives on teaching (not to mention learning) which are of potential value to us. Much of this material necessarily goes well beyond simply second and foreign language teaching. Unfortunately, the historical information we have on language teaching prior to modern times is scant.[11]

Eurocentricity of "the literature"

In drawing upon the academic and professional literature of our field and of the field of education, using mainly sources written in English, I want to recognize that this material in general, or dominant domains of it at least, tends to reflect primarily Western[12] or European academic traditions and world views. The ELT field is, however, international, and so I have tried to struggle for some sort of balance. Probably I have not achieved enough of a balance; perhaps the source material and my own cultural background makes this impossible.

There are at least two initial approaches to make in this difficult area. First, coming at the matter from the angle of actual teaching practice, let me again recognize that, given the international character of ES/FL, we should begin by assuming that ELT specialists from differing cultural backgrounds, just like any other teachers, are likely to be different in their beliefs. For example, Genishi et al. (2001) report on a study (Hyson & Lee, 1996) which

> sample[d] 175 Korean and American EC [early childhood] teach-
> ers across 10 domains of beliefs about children's emotional
> development. The majority of American EC teachers believed
> that children need warm, physically affectionate bonds with
> their adult caregivers and that teachers have a responsibility to
> scaffold children's emotional expression. In contrast, Korean
> teachers were more likely to believe that teachers should avoid
> endorsing children's emotional self-expression, developing emo-
> tional closeness with children, and demonstrating emotional dis-
> plays of affection to children.
>
> (Genishi et al., 2001: 1184)

Addressing the matter from a more general, research-oriented stand-point, Breen et al., reflecting on their observations of ESL teachers, note that "varying social conditions" would likely result in different relationships between thinking and action:

> However, much current research on English language teaching... is not comparative in this way and it tends, at least implicitly, to affirm western educational ideologies concerning the relationships between subject matter, teacher, student, and classroom practices.

(2001: 499)

Accordingly, they naturally recommend more work that is "cross-cultural and inter-cultural" in investigations of the role of teacher beliefs in language pedagogy; something we are just beginning to see more of (e.g., Butler, 2005).

The second perspective concerns philosophy and philosophy of education as it is perceived through the lens of an English-speaking, or English-dominant, field. Insofar as formal, institutionalized, mass education – the context for most classroom language teaching around the world – is in a sense of European origin, a large part of the philosophy that might be seen as going along with it could be said to be of Western origin. However, on the other hand, insofar as the teaching of English, as an international operation, must inevitably reflect different cultures, it must reflect culturally different philosophies to some extent. Non-Western philosophies of education, however, are not particularly well-developed or substantial bodies of literature (though see Herrera & Torres, 2006; Reagan, 1996). It could also be noted that whereas much Western philosophy, and indeed philosophy of education, is secular (though this has only been the case in the last 100 years or so), much non-Western philosophy has stronger ties to its religious inheritances. I will allude to these aspects of the picture from time to time (particularly in the next chapter where the ancient history of schooling around the world is touched upon), but I will not discuss them in detail, given the currently secular nature of most mass education and the TESOL sectors of it. That being said, I recognize that as the vast majority of TESOL or S/FL professionals are non-Europeans, these perspectives will be important in the development of many language teachers' philosophies of teaching.[13]

Finally, let me emphasize in advance a slightly different spin on my line that the context for most classroom language teaching around the world is of European origin. That may be true, but it may obscure the fact that we not only live in a global world these days, we have been doing so for some time. Once we arrive at modern times, it is clear that flows of ideas in education have moved rapidly across borders, even between countries that have been politically opposed (Spring, 2006). This is yet another reason why dichotomizing East and West is a dangerous oversimplification. I will highlight some aspects of this in Chapter 3 especially.

Processes

What are the processes that are likely to be involved in developing a philosophy of teaching? In the abstract, they seem to include at least "clarifying educational issues, justifying educational decisions, interpreting educational data, and integrating that understanding into the educational process" (Wiseman, Cooner, & Knight, 1999: 24). Little research[14] is available to assist us to specify firmly what is involved, so let us proceed on the basis of a (somewhat) logical (rather than empirical) analysis.

One approach in developing a philosophy of teaching that is widely used is for teachers-in-development to reflect and try to bring their views about teaching to consciousness, as a starting point. Personal narrative writing may be a way into this for some, perhaps many, teachers. For others, in my experience, a listing of values or beliefs about one's own teaching is a good starting point, as well as moderately challenging (perhaps particularly for those with less teaching experience). Another way is to use some kind of checklist or responses to a diagnostic questionnaire (e.g., Zinn, 1990; cf. Pennington, 1990), though clearly in this case one is at the mercy of the person who created the questionnaire and their understanding of certain philosophies or positions.[15] As with a number of other areas of professional development, analysis of created or "authored" cases that call for professional judgment is a possibility (e.g., Heslep, 1997). More difficult is the consideration of real cases where teachers must exercise judgment which would be informed by their personal philosophies of teaching.

Presumably some of the processes or methods of the field of philosophy of education might also be used, or perhaps we could say that they overlap with those used by teachers trying to develop their own philosophies of teaching. One of the most obvious of these would be a general process of conceptual analysis – the attempt to analyze what we "really mean" when we refer to key terms in our area, such as "teaching." This is the process characteristic of analytic philosophy of education (White & White, 2001). A second and opposed approach is to accept that the use of a given word in practice *is* its meaning (Wittgenstein, 1933: 69, cited by Gilroy, 1999: 29). This approach to the meaning of educational concepts means that we consider contexts and actual investigations of concepts in practice, and Gilroy terms this a functional approach. Taking this a bit further, and applying a more probing or skeptical spin, we arrive at what Ehrenspeck and Lenzen (2001) call the "structural method." This "attempts to discover the historical and structural foundations" of claims about educational processes and concepts. "This is achieved through an analysis of the 'deep-structures,' the history of discourses, the myths, prejudices and ideologies which are all to be found hidden inside of the investigated claim," they remark (p. 89). Briefly put, "in philosophy no assumption is unquestionable" (McBride, 1994: 86). Talk of ideologies or myths and prejudices suggests that, as we try to develop a philosophy of teaching, we should probably try to examine, in a critical and skeptical way, the views about teaching, learning, schools, and so on, that we have inherited, unless we believe we have arrived at them already through a rigorous process. So critique and deconstruction would be processes that we should avail ourselves of as well (cf. Biesta, 2001).

The practices just mentioned can be done alone, through introspection, though again there is a long tradition in philosophy of reasoning together, as in the Socratic dialogues. So, like other aspects of teacher learning, "the process [can be seen as] a socially negotiated one, because teachers' knowledge . . . is constructed through experience in and with students, parents, and administrators as well as other members of the teaching profession" (Freeman & Johnson, 1998: 401). Pike, Bradley, and Mansfield (1997) concur, emphasizing the importance of talking with veteran teachers (not only in school, but at conferences) or convening a group of sympathetic colleagues for this purpose.

Difficulties

Many of the teachers I work with comment that they find developing and/or articulating their philosophy of teaching to be difficult, even though they may be somewhat experienced as teachers and even though they may be presently teaching. If you are an experienced teacher, you may have so thoroughly internalized some principles related to your practice that it may be difficult to express them. Whether or not you have extensive teaching experience, if you are currently teaching, you may be so much involved in teaching every day that getting the distance that may be needed to articulate your principles may be difficult, too. Also, while it may be possible to state certain views or values about teaching in general and about specific practices, the idea that they have to tie up, be fully coherent, somehow be part of a "system," may be inhibitory. Finally, some of the teachers I have worked with have found that the concept seems to suggest some fixed and final articulation of their views, and this also presents an obstacle. I entirely agree that it is a difficult thing to construct; I think such conceptions are probably hindering the construction process. From a teacher development point of view, it seems to me that it should be considered an *interim* statement, subject to revision and extension. Some of the research literature on teacher development also indicates that the journey contemplated here is not an easy one. Gomez, Walker, and Page encapsulate some literature to that effect as follows:

> The learning-to-teach literature (e.g., Bullough & Knowles, 1991; Bullough, Knowles, & Crow, 1992; Calderhead & Robson, 1991; Elbaz, 1983; Holt-Reynolds, 1992; Tabach-nick & Zeichner, 1984) tells us that it is difficult to interrupt or alter notions about self and others that prospective teach-ers bring to classrooms. As Kagan (1992) summarized in her review of research on the professional growth of prospective and novice teachers:
>
>> the personal beliefs and images that preservice candidates bring to programs of teacher education usually remain inflex-ible. Candidates tend to use the information provided in course work to confirm rather than to confront and correct their preexisting beliefs.
>
> (Gomez, Walker, & Page, 2000: 154)

Clearly the domain of philosophy of education, if handled appropriately, can present material that will both confirm as well as confront teachers. My worry is less with inflexibility (though that is a worry) than with a preordinate lack of consciousness. It is not easy to know what one thinks. A lack of a sense of the range of possibilities is part of this lack of consciousness. Given the working conditions of teachers and the components of many teacher education programs, both junior and senior teachers may not have been encouraged to think within the full range of possibilities that exist in this area. Also, where a philosophy of teaching statement is concerned, an absence of models or guidance concerning the components of one is also a problem (though too strong an emphasis on one particular model or set of components would equally short-circuit thought, I believe).

Duration and contexts

We should accept that the development of a philosophy of teaching, like any other complex cognitive structure guiding professional practice, will take time. Teacher educators Wiseman, Cooner, and Knight (1999: 24) comment, "The development of a personal philosophy requires self-examination and honest comparison and consideration of what we are about as teachers. It is a continual process that involves seeking answers to hard questions over a long period of time." And in a study of preservice teachers' development, Loughran and Russell comment,

> [D]eveloping and articulating a teaching philosophy is [a] valuable outcome... that cannot be transferred in any simple way from teacher educators' minds to their student teachers' minds. A teaching philosophy is something that must be individually cast and recast as it is constructed from and translated into the experiences of practice.
>
> (1997: 176)

On the basis of a study of the development of preservice teachers' practical philosophies of teaching, Goodman recommends that this be an integral part of teacher preparation programs, but that

> this reflection must include more than just what individuals 'believe'.... It is important for teacher education to help students consider the meaning they give to their words, how these meanings may differ among a given group of individuals, and what experiences influence their ideas and actions.
>
> (1988: 134)

Of course, teachers presumably also develop, and continue to develop, their philosophies of teaching within the schools where they teach; though Beijaard, Verloop, and Vermunt (2000: 749) comment that to arrive at "conceptual frameworks that guide their actions in practice" is more difficult for teachers compared with many other professionals because they are in a "doing" rather than a "knowing" environment. One might say they are in an unreflective environment – the difficulty in finding time or encouragement to reflect, given the poor working conditions of many teachers, particularly language teachers, remains an unsolved problem.

Users and sectors

It is common in material of the present sort to provide some indication of the typical reader. This can in particular head off misunderstandings and perhaps wasted time that would occur if the work were picked up by someone who is not part of the central readership. The major group of users of this material are likely to be language teachers pursuing formal qualifications in TESOL, ELT, Applied Linguistics, or education with a focus on second, foreign, or heritage languages (S/FLs). Most of these individuals will be in what Americans call "graduate" courses, and what the British call "postgraduate" courses.

Let me also recognize the rather large set of diverse sectors of the ELT "market," because teachers (not to mention researchers) who specialize in these different sectors tend to have different orientations and values, as well as different prior training.[16] Technical labels for these areas also vary a bit across different varieties of English, but we can talk about "higher" and "lower" education to start with (although the latter term, which may seem slightly offensive, is comparatively rarely used). I will expand that initial two-part distinction, to arrive at "elementary" and "secondary" education (the lower sector) and "tertiary" (*Br. E.*), that is, "post-secondary" (*Am. E.*) education. "Post-secondary" usually means "university," though on the semantics of it, it ought to include "adult education." (Are not university students adults?) Adult education, however, is usually reserved for those part-time, after-work kind of courses that ESL is actually heavily involved in (and is also known as "further education" in British English, which lately has become "continuing and/or life-long education").

Now since this material is concerned with values and beliefs, distinctions in the degree to which teachers are concerned with such matters across sectors could be important. I will assert that elementary and secondary teachers, because they work with children, are more accustomed to dealing with the idea that they have moral responsibilities to their charges. University teachers and adult educators deal with fully formed individuals (some might say). They are less accustomed to thinking in value terms, on the face of it. Along with this pattern goes, perhaps, a greater degree of concern with the subject matter than with the student. Many elementary teachers are not "subject specialists" – they teach young children many things. High school teachers identify more with subject areas, and university teachers may also research, which is to say, *create* knowledge in or across disciplinary areas. At the extreme, a university (post)graduate seminar may be built around the efforts of a professor whose position could be, "I can tell you about my research and related studies, and I can direct you in your research or studies in that same area. I am not responsible for doing anything else instructional, since my primary responsibility is research."

Now let us make a cut horizontally, rather than vertically. We can distinguish between state and private institutions of education. In these times of powerful centralized states, education is substantially controlled by government, though around the world the private sector of education is growing rapidly, notably in nations where it had been eliminated or weakened, for a time. Because of this control, the values of the state permeate state schools; on the other hand, parts of the private sector may have very strong values of their own – consider religious schools, for example. Even universities may respond to such concerns, and in private universities, again because of the religious affiliations of many of them, this is clear.

ES/FL has some odd characteristics within these sectors. In EFL countries, until recently it had little visibility at the elementary level. On the other hand, probably the numerically greatest part of ES/FL as a whole is at the secondary level (whether public or private). At the postsecondary level, it is not a discipline, and so is not part of the mainstream. In my own university, it is labeled "remedial"; in some institutions the area has the slightly more dignified "service courses" status. However, at this level (adult) it has an enormous presence in the private sectors of many countries, both in "cram schools" and in the ubiquitous "conversation schools."[17] Many teachers working in such institutions are not aware that there is a technical term for an oddly assorted set of subject areas which have their own freestanding commercially operated schools: the "proprietary sector." Within it, conceptually, ES/FL schools find themselves cheek by jowl with schools of hairdressing, music, automobile driving, business, and plumbing. This is the vast and shadowy "private language school" sector of ELT, which is clearly a moneymaker of considerable size in both EFL and ESL countries, but concerning which there is so little research or empirical description. What formal values do such schools espouse? More than anything else, they provide a service in exchange for a fee. Outside the most prestigious institutions, *caveat emptor* may be the order of the day: You pay your money and you take your choice. Many who begin teaching in this sector do not do so because they wish to be teachers, primarily. They may be native speakers, temporarily resident in a non-English-speaking country by accident, or pursuing other vocational goals. Yet the best teachers in it aspire to professional status and the values that accompany that. (The discussion of the conceptual inheritance of the conversation school in Chapter 3 may be of particular interest to them.)

Insofar as the present text has the goal of fostering teacher development, it should also be of interest to teacher educators, some of whom (along with some teachers) may also be researchers, or have a research orientation. These readers will already have registered the point that the source material is primarily not derived from research as the term is conventionally understood. But the area of language teachers' values and beliefs is one that is gradually acquiring greater prominence, and the studies reviewed at the end of the work (Chapter 11) may suggest the need for more.

Finally, and importantly, I would like to make one more distinction among users of this material, which has particular implications for the content of the material. Although the terminology is (rightly) disputed, a distinction between native and nonnative teachers of ES/FL is still often made, and it may be pertinent to the background that TESOL specialists bring to their development. It is quite common for the former group *not* to have a relevant bachelor's degree, and it is not unusual for them *not* to be employed in lower education. Nonnative teachers, in my experience, are more likely to have studied English beginning with a first degree and to begin their careers in lower education, whatever they may do later. I want to link this dichotomy with a second. Within a substantial part of the EFL world, associated somewhat with the NS/NNS (native speaker/nonnative speaker) distinction is a West/East distinction. (This does not apply to the Americas or Europe.) I should say immediately that this distinction is only accepted or used at a preliminary level, as an extremely loose way of talking that could not possibly do justice to details, and indeed has often been identified as pernicious and dangerously essentializing (also "orientalizing" – Said, 1978; see *inter alia,* Holliday, 2005; Kubota, 1999). Because of the association between economic development, the West, and English as an imperial international language, one large and increasing sector of our field parses "new" ways of teaching English as "Western" ways of teaching English, and associates them with "native speakers" as opposed to indigenous "nonnative" teachers. Considerable clashes of values and cultural tensions occur as a result, and these are exacerbated by lack of an historical perspective concerning education, schools, philosophies of education, and contact among such major international sectors. My sense is that a great ignorance prevails, on the part of the "West" and ELT teachers who see themselves as representatives of the West, concerning education in the "East." I suspect this is also related to the lack, in the case of some in the NS camp, of a relevant first degree. For that reason, a fairly extended treatment of the *world* history of school appears in the immediately succeeding chapter.[18]

Organization of the rest of the text

We have taken a preliminary look at terms and said something about sources and processes that will help a person develop a philosophy of teaching. I have attempted to recognize the rather different groups of teachers (and other readers) to whom this work is addressed. I move now to close these preliminary ground-clearing introductory remarks. From now on I will be taking it for granted that while it is clearly true that key areas for developing a philosophy of teaching include empirical evidence, scientific theory, personal life and teaching experiences, and so on, one potentially useful area is also the domain of philosophy and the special components of that region that pertain to teaching, education, and the subdomain of ES/FL education. My final move in this introduction is to set out a map, perhaps sketchy and partial, of the terrain. This is the ground from which we might excavate material that will contribute to our philosophies of language teaching.

As I go on now to present a quick idea of what is to come in the body of the text, I suppose I am also "tipping my hand," since by my selection of these areas as domains of thought that I think are potentially important, I am also implying what I think should go into a philosophy of (language) teaching. I will be going mainly from "out" to "in" – with the exception of the brief preview subsection earlier in this chapter, I am working from the history and philosophies of school (and of learning, teaching, and teachers in society) in toward you, the reader, with the assumption that you – yourself a teacher of language – will appropriate those aspects of this material that you find useful and meaningful. Along the way, we do encounter language-teaching traditions and perspectives, but in their historical contexts. At those points I will try to highlight or exemplify philosophical concepts that were central to these perspectives.

Chapter 2 and Chapter 3 are intended to fill in the historical background to SL teaching. If a philosophy of teaching is something in which you articulate what it is you are doing, I don't see how you can have such a philosophy if you don't know *where* what you are doing came from. Teaching is a social practice embodied in (and made possible by) a social institution – school. Like any social institution, it has a history. In this context, the famous maxim, "Those who cannot remember the past are condemned to repeat it" (Santayana, 1905) seems pertinent. I take it to indicate that in order to be an active agent in the world, you have to have a sense of what has come before. When social institutions are seen as having a human history, that is, as being created, we are in a position of agency vis-à-vis those institutions. It is when the social order is presented as God-given or immutable that humans are disadvantaged. The social institution of school has remarkable stability, but it has *not* always existed. Also, on the other hand, L2 instruction was there from very early days, even if the historical record is quite patchy. English is an international (some would say imperial) language; but it is not the first such.

The field of applied linguistics, SL Studies, or ELT indeed has a very poor record when it comes to history, its own history. There is always *great* interest in "what's new"; and by contrast, histories of S/FL teaching are extremely few. One might suppose a conspiracy here, because the few histories that do exist demonstrate vividly that there is very little new! They undercut, that is, the efforts of showmen and publishers to persuade the paying public (S/FL teachers and their students) to invest in the latest "approach." But, in fact, the other part of the problem is at the research end of our field. Researchers in our field until recently have had little sense of the history of the social sciences. Since there has been a willingness to believe that there was no good old research, there has been, effectively, no research history (see Thomas, 1998). The ahistorical view of the field is not satisfactory by any means, given the field's current sociopolitical situation – namely its involvement in the clash of cultures, of civilization contact that has been going on since the 19th century with great and dangerous repercussions that continue into the 21st (alluded to briefly in Chapter 5). So another part of the point of Chapter 2 is to head off West versus East ignorance as well.

There is a similar thrust behind Chapter 3. Major options in S/FL instruction have historical roots; at one remove these go back to the mid- to late 19th century. At a more extended level of analysis, major methodological positions in SL teaching have associated positions on the nature of humans and of learning, which have roots at least in the shift to modern times from medieval times. Also, many S/FL teachers work in state education systems, whether lower or higher education. This puts them firmly in the grip of the state, which is primarily responsible for the phenomenon of mass education. A teacher who works for the state inevitably has to take a position on what it is the state expects of her or him. This can be aided by understanding where this phenomenon of mass education has come from and what have been some of the characteristics it has exhibited.

In Chapter 4, we shift from the primarily historical to the primarily philosophical. Certain major contributions to the world of philosophy have been systems of philosophy. Anyone who is drawing on philosophy to develop his or her own ideas must have a basic familiarity with these systems. So this is a basic, almost terminological review. In dealing with core material in the philosophy of education, a long-standing though not entirely satisfactory way to organize material in this area is to consider *systems* or *schools of philosophy* as applied to education. The second organizing theme I will use in this chapter is *movements* or *trends in the field of education* ("philosophies of schooling"; Power, 1982). One or more S/FL Methods partially lie within these. Rather than seeing them exclusively as ahistorical phenomena driven by linguistic theory, we should, I believe, be able to trace the descent of SL Methods from larger educational approaches so as to use them as sources for the development of a philosophy of language teaching. We should at least be able to recognize their affinities to such movements and discern their associated philosophical assumptions. This chapter closes by examining several curricular initiatives in TESOL and S/FL teaching for their philosophical issues or characteristics.

Much is made, in our field, of research- or "evidence-based" approaches to S/FL teaching. We are accustomed to judging some of our procedures against "what is known" about SL learning. But what *can* be known? Can facts be known, absolutely? How does truth come about? These sorts of questions certainly sound like the kind that philosophy would tackle; and one might hope that its answers to them would inform researchers and teachers. However, the answers to such questions have never been simple or settled ("What is truth, said jesting Pilate, and would not stay for an answer"; Bacon, 1625/1985.) This is even more the case now, following recent developments in the world of ideas reviewed in Chapter 5. This leads into Chapter 6, which addresses the matter of epistemology directly. This chapter may be somewhat removed from immediate contact with teaching; instead it is concerned really with the research bases for teaching, with teachers' knowledge, and the matter of what can be known about language. I hope it will be agreed that these are important questions to address in developing one's philosophy of S/FL teaching.

Chapter 7 tackles more human concerns. Teaching is very much tied up with doing the right thing by our students. And as teachers, we are also enjoined to be professional. And we have a duty to society; perhaps also society (the state, our employers) has a duty to us (pay us properly, not exploit us). Do we as teachers of the world international language perhaps have rights and duties of an international nature? These very value-laden matters are arguably a part of developing a philosophy of S/FL teaching. This line of thought extends into the next chapter, Chapter 8, which looks at values in their sociopolitical philosophical context.

Chapter 9 will be of interest, or not, depending on one's answers to questions addressed in Chapter 8. But to foreshadow just one issue here: Do you agree that teaching is a "woman's" profession? In your part of the world, or teaching vicinity, are there more women teachers than men? (If so, you are in a typical context.) Then, how about the principals, administrators, and so on – are there more women than men? (If the answer is no, you are again in a typical context.) Do you think this is normal, or the way things should be? If your answer is yes, you should probably skip this chapter. If your answer is no, you may find the chapter useful to develop your philosophy of S/FL teaching.

Chapter 10 tries to recognize that most of us are unlikely to be able to implement or act on our philosophies of teaching all the time, and unfortunately, in some circumstances our actions may be extremely compromised. I think we should face up to the tensions between what we might wish to do, as teachers, and what we can do, and if at all possible use that tension for growth and change – if not immediately, then as the basis for plotting a course for the future.

Finally, in Chapter 11, I take a look at a small but growing body of empirical work on teachers' statements of beliefs, principles, and so on, that seems relevant to the topic of the notes as a whole. This is contrasted with further philosophical analysis of the matter of aims, which I believe is central to one's philosophy of teaching.

Let me recap this preliminary disclosure of areas I think are important for the development of a person's philosophy of language teaching. Clearly I think that knowing where one's ideas about how to teach and how to teach languages have come from is very important. Allied with that, at a more explicitly philosophical level, is the view that the positions one takes as a teacher can relate to quite abstract ideas about the nature of the world, which often in turn allow for considerations of human purpose and agency. A sophisticated teacher, too, would be able to reflect on the nature of his or her professional knowledge, in general (and as derived to some extent from scientific knowledge), as well as in regard to knowledge of language and conceptions of learning. Given the restrictions that we often face as language teachers, I think it is important that we have a sense of our role in society, both as individuals and as professionals, and of the good we can do not just for individual students but for society as a whole. At the same time I recognize that we cannot always do so much (particularly if alone); and this also deserves a considered, analytic response. And finally, though it could equally well be in initial position: An understanding of the crucial concept of "aims" in education, in language teaching, and in life, is of particular value. While this does not exhaust the domain, it is perhaps as much as there is space for in the present work!

Discussion questions

1. Go over the range of sources and processes for developing one's philosophy of teaching and take stock. What material do you have available to you? What other individuals can you turn to for assistance? What techniques of idea generation, idea "surfacing," and idea development could you use?
2. In what senses is teachers' knowledge theoretical?
3. "Methods do not exist." Discuss.

Notes to Chapter 1

[1] For example, Kettle & Sellars (1996: 3): "Reflection is strongly linked to the process of practical theory development."

[2] Beck (1979: 2) provides "a statement of the chief activities in which philosophers have been engaged over the centuries... First is the *speculative* activity... develop[ing] a comprehensive vision or picture of the universe.... A second activity is generally named *phenomenological*... seek[ing] to provide a complete and unbiased description of basic experiences... like guilt, obligation, and fear.... A third activity is *normative* and evaluative, for philosophers try to act as critics by providing standards against which individual and social conduct may be judged and guided. Fourth, in what may be called the critical or *analytic* activity, philosophers strive to achieve clarity about the meaning of basic concepts like true, false, good and just."

[3] And who am I to do this? I believe it is important that readers have a sense of the positionality of the author as soon as possible. The credibility of this material to a fair extent depends on who it is that drew it up. At time of writing, I'm a white middle-class

male, 53, a British-American immigrant, long resident in the central Pacific islands of Hawai'i, married to a Colombian woman and father of a son whose first given name is Hawaiian. I have been involved in ELT for 30 years, with extended experience in the "Third World" (Malaysian Borneo), East Asia (Japan), and shorter visits to a variety of EFL settings in Central Asia and South America. I mainly work with teachers in the academic setting of my home department, the Department of Second Language Studies, University of Hawai'i.

4   For example, Johnston (2003), who introduces his book by saying that "In a way, the book falls under the category of philosophy of education" but hastens to note that it "is not the dry, abstract philosophy with which the word is often associated" (p. ix). In fact, it focuses on the subarea within philosophy, of ethics or morals, and Johnston comments that he has "not found the philosophical literature to be very helpful in [his] goal of seeking to understand the moral foundations of language teaching" (p. 12).

5   Discussing "whole language," Black refers to it as a philosophy of teaching, a method, and a strategy, using the terms interchangeably.

6   Like some other writers, I am using the "capital-M Method" to make explicit this particular use of the term, since the word is otherwise ambiguous.

7   Halkes (1986: 211) notes, "The study of teachers' thought processes was more or less officially initiated at the 1974 Conference of the NIE [National Institute of Education]."

8   On the personalization of professional knowledge in our area see also Burns (1996), Moran (1996), and Ulichny (1996).

9   This is implied, for example, by the definition of the area that ERIC uses: "Critical examination of the grounds for fundamental beliefs and analysis of the basic concepts, doctrines, or practices that express such beliefs" (ERIC Thesaurus 07/01/1966).

10   It is possible that a handful of book-length studies in our field could usefully be reviewed to stimulate the individual teacher's development of a philosophy of teaching: for example, Stevick (1980), or more recently Brumfit (2001). Given the length of the works, I have reluctantly decided not to include a detailed review of such extended discussions within the present text.

11   The small number of book-length historical treatments of S/FLT are Howatt (1984), Howatt & Widdowson (2004), Kelly (1969), Musumeci (1997), Titone (1968); cf. also Newmark (1948) and Pugh (1996). Surprisingly relevant too is Thomas (2004).

12   On first use of this term, I note that it and its opposite, East/Eastern, will be used in this work as shorthand or "strategic essentialisms." In fact, on the one hand they are obviously Anglocentric (east or west of what?), and on the other hand do no justice at all to the interpenetration and nonhomogeneity of ideas in philosophy and education since earliest times.

13   This is yet another area where change is clear, including in our field. Discussions of spirituality or religion in TESOL would have been very rare and looked on with extreme skepticism until only a few years ago; yet now they are appearing as well as rather directly challenging investigations of this area (e.g., Johnston & Varghese, 2006).

14   Surprisingly little empirical investigation appears to have been done concerning this enduring topic. An ERIC search produced only 17 entries which contain the phrase "philosophy of teaching" in the title, and only 110 occurrences overall, from 1966 to present. Almost none of these are substantive empirical investigations. (See Chapter 10.)

15 See also Morris (1961), Van Scotter et al. (1979/1991).

16 For a helpful dissection of the field from the point of its diverse institutions, see McKay (1992, Chapter 5).

17 This whole sector is remarkably untouched by the research enterprise – from a research point of view we have few studies of practice in these areas.

18 Honesty and modesty compel me to admit that I resemble this remark, as my own first degree in Economics equally did not prepare me for a subsequent career in TESOL or a lifetime in Asia/Pacific education.

2 The early history and philosophies of school

Introduction

There are several points I would like to make in introducing this chapter, so as to explain why the chapter exists and why I am tackling this material. First: The long-term goal of this material is to aid the development of philosophies of ES/FL teaching that relate to teaching *within its social and educational contexts*. Put more narrowly, that means within the context of formal education. There can be some philosophizing about learning and teaching of S/FLs that applies regardless of context, perhaps, or concerns only informal learning. But as most S/FL teachers teach in schools, I intend to focus on philosophies of education in context, which usually means education that might be embodied in school systems. What is implied by an emphasis on context? Many (e.g., Meijer, 2001) would argue that culture is a highly relevant interpretation of "the context" of education; and cultures are time-bound. So, for me, the history of education and the philosophy of education are fields which naturally go together. In the present and succeeding chapters, a historical approach will be uppermost. Putting a tangled web of ideas and concepts in a temporal sequence is one way to straighten them out, and the analytic scheme in question (time sequence) is one we are all familiar with and – unlike other analytic schemata – requires no extra explanation.

My second initial point is a caveat: In considering ideas of teaching and learning that will eventually show up in S/FL contexts within a cultural and historical framework, I will emphasize as much as possible a world perspective. I do so against a bias that has often been perceived in the literature of ES/FL teaching (applied linguistics, second-language studies, etc.) as well as in studies of education generally. Hampered by the fact that the preponderance of studies of teaching and learning, and associated journal indices[1] relate mainly to the English-using parts of the world, much research in our area could be said to be "Anglocentric" or "Eurocentric." These terms are now widely understood to point to a limitation of vision, a parochial vision, that, though previously widespread in the English-speaking world, is not adequate at the beginning of the 21st century for studies of the present sort. It is particularly unsatisfactory in any international field of endeavor, and the study of S/FL teaching is one such; in addition, it is equally unhelpful when we are dealing with the primary international language, English (cf. Marks, 2002).

My third point is closely related to the previous one: So long as English is the primary international language, teachers of ES/FL, more than teachers of any other subject area, are engaged in practices of cultural contact. At the same time, two major driving forces of ELT, the publishing industry and the academic industry of applied linguistics, continue to be dominated by what Holliday (1994a, 1994b, 2005) has called the "BANA" perspective of individuals closely associated with Britain and North America, academics and materials writers of the English-speaking developed world. Meanwhile, though, major consumers of this industry include countries that for historical reasons are categorized as "non-Western." A massive contact zone of particular importance for the 21st century, in which native and nonnative teachers of EFL mix, and in which different approaches to learning and teaching jostle, is constituted by East and Southeast Asia (with its Chinese heritage),[2] with Central Asia and the Middle East (with its Islamic heritage) rising on the geopolitical language-teaching horizon.[3]

Finally, a further word of justification concerning the historical material upcoming: Within the contact zone just mentioned, I believe many ES/FL teachers could benefit from a review of the educational histories they are heir to. For those who are currently "top dog," history can teach us a welcome modesty about how recently that position was obtained and how short the status of "king of the hill" is among historical civilizations. For those whose access to their own indigenous traditions has been made difficult by political instability and Western hegemony, a little historical excavation can provide a more balanced perspective concerning what "new" ideas to accept, what to reject, and what to resuscitate and renovate. For all teachers of English as the current international language, a little history of previous international languages can prove salutary, as we come to realize that this is *not* the first time that some of the issues we grapple with have been visible on the globe. Finally, becoming aware of the history of social institutions, indeed discovering that they *have* a history, is very important for their revision. If we do not examine the history of things, we have a tendency to take them for granted. So, though the reader may feel that the upcoming excursus into the history of school takes us a long way from the world of ELT, there is a reason for this.

The beginnings both of schooling and of S/FL literacy

It is not easy to determine when schooling, in anything approximating the modern sense, began. At one level, such beginnings might be seen as closely associated with the development of literacy; something again not easy to pin down historically. Currently, many specialists are willing to consider that writing systems may well have developed independently at several times and places in the history of the world, although Mesopotamia and its associated Sumerian civilization seems likely to be the earliest case (Glassner, 2003). Such early writing systems often go together with the needs of rulers for taxation and records, and of institutionalized religious systems as well. So the earliest formal schooling is associated with elite palace or temple operations; and in this association we can also find very early bilingual word lists (for Akkadian; Kelly, 1969: 24) and thereby deduce the existence of the first formal L2 teaching. But the specialized training of scribes and accountants is not school in the modern (mass) sense. "The schools of Mesopotamia, Egypt, and China trained specialists for the service of the state, but left the citizenry untouched" (Smith, 1955: 131). The question is, at what time, and where, did literacy, whether of first or second languages, cease being confined to the specialized groups of scribes and priests and become associated with the basic training of, at minimum, some part of the population (most likely the sons of the aristocracy, to start with)?

When we focus on the matter of the earliest formal school systems, Chinese civilization has a very early claim. It eventually came to constitute the first manifestation of state-supported education encompassing a meritocratic test-based use of education as a system for personal advancement in society; an effort that was to be repeated much later in Europe more or less coincident with the beginning of modern school systems in the West. Scholars used to accept the claims of ancient Chinese historians (Cleverley, 1991: 1–4) that by 1000 BCE, or even earlier, schools as we know them were already preparing students for exams for the civil service. However, Walton comments:

> Despite rhetorical allusions made by many Sung writers to a hierarchical network of schools in antiquity that extended from ruler's court to rural village, before the Sung [AD 960–1127] most schooling took place within the home and family, through private tutors, or in religious establishments, such as Buddhist monasteries.
>
> (1999: 12)

Although writing systems of Mesopotamia, Egypt, and China appear to date from the 4th to the 2nd millennia BCE, it seems unlikely that schools that got beyond the confines just mentioned came into existence earlier than the "Axial Age" (Jaspers, 1953) of the 6th century BCE. Independent evidence (as opposed to claims concerning a past Golden Age) seems slim for earlier starts.[4]

Around that time, across most of the ancient world, something approximating school was developing at a greater or lesser speed, as basic literacy and numeracy training gradually moved among or across individual house and family schools, religious institutions, and temple schools. Eventually, small private schools also began to occur. In India, young children, mainly boys, learned their letters and also to memorize the Vedas within the homes of religious teachers. With the rise of monasticism (the first religion to make heavy use of this structure appears to have been Buddhism), some of this schooling shifted from the teachers' homes to monasteries. Early Chinese schooling began with boys learning characters from about the age of six.

A broadly similar picture seems to hold for Greece and Rome, wherein home tuition moved to small schools (without the direct involvement of religious institutions, it seems). Concerning Greece, Morgan (1998: 10) explains that even though there was a sudden upsurge in literacy associated with Athenian democracy, "there was no such thing as 'education based on literacy'" until about 450 BCE or later. The transition from tutors teaching in the homes of the rich to schools was a preliminary step in this geographical area too, as it had been earlier in the East. In Rome, the teaching of literacy in schools was not at first thought desirable. Only by about 100 CE,

> the Roman Empire quickly moved to support schools with public money and, in fact, used the schools as a means of Latinizing their conquered lands. The acceptance of standardized teaching methods made it possible for Roman schools scattered around the world to have substantially the same classroom regimes...
>
> (Murphy, 2001: 2)

Elementary schools were naturally more numerous:

> At the height of the Empire, around [the first century CE], elementary schools existed in even the smallest towns.... The elementary curriculum consisted of reading, writing, arithmetic, grammar, and history, with heavy doses of patriotism....
>
> (Sharpes, 2002: 82)

Some students (male and female) went on at the age of 13 for three more years of secondary education. Sharpes (2002: 82, citing Durant, 1944: 367) states that "by 130 AD there were twenty secondary schools in Rome."

It is with Rome and Greece that we get the first hints of schooling (for the young) that encompasses a concern with more than one language. Greek was a very important aspect of the Roman world, culturally and administratively, and the Roman administration made heavy use of it, inheriting this from the international, Greek-run empire of Alexander.[5] However, as Morgan tells us, there is little detail in the early record:

> Evidence from the ancient world as a whole about language learning is scanty. From the Archaic period to the end of the Roman Empire, across a region in which dozens of languages were spoken, it is remarkable how infrequently we hear either of interpreters or about individuals learning other languages, let alone about how they learned. Such slender evidence as we have, however, suggests that spoken languages were learned by ear, probably supported by glossaries, and that texts in languages or dialects which were not spoken were approached through glossaries alone. A few shreds of evidence from educational texts confirm this: [early educational theorist] Quintilian [expected his] pupil to learn Greek by ear, which is why Quintilian insists that he do so as young as possible. The bilingual schooltexts from Gaul [3rd century] appear to be exercises in translation from Latin into Greek ... [though] Augustine implies that he learned Greek without speaking it ... [through] formal teaching and with reading Homer.
>
> (Morgan, 1998: 165–7)

Analyses of what historians of European antiquity call "schooltexts" show that the first indications of school training for bilingual literacy are associated with the spread of the Roman Empire. Latin was the international language of the imperium, and techniques for teaching Latin in many different domains of the empire appear to have been somewhat standardized, turning out a product (Latin as a second or foreign language) that presumably had international or interprovincial communicative capacity as its main concern. Referring to the pedagogue and grammarian Priscian, Kelly comments: "it must be remembered that he was teaching Latin in Constantinople, the capital of the Greek East" (1969: 117) – he was thus presumably one of the earliest expatriate S/FL experts we know of (fl. 500 AD).

The most acknowledged form of bilingualism in the Roman Empire was with regard to Greek. Upper-class Romans acquired Greek as a second language through elite schooling and tutoring (mostly from native speakers, often slaves); it had come to be regarded as the language of culture, philosophy, and learning quite early, by, for example, the time of Cicero (1st century BCE). More broadly, we can certainly say that early Europe, particularly as a result of contacts between cultures caused or fostered by the empire, had extensive zones in which bilingualism was common (Adams, 2003). The army was made up of individuals from many language backgrounds, not all of whom spoke Latin well, and some units of which operated mostly in Greek. "Interpreters were an important group...and these will have combined Latin with a variety of languages, such as forms of Germanic and Aramaic" (p. 760); the Roman Empire was administered in two languages (Latin and Greek). Adams deduces the existence of formal instruction in Latin within the army (p. 632), but has no direct evidence or description of practices. Millar (2006: 86) comments that "the Imperial [civil] service...made the learning of Latin a necessary qualification [for] everybody...who entered" from Greek parts of the empire, and deduces that those who entered public service either learned the language in school or "sought a special training in Latin" but "our evidence for the process of learning Latin...is remarkably poor" (p. 90). Again there is little evidence. Possibly much of the development of bilingualism did *not* occur in schools, except through a process of submersion.[6]

With the decline of the Roman Empire, the need for a bilingual bureaucracy (or a multilingual army) died out. The center of power and civilization in the West shifted eastward to Constantinople and southward to the Islamic world, and monastic and religious institutions played a larger role in education again from then on. Text-based translation became for a while the main driving force for any kind of S/FL literate learning.

The beginnings of higher education and of philosophies of schooling

With respect to early institutions of education, more is known about what we might call "colleges," rather than schools.[7] After a period of prolonged social and political unrest, and with the intent of improving social conditions, one of the first private colleges we know much of was opened by Confucius late in the 5th century BCE. Some time later, Confucian philosophy became the thinking most valued by a succession of Chinese rulers, and a long-standing pattern eventually emerged that the administrative elite of China were to be prepared for their work through the study of what was basically a system of ethics (as opposed to techniques of management, for example). By 124 BCE, the Imperial College was set up to train scholar officials in Confucian ideas. For a comparatively short span of centuries, Confucian ideas were either repressed completely (by the Legalist school and a dynasty that favored them) or diminished by comparison with popular (and imperial) interest in Buddhism and Taoism. But by the end of the Sui-Tang period (581–907 CE), national examination procedures were increasingly well-established, and scholars had to focus on classics or on law, with emphases also on calligraphy or mathematics. The national examination system, with its meritocratic orientation, seems comparatively modern in tone, and there is evidence that this system was introduced at least partially to weaken the power of aristocratic elites and aid the efficiency of the civil service (Holcombe, 2001). There were many examples of it being corrupted or subverted, however; furthermore, the entire system discriminated absolutely against women, and its economic demands meant that generally only the well-to-do could participate.

Formal institutions of learning for young adults and scholars were also to be found in other ancient civilizations, and from perhaps as early as 700 BCE started to take a shape that would be somewhat recognizable even now, though with a much heavier emphasis on religion and philosophy than science. The cities of Takshashila[8] and Nalanda are often identified as among those institutions of higher learning that have a good claim to being the first universities. Around 700 BCE, Takshashila offered an eight-year program of study, and though the Vedas were prominent, topics also included accountancy, agriculture, commerce, medicine, astronomy, and military arts. Starting somewhat later (from 425 CE), Nalanda offered a more Buddhist curriculum, though including logic and astronomy (Anon., 1969). And a little later, Plato's Academy and the Lyceum of Aristotle came over the time horizon (beginning around 387 BCE and 335 BCE respectively).

Greek learning and institutions continued to flourish during the Roman Empire, with Alexandria gaining over Athens. But the rise of Christianity was the downfall of higher learning in the east of the empire (though it preserved it at the western end):

> In 529 the Emperor Justinian...closed the Museum of Athens [the Academy].... He thus terminated an institution that had survived for nearly 1,000 years. Justinian confiscated the endowment... – depriving the faculty of its salaries – and decreed that pagans could no longer teach there.... Philosophers and rhetors migrated to Byzantium and then to upper Mesopotamia and Jundi Shapur, where they joined Nestorian Christians.
>
> (Stanton, 1990: 54)

The Nestorians were followers of Nestorius, the 5th-century patriarch of Constantinople who had been exiled for articulating humanistic beliefs about Jesus Christ. "To escape persecution they fled to the Sasanian [Persian] frontier... where they founded monasteries and schools to promote Neoplatonism in its Christianized form" (ibid.). In due course, the scholars of Alexandria, persecuted by the Christian Byzantines who conquered their city, also packed up and moved to the same region, bringing their manuscripts and their traditions of learning and teaching. Here the language of learning was Syriac, so this phase of higher education is associated with a specialized form of bilingualism, held narrowly among scholars, it seems. Over the next hundred years or so, bilingual Nestorian scholars translated enormous quantities of texts from Greek to Syriac, and then, funded by Muslim rulers, from Syriac into Arabic. Thus was preserved the learning of the ancient West that otherwise would have been completely destroyed by Christian intolerance and the economic devastation that followed the fall of Rome.

The rise of Islam produced new institutions of learning. The mosque itself was something of a new development. Springing from it (though somewhat separate) was the *madrasa*, the Islamic university emphasizing legal and philosophical studies. By the 11th century CE, this entity had become the dominant institution of higher education in much of the world.[9] Between, say, the 7th and the 13th centuries (CE), institutions of education in the Islamic world, particularly higher education, were certainly stronger than in Europe (cf. Nakosteen, 1964; Rubinstein, 2003). During this period, though similar institutions in the Indian subcontinent were in some decline because of political instability, academies in China also flourished, with some ups and downs.[10] The 11th and 12th centuries were a time of educational development in China, starting with the expansion of the examination system in 977:

> The educational program of later reformers, from its abortive inauguration in the Ch'ing-li period (1041–1048) to its fruition under Ts'ai Ching (1046–1126) can be viewed in large part as a complex reaction to that expansion. In their attempt to create an empirewide system of schools the reformers responded to both the demands for more schooling and the growing tendency, from the 1020s on, of local officials to establish government schools.... For a time in the late Northern Sung [dynasty] the government's ... system of schools stretched from county schools to the Imperial University in K'ai-feng and came close to supplanting the examinations themselves.
>
> (De Bary & Chaffee, 1989: 8–9)

The period right at the end of the 12th century is also important because it was at this time that the great reformer and educator Chu Hsi (Zhu Xi) was codifying Confucian texts and establishing them as the basis for neo-Confucianism, the version of Confucianism that was to maintain something of a stranglehold on the Chinese cultural area, and schools within it, for the next half century or more.[11] During this period, of course, and well through to the 1500s, Chinese civilization far outstripped that of Europe. Major cities in China were larger and more prosperous than many in Europe; knowledge of medicine and early science was probably better in China than in Europe as late as the 14th century; and the extent and systematicity of the Chinese education system was presumably greater as well. The Indian education system, later destroyed by colonization processes, was also probably more extensive than that of Europe during this time (Dharampal, 1983; Kumaravadivelu, 2003).

The first movements toward a university in Europe surfaced much later than in China – around the 12th century (Bologna and Paris; cf. Pedersen, 1997). Some suggest that institutionally they were influenced by the Muslim *madrasa* (Makdisi, 1995). At any rate, the period between 1000 and 1200 is conventionally accepted as the time when the classical learning (of the West) was handed over from the Islamic world to Europe, by way of Arabic manuscripts arriving in Portugal and Spain (although the process continued for some time longer), and the time when European colleges and universities developed (again, drawing on scholarly bilingual and translation capabilities). In this area, higher educational systems were strongly associated with the Christian Church, institutionally and conceptually. The universities, such as Paris and Bologna, were dramatically different from their modern versions. They had no regular administrators or bureaucratic staff; in southern Europe (e.g., Bologna) they were student-run; undergraduates could be as young as 14 years old, and some teachers with bachelor's degrees in hand might be aged 19; "the average age of those in authority at Paris or Bologna... [was] mid-twenties" (Courtenay, 1987: 25).

Conceptually, over several centuries, these institutions had to grapple with the challenge to Christian thinking presented by "Greek learning" and the logical, empirical, and rational views of Aristotle and others. The short-term result was "scholasticism," a somewhat defensive interpretation of Christian doctrine and concepts consistent with Aristotle's views, developed by Aquinas. In the long term, the challenge was too great and (as sketched briefly in the next chapter), the universities and their ideas shifted to the more clearly modern stance of humanism from the 1400s on.

The philosophies of early schools

This has been a brief review of the first phase of the worldwide rise of the institution we call school, emphasizing, where possible, the role of additional languages. Let me now ask what concepts of education these manifestations of school actually had and what ideas they were transmitting. Though recognizing the paucity of the historical record, we may ask if there were any aspects of the record that bear on our basic concerns.

There is a tendency to assume that the general pedagogy of premodern schools was memorization. This is not necessarily correct. Confucius's own remarks on teaching emphasize the importance of students' questions, for example.[12] Discussing Chinese schools and education, Nylan is vigorous in his revisionism, referring to "cherished stereotypes":

> A surprisingly high percentage of children in pre-modern China acquired "basic literacy" ... through a wide variety of educational opportunities, including home schooling, charity schools, and cheap "private schools" (*sishu*) ... where two to twenty-five pupils at different levels trained under a single schoolmaster. Three standard primers were all that was needed ... the primers could be finished in less than a year, giving the child the necessary tools to read for content in advanced texts. ...
>
> In traditional instruction, the tendency was – contrary to prevailing stereotypes – not to have the entire school chanting a single line of text, but to allow each student to progress at his own pace, a tendency made possible by the small size of the typical school. ... It was the Chinese, ironically, during their initial contact with the "West," who were startled to find the Euro-American system of "grades" based on the regulated factory or army model, for the Chinese never used to presume (a) that at the exact same age all children can be socialized to engage with virtual strangers in a classroom or (b) that all children will advance in their subsequent studies at the same speed.
>
> (Nylan, 2003: 140–41)

While memorization of these readers, and of other texts by more advanced students, certainly took place, Nylan follows analyses of memorization in modern Chinese schooling (e.g., Biggs, 1996) to dispute the implication that this practice stifled the development of creativity or individuality.

Underlying the practices of early Chinese pedagogy were some philosophical positions about the nature of man and of learning. One of the most notable is implied by Confucius's statement that "by nature men are nearly alike; but through experience they grow wide apart." This is a progressive, rather than conservative, understanding of intelligence as something *not* hereditary, nor fixed. He also similarly articulated a class-neutral position, providing instruction for a flat fee and reflecting the fact that some (admittedly, not many) of his students came from poor backgrounds. Finally, one way that language was implicated in Confucius's philosophy was by a sense that it was itself powerful, through the power of naming:

> And here one is reminded of the Confucian doctrine of Rectification of Names. In essence this states that if a name such as *school* has come to be applied to an organization which is *not a*

school in the original sense, but rather some sort of arrangement for childholding, job preparation, or social conditioning, then one of three things should take place. Either the school should cease to call itself a school and instead call itself what it now is ... or the shift in language should be recognized so that all now understand what the name properly signifies and denotes, or it should change to fit the original definition.

(Hodgkinson, 1991: 111)

Confucius repeatedly advocated the rectification of names as part of the reform programs he urged on a series of not very sympathetic national leaders.

Pedagogically, at least at the "college" level in ancient Greece, an emphasis on debate and dialectic was apparent early. Language, in the form of rhetoric, was crucial, though as we have noted, second languages only come in with the rise of Latin and the Roman Empire. Morgan (1998: 19) comments that "we know almost nothing about the institutions of education in the Classical period" but "what the fourth century [BCE] did develop was a range of theories about the relationship between education and political power and authority."

Aristotle and Isocrates formulate for the first time an educational system in which literacy is a fundamental requirement ..., literature and literary culture [are] essential elements and political power the final aim.

(Morgan, 1998: 20)

Most commentators on Chinese education would agree with Zheng (1994), who remarks that Chinese rulers always saw schools in political terms and from the earliest times made serious efforts to control them accordingly. The system was elite-oriented, channeling scholars to government service. However, during neo-Confucian times it contained specialists who advocated mass education and inquiry (at a time when theocracies in Islam had closed down the early promise of Islamic education, and at a time when most European monarchs were illiterate). In this respect, note the example of the famous revisionist scholar Wang Yangming (1472–1528) who represents a dissident response to the reinstatement of Confucian thought following the establishment of the Ming Dynasty (1368). He held that knowledge and wisdom could be attained by individuals without extensively engaging with the Confucian classics, depending instead on experience and innate knowledge. His followers pursued the implications of this in the direction of individualism and egalitarianism. With reference to child development, he proposed

an analogy of child growth similar to that of the [later] Europeans Froebel and Pestalozzi: "Child nature enjoys freedom and fears restriction. It may be likened to a plant in its state of germination; left to itself, it will grow, but interfered with, it will wither and decay. In instructing the child, if his natural inclinations are stimulated, and his innermost self is made happy, there will be no end to his growth."

(Cleverley, 1985: 25)

Almost at the same time in the same area, another nonconventional thinker, Chen Xianzhang (1428–1500), advocated schooling forms that combined work with study in ways that would have appealed to some communist educators in that area much later.

Similarly, Aristotle and Quintilian suggest that schools most certainly were intended to transmit the values of the dominant culture so that young people (or more obviously, young men) acquired the civic virtues (dispositions that support participation in civic life and government). To turn this around, we may note that Confucius, and all the senior scholar–teachers who came after him, explicitly had a political agenda: They hoped to improve the state and the conditions of the people by improving the virtuousness of the rulers and of the administrative elite.

There are indications of tension and dissension, too. After the Romans had conquered Greece, they relied heavily on educated enslaved Greeks as teachers in their schools, but at the same time actually tried to ban the Greeks from delivering instruction in certain ways or in certain areas, it seems (Adams, 2003). And again, in Rome, as traditional Roman religion was giving way to Christianity, Emperor Justinian (for example) promulgated edicts that prohibited the teaching of the early literature of Christianity in Roman schools. This suggests that there were indeed teachers who were using the schools as sites for ideological subversion.

S/FL learning in ancient schooling

There is a danger of assuming that, because our present-day systems of education are (of course!) enlightened, by contrast, those of antiquity must not have been. At first blush, it seems that concepts of learning in both ancient East and ancient West may have been concerned with memorization and habit (from the point of view of the present de-emphasis of this in some areas of S/FL pedagogy), and it is tempting to immediately draw conclusions about associated values. However, close inspection is warranted, and assumptions should be questioned. Kelly's (1969) magisterial history of language teaching presents a picture of a continual oscillation between formal and functional approaches to S/F languages. For example, referring just to the introduction of new language material, he says:

> [D]uring the classical era...it was intuitive command of the target language that was required, formal knowledge being seen as a mere reinforcement of practical mastery.
>
> (Kelly, 1969: 7)

Kelly places the concept of induction as central to concepts of learning and exploration in ancient Europe. He then attributes to St. Augustine the application of this principle in education and the learning of words:

> In language, this implied that one was to seek a practical command of linguistic skills rather than memorize the rules. To meet this aim, St. Augustine popularized dialogued methods of teaching, making the pupil's role in the dialogue part of the act of discovery.
>
> (ibid.: 35)

Kelly does not mention that Augustine had knowledge of several languages. Though born in Africa, his first language was Latin (and of course he also knew Greek); in addition he had an extensive knowledge of the local language, Punic. In one of his letters, he chastised a colleague who had sneered at that language. Augustine comments that his colleague had "forgotten your identity, as an African writing for Africans" if he thinks "that Punic names should be criticized" (Adams, 2003: 239).

At some point after the development of Nalanda, there must have been a concern for translation in most of these universities. The spread of Buddhism was heavily associated with the work of translators, particularly between Sanskrit and Tibetan in one direction, and Sanskrit and Pali in another. And later, of course, translation from Greek to Latin and to Arabic was necessary. China did not have a need for bilinguals for administrative purposes during most of its history, and even invading tribes learned Chinese or took on Chinese characteristics. However, during this period, translators arose who had developed multilingual capabilities through growing up in "cultural borderlands" (Hung, 2005: 47–8). Hung notes that while "most of the Indian monks preaching in China during this period had little command of Chinese, the leading Central Asian monk-translators...master[ed]...Chinese.... Translators of Central Asian origin who grew up in China... received a bi-cultural education" in Buddhist as well as Confucian literature and languages. But overall, as Hung comments,

> Because of China's traditional sense of cultural superiority, translation activities were never the concern of the intellectual mainstream before the mid-19th century
>
> (2005: 56)

and this probably extends to a lack of foreign language emphasis in schools or colleges in this area as well.

In medieval times, Europe tended to access L2s by way of Latin. Courtenay remarks:

> Fourteenth-century education [in England] at the beginning level would seem strange and ill-conceived to the modern observer. The beginning student, usually about the age of seven, would first be taught the alphabet and then would be immediately introduced to the recognition and proper pronunciation of a useful but foreign language, Latin. . . . The child's [home] language would have been French or English. . . . French had commercial, administrative, and legal uses and, if not learned as a child, was taught at a later stage by way of Latin as part of a "business" curriculum.[13]
>
> (1987: 16)

Courtenay identifies education up until the 12th century as "almost exclusively for future ecclesiastics" (p. 17), but,

> by the early fourteenth century primary and grammar education were available throughout the cities and larger towns of England for those of even modest means and, in certain circumstances, for those with no financial means at all.
>
> (ibid.: 19)

Modern school

While I do not wish to suggest that the schools (as opposed to universities, academies, and colleges) that I have alluded to were totally different to school as we know it, one might want to ask whether there was somehow a smooth transition everywhere in the world to the institution we know as school these days, or whether there was to some extent a rupture of continuity. If we take the second viewpoint, it would be allied to a conception of the modern school as primarily associated *only* with those rapid and somehow distinct developments in Europe from the 16th century on, which directly or indirectly are associated with upsurges in science, technology, economics, and in due course political influence and colonialism.

One way to consider the changes is to recognize that the dominance of the West in political, economic, and educational arenas is a recent (and perhaps temporary) phenomenon. Prior to the 1500s, major cities in China were larger and more prosperous than many in Europe; knowledge of medicine and early science was probably better in China than in

Europe as late as the 14th century; at this time Damascus was perhaps a more civilized city than Paris. And later, around the time of the European "Enlightenment," the degree of development of Western and Eastern economies was similar. But according to the dominant interpretation, laws and societal values in China seem not to have encouraged the inquiries which led to the further or disparate growth of science in Europe; and commerce and communication, along with military and colonial exploration, seem to have been supported more outside of China at this crucial time.[14] So despite the establishment of a world system (e.g., Wallerstein, 1974), one increasingly distinct sector of the globe rapidly diverged from another that had previously been its equal or greater in economic development. In due course, some conceptions of school in the European sector also diverged to some extent from the early conceptions of educational institutions in Central and East Asia. When these two versions of school later came into contact again in the 19th century, what had perhaps been fairly similar to start with had by then come to be seen as different.

With the rise of the modern world and the associated European colonial and financial structures I have alluded to, many non-Western countries revised their existing concepts of school and took on board those circulating in Europe and European ex-colonies such as the United States. In many cases, this was the result of innovation-oriented local elites identifying school and the kinds of learning that followed it as implicated in the power of Western nations and trading networks. In other cases, of course, this was also the result of direct European colonialism. This continued for quite some time, in many cases up to the present day. As Spring comments:

> Formal Euroamerican school structures remained in place after independence from colonial rule in the Middle East, the Indian subcontinent, Sub-Saharan Africa, and Korea. The impact of imperialism transformed [Koranic] schools and madrasas and enfolded religious instruction into formal Euroamerican school structures, curricula, and pedagogy.
>
> (2006: 189)

Nonmodern philosophies in language teachers' developing philosophies of teaching

But what about the majority of present-day teachers of English who do not associate themselves with a tradition of ideas that has a European ancestry? Just because non-Western countries took on board, with mass schooling, "modern" ideas that were not part of their cultural inheritance, surely this does not mean that there is no room for, say,

42

Buddhist or Islamic philosophy within the philosophy of teaching of a non-Western teacher of English. Indeed, what about other ancient, rather than modern traditions, most obviously that of Christianity, within philosophy and the philosophy of a language teacher?[15] All major religious philosophy is premodern in origin, after all.

This is pretty difficult territory, particularly difficult to handle in a work of the present limited scope. The dominant traditions of the field being modernist, they have no particular connection with expressions of spirituality per se, and they are not familiar with religious philosophy, even though it stands just behind various important aspects of mainstream philosophy of education (in, for example, the thinking of Descartes, Kant, Hegel, and Dewey, at least). It is also difficult because within what might be presented as a single tradition, such as Buddhist philosophy, there are widely differing perspectives (both materialist and idealist, for example); Islamic perspectives clearly include both fundamentalist and speculative approaches, both historically and at present. I will in some places allude to the possibilities that the non-Western traditions of philosophy offer (for example, Confucian ethics), but I will not have space to fully develop them. A crucial point is that while these philosophies are certainly rich and diverse, they have usually not devoted themselves much to the institution and traditions of mass schooling. Thus, while Buddhist philosophy, for example, is extensive, Buddhist philosophy of education is not.

Concluding remark

For some readers, this detour through ancient history will mainly have restated familiar truths; for others, I hope that my revisionist emphasis with its orientation to the legitimate claims to early priority of areas *not* associated with English will be of use to current English language teachers. In brutal brevity, some of my main points and their implications are the following:

- School is not an inherently Western institution.
- Formal higher education is not necessarily Western in origin.
- A meritocratic, exam-driven education system feeding the state is not a Western invention.
- S/FL teaching has been involved in the processes of empire building (and maintenance) on various occasions.
- Right from the start, schools had a political role and were ideologically contested sites.
- Neither Western nor Eastern traditions of education are homogenous. The past of S/FL learning is not all memorization and translation, just as the past of child learning is not all beating and brutality.

43

- Mass schooling is only by accident "Western"; had China not turned away from science and technology, mass schooling by now would be an "Eastern" phenomenon.

Discussion questions

1. What is the significance of the fact that, during the history of China, Confucian ideas were submerged for a thousand years, for the concept of a Confucian heritage in certain education systems?
2. In what senses, in what contexts, or under what conditions does English manifest some of the characteristics of a "classical" language?
3. What do you think of the idea that school structures in countries such as Korea or Egypt could be said to be "Euroamerican"?
4. Why is it important to recognize the nonhomogeneity of trends in the history of language teaching?
5. Is it fair or unfair to draw parallels between Latin as an imperial language and present-day English? Was Chinese ever an imperial language? (Is it now?)
6. What is the role of second/foreign language teaching in the creation of a meritocracy? (Can a meritocracy exist?)

Notes to Chapter 2

[1] In a research review in a recent high-profile publication of the American Educational Research Association, Richardson and Placier (2001: 907) note that "ERIC...cites primarily studies of North American schools and classrooms." They go on to reference Fuller et al. (1994), remarking that "studies of U.S. schools and teachers cannot be generalized to nations with different political structures and cultures" (ibid.). For anthropologists this is a credo, but it is sometimes neglected in general reviews of ELT (or educational) research.

[2] Holliday (2005: 20) refers in a slightly jaded tone to the "current preoccupation among English-speaking Western ESOL educators with students from the Far East." This is unlikely to be merely a passing matter of fashion, if a geopolitical view is taken.

[3] There have to be some limitations on the international orientation and derivation of a work such as the present, however. I have chosen to emphasize an East–West perspective, with particular emphasis on the Chinese cultural area as the primary exponent of "East." This is at the expense of Indian and Islamic historical traditions (let alone others such as Central American or African), partly on the grounds that the Chinese cultural area represents the most active challenge of the early 21st century, and certainly an area in which the learning and teaching of English is particularly substantial.

There is one other divide similar to East–West, and that is "North–South," which refers to the divide between rich and poor countries. ELT is definitely involved in this, and it might play out in the philosophies of education of English language teachers.

For reasons of space I have chosen not to deal with this directly, even though I think it is important. (See Kenny & Savage, 1997.)

4 See also Lucas (1972), who is very much of the "nothing new under the sun" school, and Bowen (1972).

5 The letters of Cicero are one of the best-known literary sources of evidence for this, besides bureaucratic archives, etc. See Adams (2003).

6 Bilingualism, in the form of the preservation of local languages while elites acquired one of the classical administrative languages, is attested to repeatedly (Harris, 1989), again without evidence concerning how this happened.

7 We should recognize that during most of the history of formal teaching, elementary education and higher education have been by no means completely institutionally separate. Palmer (1985: 252) comments about much later times: "The pre-Revolutionary university colleges had admitted boys of twelve. The lower faculties of continental European (and Scottish) universities in the eighteenth century often did the same." The bulwark that has come between them, known as "secondary education," is a recent development. The term is attributed to the French mathematician, philosopher, and educational planner Condorcet, around 1792 (see Baker, 1976); however, a middle-grades–focused education was also to be found in the *colegio* of the Jesuits, from around the 1550s onward (Musumeci, 1997).

8 Now known as Taxila, presently in northern Pakistan.

9 The first instance of a madrasa was the Nizmiya, founded in Baghdad around 1064. This institution was set up particularly to be independent of mosque-based centers of learning, providing a higher education structure under the control of the civil power.

10 "The first seventy years of the Sung dynasty comprised a period of growth for the academics . . . the [next] century was a desolate phase in which all influential academies lay in ruins. . . . 1163–1194 [was] a revival phase in which some neo-Confucian officials rebuilt several famous academies and made use of the strength of local governments to support them strongly, even though the central government disliked them." (Zheng, 1994: 201).

11 This was a classicizing return to supposedly ancient traditions, after a thousand years during which Buddhist philosophy was the dominant tradition in China (cf. e.g., Van Norden, 2004).

12 Though Cleverley (1985: 8) notes that the *Book of Rites*, which of the nine basic Confucian texts was the one most focused on education, mentions that *young* students were forbidden to ask questions.

13 See also Pennycook (1989) on 14th-century French for Business Purposes.

14 Chinese maritime adventuring and trade had become quite extensive. Voyages of exploration under Admiral Zheng He involved resources a hundred times greater than those of the Europeans and reached as far as the Middle East. However, they came to an abrupt and complete end after 1433. This inward turn was greatly to the advantage of the West.

15 There is also the matter of the practical association of the proselytizing practices of one specific religion, Christianity, with the teaching of a specific language, English. The academic part of the field of TESOL is just starting to come to grips with this in print, but as this discussion is only just beginning, I am not going to address the topic in the present work. See Johnston & Varghese (2006) and Pennycook & Coutand-Marin (2004), for the beginning of what looks to be an extended debate.

3 Language teaching traditions in historical and philosophical context

Introduction

The present chapter continues the historical focus and brings the periods under consideration to the immediate recent past. Schooling in antiquity was a phenomenon thinly spread over all literate civilizations. For the modern period, by contrast, most scholars would see it transfigured into "mass education," a social innovation emanating from Europe, spreading rapidly throughout the rest of the world, and involved in the clash of civilizations that characterizes this period. Thus this chapter will start with a Western focus.[1] Now, let me emphasize a crucial part of the rationale for this chapter. Our field has been bedeviled by ahistorical, decontextual presentations of "Methods," from which otherwise teachers might derive some aspects of their philosophies of teaching. The field also continues to be vitiated by the expectations (fostered perhaps by textbook publishers) that there is something "new" on the horizon that will solve our present problems. Consideration of the historical record of language teaching (rare in itself) rapidly shows how false these positions are. It is very important for teachers who want a well-grounded philosophy of teaching to see something of the complex but not inherently progressive history of our field. In addition, such a review will demonstrate how some of the philosophical issues are always present to be grappled with in the work of teachers and the structures of education.

Humanism (from the 1400s forward)

The development of some (though not all) concepts of education to be found in modern times can be identified in the history of education in Europe beginning with the period known as the Renaissance (1400–1600), and continuing with the period following it, self-described as the Enlightenment (1700–1800).[2] During the Renaissance in particular, philosophers, educators, and literati benefited from, and continued, the recovery and reworking of the ideas that Islamic scholars had transmitted to Europe from ancient Greece and Rome. In doing this, they developed a modern version of humanism: the position that values positively the capabilities of human beings as rational, capable of self-determination, having the potential to make the world a better place, and other optimistic understandings of humans that had been very much absent in the immediately preceding centuries in Europe.

For our field, Musumeci's (1997) work provides a detailed discussion of FL educators in the European tradition, and initially picks up the story at the time of the European Renaissance. S/FL education in Europe after the fall of the Roman Empire can be seen as first a loss, and then a regaining of, (elite) L2 literacy. The Renaissance begins with the rise of political and economic strength in the 1400s, the development of printing in the West, and a time when "Latin and Greek manuscripts were discovered almost daily" (Musumeci, 1997: 11). These writings were seen as containing knowledge of other, older cultures, which were actually in some respects much more advanced than European cultures of the 15th century. Thus they were sources of considerable potential power. As Musumeci says, "Learning Latin in the fifteenth century was not very different from learning English today" (p. 10). That is to say, Latin then was as English is today, an international "auxiliary" language of power, spreading well beyond any one nation–state.

The development of S/FL abilities was central to the development of a philosophically distinct and new (or at least, newly rediscovered) position in education. In this context, "Renaissance humanism" was a reaction against the existing systems of education, which were theocentric, oriented to faith and authority rather than inquiry, and of course, entirely dominated by the Christian Church. This response was generated and made possible by the sudden availability of sources from Greece and Rome that presented alternative ways of thinking and being. Somewhat new curricular areas, such as history, literature, and moral philosophy, became known as the humanities and were advanced partly "as a course of study whose function was the formation of good citizens . . . especially those who would be in authority" (Musumeci, 1997: 12–13). In this period, S/FL learning of the main international language was not just for instrumental purposes, then; this appears to be an accurate description of the immediate subsequent developments. Humanism, or at least the humanities, were a central part of the curriculum in Jesuit schools; these schools were the most advanced in Europe in the 16th century. Second-language teaching (of Latin) continued to be proposed because its content (the wisdom of the classical authors) was an aid to individual development. The intent of Jesuit humanistic bilingual competence was that it should contribute to producing a "more widespread good" than that of the preexisting scholastic tradition (Loyola, 1547/1959: 134).

In looking at the history of S/FL teaching, even the briefest inspection of early sources shows us that much that we might think of as new is just old wine in new bottles. Kelly's (1969) exhaustive analytic treatment makes this point repeatedly. A related position is that trends or concepts that one might have thought preceded or followed one another are, on closer inspection, to be found concurrently. At one particular time, first one position may be dominant and the other more marginalized; then these positions may reverse themselves. Musumeci follows Titone (1968, 2000; see also Mackey, 1965) in identifying two poles between which advice to S/FL teachers has oscillated during the whole of the modern period in European history – Titone calls them the "formal" and the "functional" approaches. For much of the period between the 15th and 17th centuries, S/FL teachers emphasized natural language learning for and through communication – Titone's functional pole. However, the formal pole was quick to reassert itself. Musumeci provides the example of a Renaissance S/FL teaching specialist who emphasized a functional perspective – this was Xavier Guarino, a teacher (and author of S/FL teaching handbooks) who focused on meaning and communication. However, his son, also a well-known language specialist, emphasized the minutiae of grammatical detail. Similarly, though according to Loyola's initial conception, Jesuit bilingual education was to take place through extensive use of the target language throughout all instruction and student activities and discussion, his immediate successors promulgated a detailed interpretation of his ideas in a way that violated their spirit, rigidifying them away from learning through use. In particular, as the Renaissance moved toward the Enlightenment, the power of Latin as a means of international communication faded, and schools no longer functioned in Latin; in the absence of a communicative or functional orientation, instructors fell back on rule learning and rules for learning. These rules were enumerated and prescribed at inordinate length in the Jesuits' *Ratio Studiorum*, officially issued in 1599. In Musumeci's account (based on Fitzpatrick, 1933), this exhaustive and tedious *Plan of Study* explains to a large extent the reputation that schools had prior to the reforms of the Enlightenment period: as places of repetitive routine and ineffective schooling, particularly with the study of Latin as a second language reduced to a boring and unsuccessful treatment of grammatical rules and errors.

One of the greatest early specialists in second or foreign language learning and teaching appears on the scene in Europe just as that part of the world ceases to be unified by a commitment to Latin as the widespread second language of scholarship and international commerce. Johannes Comenius, from Moravia (now part of the Czech Republic), wrote widely during the 17th century (*floruit* 1630–50), and his works continued to be republished during the next two centuries, as S/FL teachers found them inspirational. His long career had many ups and downs, and he moved across Europe and resided for some years in a variety of countries, including Hungary, Poland, and England,[3] and had what we would these days call consultancies with authorities in Sweden. Besides running schools, Comenius gained fame as a textbook writer (introducing almost for the first time the use of visual aids in support of language teaching); he also wrote about the theory and practice of language teaching. The quick swings of the pendulum that were found, between, for example, the first works of Loyola and their subsequent codification, Musumeci also finds *within* Comenius himself. Although he certainly expressed a strong preference for language teaching that began with meaning and content (rather than grammar), and attacked memorization, he also backpedaled on these positions. And as someone heavily committed to the textbook, perhaps the first really successful textbook writer in our field, he left little room for the professionalism or independent practice of the teacher, it seems. Titone, discussing Comenius's ideas, is less concerned with their contradictions, and sees them, together with those of Rousseau, as to be found in the S/FL specialists who represented the best of the functional tradition, especially in Germany, before the pendulum swung against them in the 1800s. This position is echoed by Musumeci (1997: 116) looking back on all three of her founding figures of applied linguistics: "the second language teaching theory advocated by educational reformers of the fifteenth, sixteenth, and seventeenth centuries bears a remarkable resemblance to what the profession knows today as 'communicative language teaching.'"

The philosophical positions of Comenius echoed two broader educational developments that were just beginning in his time: first, the move to mass education, and second, the concept of the "whole child." More than his immediate predecessors in language teaching, he clearly foreshadowed the democratic tradition in schooling; he cites Martin Luther in calling for mass education. In fact, he claims that "with the proper method one teacher can instruct many children, hundreds in fact, simultaneously, just like the printing press turns out books" (Musumeci, 1997: 84, paraphrasing Comenius, 1657). The emphasis on mass education is important for us; at this point in time we see a move in the world of ideas that shifts the teacher's responsibility from serving the elite to serving the people. Comenius, it seems, was part of the tide of the times that wanted to see general education in literacy, partly in his case for religious reasons,[4] and he had a vision for a new society in which every village would have a school.

On the second of these developments, the idea of educating the "whole child," two early advocates of this concept in education besides Comenius were Montaigne (1533–92) and Locke (1632–1704). Though each wrote only briefly about education, their views were influential.

The former, "under the influence of humanism... broke away from the classic intellectualism.... Children should not be filled with book wisdom but be able to form their own opinions" (Koops, 2003: 6, concerning Montaigne, 1575). Locke's position that we begin as blank slates provides important epistemological support for the crucial role of the teacher. His position that "every man was born with the perfect freedom to enjoy rights to property, liberty, life, and choice of religious belief" was enormously influential on educational (and political) experiments and initiatives, including the American and French Revolutions (Dupuis, 1966: 112). Particularly intriguing is his critique of some aspects of the humanist tradition that preceded him (of Guarino, Loyola, etc., discussed above). Humanists had tended to concentrate on the development of intellectual talents alone. Locke

> had intimated that the school had failed to educate a person if his physical, moral, and emotional development had not been cared for.
>
> (Dupuis, 1966: 103)

Even though it was Rousseau and his followers, a century later, who really took up the implications of this, some would attribute to Locke the first articulation of the "whole child theory," the idea that "the division of the child for educational purposes... violated nature" (ibid.).[5] Lawton and Gordon comment:

> Locke believed that unhappy experiences caused children to dislike those aspects of learning with which the experience was associated. Though the teacher's authority was to be firmly established, he urged that "playing and childish actions are to be left perfectly free and unrestrained"... Latin should be taught colloquially, learning by heart was "useless."
>
> (2002: 202)

It is true that Locke differs from Comenius and indeed from many others in this child-oriented line by his assumption that the child's mind is initially a *tabula rasa* or "white paper on wax," but he was "one of the earliest educationists to make a link between pedagogy and theories of childhood" (Lawton & Gordon, 2002: 203).

Even in this early phase of modernity, then, we can see second and foreign language teaching specialists in tune with the advanced pedagogical ideas of their times (many of which are also still current). And we can see language teaching as naturally incorporating particular philosophical understandings of the learner, of the mind, and of the role of school in society.

The 18th century in Europe

Mass education

Throughout the 18th century, the modern nation–state was beginning to take shape. Arguments for universal public education were increasingly made by what we would now call "right" and "left" (respectively, Smith, 1776;[6] and Condorcet, e.g., 1791; cf. Rothschild, 1998). Reforming administrations began to see the need for developments in science and technology as a way of strengthening their countries. The state began to reform the universities. At the beginning of the century, for example, in the progressive state of Brandenburg, the new University of Halle was set up and swiftly became a center of "objectivity and rationalism, scientific attitudes, and free investigation" in which German, no longer Latin, was the main language used. Electives and seminars were introduced (replacing the previous fixed curriculum). Even lectures were a new departure, replacing the study of texts; and professors acquired much greater autonomy. The curriculum as a whole was reworked to train officials and bureaucrats, rather than clergy (Ford, 2002: 27).

Between the mid-1700s and the early 1800s, almost all European countries moved to develop, reform, and expand schooling; in the forefront were Prussia, France, and the northern United States, with southern Europe and England[7] (Green, 1990, 1997; Palmer, 1985) lagging well behind. It appears that it was not the quality of the private sector that was at issue, but that it failed to provide anything beyond instruction in literacy:

> The most common objection of civic leaders to private schools was that such schools were not socializing children in accord with political, moral, or religious values that reformers thought important. . . . In Baden the official 1834 school code stated that "Children are to be impressed with the duty of loyalty to the Grand Duke, love of fatherland, obedience to laws and ordinances, attentiveness to religious and secular authorities . . . and to their duties toward their fellow citizens." (Maynes, 1985: 50). In nineteenth-century Russia, peasant-sponsored schools were labeled by government officials as "wild schools." [(Eklof, 1986) reports that] a Russian finance minister asserted that "the fact that literacy was growing more rapidly than the school system represented a major political danger."
>
> (Mitch, 1992: 37)

And the actors here were not the governments of the most-developed countries, but rather those in states which lagged in development

Values, Philosophies, and Beliefs in TESOL

somewhat yet had growing hopes of international advancement, such as Prussia, Austria–Hungary, and Sweden.

Ideas of democracy and citizenship were developing during this time, although their most formal practice (voting) was restricted to men and usually excluded the poor. In France after the Revolution, by 1803 the vote was tied to a literacy test; some intellectuals supported education to develop an educated leadership as "especially necessary in a state founded on a democratic basis" (de Staël, 1801, cited in Palmer, 1985: 224). The United States, having already had its revolution, may have been in advance of such thinking. Jefferson advocated universal elementary education as early as 1797, and also worked for the establishment of meritocratic higher education.[8] His ideas were not to bear fruit in the United States until later, but for a short period around this time the French state put into place the beginnings of progressive education.

In France, beginning in 1795, about 100 "central schools" were established, serving about 10,000 students per year at their height. As Palmer says, they were remarkably modern:

> They had virtually no admission requirements, no graded classes, and no set term of years of study.... Instruction was by "courses" rather than "classes," that is, each teacher taught only his own subject; and lecturing, supplemented by questions and discussion, was favored over drill and recitation. All courses were electives for the students, and examinations were optional for the professors. There was no religious instruction.... The planners meant to favor science and mathematics and a modern approach to other subjects, so that the student of grammar, for example, was not to learn arbitrary rules but to understand the reasons underlying them.... The faculty of each school was self-governing; there was no principal or head.... They were "comprehensive" in stressing both cultural and vocational aims, and in teaching the sons of both professional elites and artisan and shopkeeping families... The schools were likewise open to the community in that each had a library open to the public, and adults were welcomed in the classrooms to hear lectures or observe scientific demonstrations, so that instruction of the young was blended with continuing education.
>
> (1985: 243–4)

Clearly these schools were far ahead of their time, and lasted only a few years (until about 1802).

The whole child: Rousseau and his followers

At the same time as the state was taking an increasing interest in education, for reasons of national development, and while the first tinges

52

of education for citizenship were appearing, a somewhat separate, idealistic movement began to appear that was to eventually be the basis
of liberal and progressive trends associated with the writer Jean-Jacques
Rousseau and the Romantic movement. Ideas of freedom alluded to earlier were taken to a more extreme position in Rousseau's idealistic writings. His works were widely read and controversial. Though by no means
uncontradictory nor in all ways modern,[9] he articulated many ideas that
were taken up by forward-thinking educators and which can certainly
still be found in progressive educational views today (not to mention
ES/FL "learner-centered" programs, and even SLA theory). These ideas
included an emphasis on the child as the center of education (rather
than the teacher) and on the child's needs and developmental stages.
He emphasized (as Lawton & Gordon, 2002: 96, point out) ideas such
as "readiness, child-centered . . . learning from discovery and personal
experience . . . and teacher-pupil contracts." In his novel *Emile*, Rousseau
(1762) gives his account of an approach to teaching in which the inherent goodness of a child would not be ruined by the need to prepare
him or her for citizenship. This fictional narrative presented an apparent success story of the benefits of his methods. Though quite untested
in practice, the documentary-like quality of this work gripped readers
and led to the wide dissemination of his ideas. Rousseau himself never
put into practice any of his educational ideas, and there is little evidence that they were acted upon by French state educators during the
Revolution. However, some of them were tested and incorporated into
the actual practice of a few go-ahead educators. Radical writers like
William Godwin added to the developments by arguing for a conception
of the child as an inherently autonomous moral being, and thus one who
should in no way be subject to coercion while being educated (Godwin,
1793a, b).

By the second half of the century, a variety of small-scale initiatives were apparently in progress. For example, "David Manson (1726–
92) . . . ran his own private school in Belfast that had no corporal punishment and used various 'play way' techniques to encourage the children
of the poor to achieve" (Lawton & Gordon, 2002: 97). More substantial
were the efforts of the German innovators known as the Philanthropists,
associated with Johann Bernhard Basedow (1723–90) and his school
(the Philanthropium) at Dessau. This school (and teacher-training facil-
ity) included:

> a curriculum designed to meet the natural needs of the pupils.
> Physical and vocational education were central activities in the
> curriculum; only the practical aspects of science, mathematics,
> and language were taught. Even grammar, which constituted
> the heart of the classical curriculum, was practically eliminated.

> Dancing, music, and art were included for their recreational value
> or as opportunities for some pupils to follow special interests.
>
> (Dupuis, 1966: 105–6, referring to Basedow, 1770–72/1990)

> The school was based on the notion that education should be
> an enjoyable experience, and that children should be treated
> as children.... Like Comenius, Basedow emphasized the need
> to reduce memory work and instead, use children's senses to
> make acquaintance with the world. In many ways the activities
> of the Philanthropium [constituted] a forerunner of the modern
> activities curriculum.
>
> (Lawton & Gordon, 2002: 204)

That Lawton and Gordon can push the beginnings of "the modern activities curriculum" this far back is noteworthy, as it is also a close cousin of some of the most recent developments in language curricula at the beginning of the 21st century.

Other developments that seem very much ahead of their time are to be found in the first substantial effort to fuse some of the ideas of the French Revolution with S/FL teaching – this comes to us from the work of Jean-Joseph Jacotot (1770–1840), whose ideas were published in 1830. Here I rely completely on Howatt's summary of his work.

After being active in revolutionary politics as a young man, Jacotot briefly became a professor of Latin, and then joined the French revolutionary army. After the fall of Napoleon, he taught French at a university in the Flemish-speaking part of Belgium:

> Jacotot's students were asked to acquire copies of Fénelon's
> *Les Aventures de Télémaque* along with a Flemish translation.
> Unable to translate or explain, Jacotot read the first sentence, and
> then returned to the opening phrase and read it again: "*Calypso
> ne pouvoit,* ...." He asked his students to hunt through the rest
> of the book for further examples of the words he had just read.
> *Ne*, of course, was common enough, *Calypso* turned up occasionally, and *pouvoit* (or something that looked like it) from
> time to time as well. Then Jacotot returned to the beginning
> of the text and added the next phrase: "*Calypso ne pouvoit se
> consoler,* ...." The research activities were repeated, and the
> process continued: "*Calypso ne pouvoit se consoler du départ
> d'Ulysse.*" As the course proceeded, the students came to know
> the text by heart, and Jacotot supplemented the text-study with
> comprehension questions and other forms of linguistic work,
> insisting that the students should look for similarities and differences, generalize their observations, form and test hypotheses,
> and discover how the language worked.

What struck Jacotot most forcibly was the irrelevance of explanation. This, naturally enough, came as a complete surprise to him. How can you claim to be a language teacher if you cannot explain anything, had been his immediate thought on arriving at Louvain. He now realized that not only was explanation unnecessary, it was actually wrong. All his radical ideals were roused by this insight which he developed at some length in his *Enseignement universel, langue etrangère* (1830). Every individual had a God-given ability to instruct himself. The function of a teacher was to respond to the learner, not to direct and control him by explaining things in advance. This philosophy also chimed with his belief that everyone had equal intelligence, and that inherited differences in ability did not exist. His answer to the obvious counterargument that some individuals achieve more than others was that, given sufficient strength of will and determination, these differences would disappear.

(Howatt, 1984: 150–51)

The notion of teacher as facilitator, the dismissal of conservative theories of intelligence, and an understanding of self-instruction similar to that of the late 20th-century alternative method "The Silent Way" – these are a remarkable set of precursor attributes.

Pestalozzi, natural approaches, and conversation schools

Pestalozzi (1746–1827) is identified by some as just as influential as Rousseau. His accounts of educational practice, though also novelistic (e.g., Pestalozzi, 1781), were based in actual practice, with the children of the poor. After some earlier efforts, he ran a boarding school (at Yverdon, in Switzerland) for about twenty years. He took the view (like Rousseau) that the child is by nature good and has the potential to improve the world. Because of his emphasis on a curriculum that addressed intellectual, physical, and moral domains, Pestalozzi could be said to presage holistic approaches to education. For him, school was "to be a model community which civil rulers might adapt to the larger community" and thus was also "perhaps the first statement of the notion that the school should be the model for a new social order" (Dupuis, 1966: 106). In due course, he and his followers came to be called the *"vom Kinde aus"* movement ("from the child itself"). The following quotation from Pestalozzi suggests the quite radical nature of his views: "Everything you are, everything you want, everything you should [be], comes from yourself" (Koops, 2003: 6). The long duration of this experimental school allowed it to be visited by other educators who went on to develop new or at least different ideas about education, such as Froebel (the inventor of the *kindergarten*, 1837), Herbart, and Mayo.

Historians of S/FL teaching have noted the importance of Pestalozzi for modern lines in curriculum and method. Kelly attributes to Pestalozzi the first formulation of the "principle of complete reliance on oral–aural training in the first stages of a new language" (1969: 313). Howatt (1984) is more emphatic and has more to say, attributing all modern "natural approaches" to the example provided by Pestalozzi and his development of the "object-lesson." This was central to Pestalozzi's work, and indeed has become an idiom with a distinct meaning. (It was also rapidly disseminated into the English-speaking world, by Mayo, 1832.) Accordingly, it deserves a more detailed explanation:

> Pestalozzi was a sense-empiricist in the Baconian tradition whose cardinal principle of *Anschauung* (intuitive observation or contemplation) required that children focus in the first instance on objects . . . second, like Comenius, he was concerned with form in the presentation of knowledge and the structuring of teaching. Each subject had to be broken down into its constituents that were then reorganized in a logical relationship and presented to pupils in carefully graded steps.
>
> (Alexander, 2000: 310)

The development and extension of this idea by one of Pestalozzi's followers leads us in a direct route to modern practices in S/FL teaching. Howatt presents the story as follows:

> One of Pestalozzi's disciples in Germany was a schoolteacher called Gottlieb Heness who applied the object-lesson technique to the teaching of standard German to his dialect-speaking pupils in south Germany. His success encouraged him to think of broadening the method to the teaching of German as a foreign language, and an opportunity to experiment along these lines came while he was on a trip to America in 1865. . . . [This] was an outstanding success and Heness decided to extend the idea even further and set up a language school of his own. For commercial reasons he needed to offer French as well as German [and collaborated with] Lambert Sauveur. . . . Sauveur and Heness moved to Boston in 1869 and opened a School of Modern Languages in the city.
>
> [M]ost of the Heness-Sauveur courses . . . consisted of a hundred hours of intensive instruction, two hours a day, five days a week, for four and a half months. . . . [In Sauveur's course] the first five lessons are on parts of the body and obviously [he]

made considerable use of gesture in conveying meaning....He followed two basic principles. The first was only to ask what he called *"earnest questions."* What he meant was genuine questions, not in the sense that he was seeking information he did not possess, but in the sense that he was genuinely looking for an answer....

Sauveur's second principle of linguistic organization in the use of classroom language was *coherence*: "to connect scrupulously the questions in such a manner that one may give rise to another." This principle probably explains his success in communicating with his students better than anything else. They understood what he was talking about because they were able to predict the course of the conversation....

Within a decade or so the Natural Method, as the Sauveur approach was known, had become the most seriously considered new development in language teaching in America.

(Howatt, 1984: 197–201)

Some criticisms were made (Kroeh, 1887). First, that the emphasis on conversation led to exchanges on topics that were trivial. Howatt's view is that this concern persisted and "helps to explain [the] relative failure" of direct methods in regular schools in the first half of the 20th century. Second, that "the teacher is required to do a disproportionate share of the work." Accepting this point, Howatt notes that "student interaction is the most significant feature of modern versions of 'natural methods,' but it took a long time to be accepted" (1984: 202).

At almost the same time and place as Sauveur and Heness developed and succeeded with their approach, a closely parallel arrangement was begun under a much more famous name. In 1878, Maximilian Berlitz, a German immigrant to the United States in his late twenties, opened a language school in Providence, Rhode Island. Like Heness, he needed a teacher of French and hired Nicholas Joly, who, without direct input from Berlitz (who was more the administrator) began to use something similar to the Sauveur-Heness approach. As Howatt notes, it is intriguing that this partnership was working in the same geographic area as the other one. The "Berlitz Method" was basically another version of the direct or natural method. However, although

"[n]atural methods" had started well and attracted professional interest and support...the ordinary schools of America, or anywhere else at the time, would never have adopted "natural methods." The teachers would not have known what to do, and parents would have been horrified at the loss of prestige

57

> that "ordinary conversation" implied. Natural methods required schools of their own . . .
>
> (Howatt, 1984: 202)

Although before the 19th century it hardly makes much sense to differentiate between a dominant state sector and a private sector of education, and although clearly there has always been a small handful of language tutors serving business and diplomacy, it seems that along with the growth in mass state-education systems, it is in the late 19th century, and particularly with the efforts of Berlitz, that we see the takeoff into major growth of the private language school as a distinct, separate entity with its own special characteristics. The prominence of an entirely different approach to language teaching is one of these characteristics; the other is its separate development from early considerations of "the profession" of education:

> Berlitz catered for beginners. . . . The teacher's directions are very clear and straightforward. . . . His teachers were all native speakers, a cardinal Berlitz principle, and this meant in practice that most of them were young and there was inevitably a high turnover of staff. Training could not go very deep, nor did Berlitz put many resources into it. . . . Except in rare circumstances, it was not a career in itself and neither the teachers nor the schools treated it as one. The Berlitz system was intended to be a "teacher proof" system for relatively inexperienced, and not always very highly motivated, teachers.
>
> (Howatt, 1984: 205)

The changing times had produced either a new kind of language student[10] or at least enough of them so that a new kind of school was warranted and feasible. "The *Gymnasium* teachers scarcely knew such a world existed, and even the Vietor-Sweet reformers were a long way from seeing language in this straightforward, utilitarian light" (Howatt, 1984: 207). The utilitarian tradition is an inheritance that certainly persists to this day.[11]

Herbart and the rise of educational psychology

During this period we find the first cases of what has become an important pattern for S/FL teaching: the influence from the field of psychology. All the social sciences are products of the 19th century, and psychology and its subdiscipline educational psychology are no exceptions. One of the foremost early specialists was Johann Friedrich Herbart (1776–1841). Though he drew on psychology, Herbart differed from later mainstream manifestations of this discipline by giving priority to values over empirical evidence:

> Pedagogy as a science depends on ethics and psychology. The first provides the aim of pedagogy; the latter shows us the way, the means, and the obstacles.
>
> (Herbart, 1835, cited in Koops, 2003: 6)

In his psychology,

> Herbart visualized three levels in the development of the mind: first, sensations and perceptions; second, imagination and memory; and third, conceptual thinking and judgment. One special mental function . . . [was] "apperception," the linking of new knowledge with previous teaching and similar ideas already experienced by the student.
>
> (Lawton & Gordon, 2002: 206)

Clearly this was a forerunner of constructivist psychological theory. According to Koops, Herbart developed

> didactics based on developmental psychological theory. Taking into account the state of insight into cognitive development at his time, Herbart . . . laid the foundation of . . . instruction[al] technology.
>
> (Koops, 2003: 7)

Following on from Pestalozzi's principle of *Anschauung*, Herbartian lessons used "the classic scheme of motivation, creating clarity, association with the known, synthesis and application" (Depaepe, 1998: 123, cited in Koops, 2003: 8). This can also be presented as "clarity, association, system and method, in which teaching proceeded from first-hand observation on the basis of association of ideas" (Alexander, 2000: 311). The Herbartian pedagogy was, then, intended to be a direct reflection of what was known at that time (or in Herbart's theory) of human learning. Herbart's five steps, as set out in his *Plan of Lectures on Pedagogy* (1835) were:

- Preparation. Pupil's past ideas and memories relating to the topic being discussed in class are necessary for assimilation;
- Presentation. The ordering of material so that the pupil fully understands it;
- Association. Comparison with ideas previously brought up in class to be thoroughly assimilated;
- Generalization. An essential step in the development of the mind involving the analysis of sensory experiences;

> • Application. The final stage in the acquisition of knowledge by using it in the interpretation of life.
>
> (Lawton & Gordon, 2002: 206)

Overarching this was the idea that learning (and ability) were not innate; thus, education had great moral force through its effect on character. These ideas were rapidly transported across the Atlantic and manifested in manuals for Herbartian practice in the English-speaking world (e.g., Bowen, 1981; McMurray, 1903) and presumably elsewhere. In the process they became more mechanical than originally intended (cf. Alexander, 2000). Somewhat condensed, they also form the basis for a long-standing tradition in ELT pedagogy: Presentation, Practice, and exPloitation.

Reactions and other reforms

It was not the case that, because of Rousseauian and Pestalozzian ideas, all was very progressive in the 19th century. Reaction was not slow, in some cases specifically responding to political change. Poised against the child-centered tradition was a horrifyingly industrial approach to classroom instruction, developed in the black heart of the Industrial Revolution (namely, England), and called the "monitorial method."[12] Popular in both England and then France, the monitorial method was presented as an improvement over both individual instruction (common in small rural schools) and whole-class instruction. In this system, one teacher taught the material to a set of "monitors," or "pupil-teachers" – senior pupils who simply taught it in turn to the other students. Through human mechanism, subject matter was cheaply transmitted to hundreds of students using the cheapest means, the students themselves. However, in France by the mid-century, "monitorial pedagogy had been largely superseded by a return to *l'enseignement simultané* or a combination... of simultaneous teaching, more or less homogenous groups, and monitorial support or supervision" (Alexander, 2000: 57).[13]

Swift rise and fall also affected Herbart's work. Although his ideas were very popular in the late 19th century, unfortunately, as with other pioneering efforts, Herbartian ideas were traduced by their subsequent followers. In particular, these lost sight of motivation, and advocated passivity and intellectualizing. By 1900, Herbart's ideas were criticized as promoting "docile, patriotic character formation through scholastic curricula" (Strasser & Monshouwer, 1967, cited in Koops, 2003: 8), with the student's role that of repeating and imitating the teacher. And similarly, Pestalozzi's ideas along with Herbart's were institutionalized in the Prussian education system (by Ziller and Rein, says Alexander), where they met a similar fate of formalization and ritualization.[14]

The originally good intentions of the child-centered school had been led astray, and decline led in turn to a range of reform movements. The best-known reformer in the English-speaking world is perhaps Dewey, but others were Decroly, Claparède (cf. Koops, 2003) and later more extreme though perhaps better-known names such as Steiner and Montessori, Petersen of the Jena Plan, and Parkhurst of the Dalton Plan. There were also the reformers of language teaching. At the risk of over-simplifying, the perception of many language educators toward the end of the century was that the preceding period had overemphasized structure, drill, and translation. Against this in turn, the late-19th-century Reform Movement language specialists rose up. In doing so, they drew on the influence of Froebel and Herbart on educational systems and practices:

> Herbart's theories of education and learning were the basis of the teaching practice of the Direct Method. As language was a matter of organized perception, teaching it involved obser-vation lessons...which gave the pupil direct experience of the language and its reality. The five steps of the Herbartian lesson can be seen in every treatment of the Direct Method: they were preparation (revision of old material), presentation (imparting new facts), association (of the new with the old), systematization (recapitulation of the new work in its context), and application (practice).
>
> (Kelly, 1969: 312)

In other words, these reform movements, which are sometimes taken as the beginning of modern Methods or language-teaching traditions, far from being a new beginning, emerged from established if somewhat alternative lines of pedagogical thought that represented quite progres-sive thinking that had been lost sight of. In that sense, there has been much reinventing of the wheel in language-teaching traditions, it seems.

The 20th century

Western and Eastern Progressives

The ideas of the reformers of the 19th century, perhaps in decline under the pressure of institutionalization as the century closed, received fresh energy from the major movement of the early 20th century in education, the Progressive Movement. This is associated with philosopher John Dewey, and with the philosophical school of "pragmatism," and took off from the burgeoning economic and cultural power of the United States in the early years of the 1900s. In Chicago, Dewey began to explore the ideas of previous educational innovators, and also reacted against the mechanization of their ideas that had become widespread. With his daughter Evelyn, he

> visited and observed the best...experimental schools in the nation, showing how they applied various educational theories, by Rousseau, Herbart, Froebel, Pestalozzi – and Dewey....Most of the schools...[can] be considered "child-centered" schools, – that is, teaching at the place where the child's readiness resides, schools in which learning occurs by doing and doing flourishes through liberty.
>
> (Martin, 2002: 155–6)

Educators in this tradition believed that education should help the child to develop as a human being, and also that school should be a force for the improvement (in democratic and peaceful ways) of society as a whole.

To give an example of what this tradition looked like in its full flowering, here is a concise summary of the New York City "Activity Program":

> The Progressive Movement in America was the foundation for the Activity Program, a 6-year experiment beginning in 1934. Eventually involving 75,000 students and 2,200 teachers in 69 schools, it became the largest demonstration of progressive practices in the nation.... [M]ajor concepts in the Activity Program were (a) children as well as teachers participate in selecting subject matter and planning activities; (b) the program centers on the needs and interests of individuals and groups; (c) time schedules are flexible ... ; (d) learning is largely experimental and inquiry-based; (e) formal recitation is supplemented by conferences, excursions, research, dramatization, construction and sharing, interpreting and evaluating; (f) discipline is based on self-control rather than on imposed control; (g) teachers are encouraged to assume responsibility for what transpires in their classrooms; (h) the teacher enjoys considerable freedom in connection with the course of study, time schedules, and procedure; and (i) emphasis is placed on instruction and creative expression in the arts and crafts.
>
> (Gallego et al., 2001: 972)

Major elements of this initiative, notably (a), (b), (d), and (e), show up in the ELT traditions fifty years later, collectively in various aspects of communicative approaches of the 1970s, with (a) particularly visible in some of the task-based (Candlin, 1984) and critical (Crawford-Lange, 1981) approaches of the 1980s.

This growing tradition was, like other lines in Western education, rapidly exported outside its home base.[15] As Western influence had expanded, it had taken with it educational ideas implemented by the various missionary societies, directly or indirectly associated with colonialism. Many independent non-Western states, seeing the advantages that a technology-oriented education had brought Western nations, also initiated their own versions of such school systems.[16] On China, Cleverley comments:

> Modern schooling initiated by the Chinese themselves began in the 1860s when a group of reformers, fearful of long term occupation by foreign powers, introduced a self strengthening movement.... Applying the pretext, Chinese learning for 'essence' and Western learning for 'application', its leaders initiated technical and professional training for the ends of war and diplomacy. The first enterprise, the Tongwenguan School of Combined Learning, opened in Beijing in 1861, principally training interpreters in English, Russian and French.[17]
>
> (1985: 34)

A similar story can be told for Japan, which began its modernization process earlier and moved faster and with more success, beginning to emulate Western powers with military defeats of China and Russia and the development of colonies on the Chinese periphery. The influence of Prussian educational ideas was widespread.

Both these powerful Asian countries also entered phases of democratization and were actively engaged, for a while, in the uptake of progressive educational (and other) influences emanating from the West (or from dominant modernist sectors of it; although such influences came from the West, this does not mean that they were mainstream or widely adopted in that area). After 1919, some sectors of the Chinese elite were in search, according to Cleverley,

> for more democratic forms of schooling.... The Ministry of Education turned to the progressives of Europe and America for inspiration. Many innovative educators were hosted in China after World War I, among whom were E. P. Cubberly, W. H. Kilpatrick, Von Driesch, Bertrand Russell, Paul Monroe, Rabindranath Tagore and John Dewey. Experiments began with schemes like the Dalton Plan, the Batavia System, the Gary Plan, the Winnetka Plan, and W. H. Kilpatrick's Project Method. A Society for the Promotion of New Education was formed in 1919.... The society published an influential monthly.
>
> (Cleverley, 1985: 50)

Progressive traditions in these countries were strengthened by the globe-trotting of John Dewey, whose two-year stay in China (1919–21) has often been discussed.

> Two eminent ex-students of his from Teachers' College
> Columbia, the leading intellectual Hu Shi and Jaing Menglin,
> Professor of Education at the National Beijing University, orga-
> nized his tour, seeing to it that journals published his articles in
> advance, and that translations of his lectures were readily avail-
> able and his meetings well advertised. They had high hopes that
> Dewey's liberal democratic thought would take hold and help
> force the militarists from political office.
>
> (ibid.: 51)

Of course, Western influences were resisted by conservative forces, but it
is more interesting to note that they were not necessarily accepted even
by local progressive educators. In China,

> Dewey's doctrines were reformulated for Chinese conditions
> by a remarkable disciple, Tao Xingzhi.... Tao declared that
> good teaching was "the union of teaching, learning, and doing."
> Instead of the Deweyan concept "education is life" he suggested
> "life is education," arguing for the full utilization of educational
> opportunities outside the school...
>
> (Rawski, 1979: 168)

It is important to note how Tao also drew on older Chinese philosophy:

> From Wang Yang-ming, [he] took the notion that knowledge
> and action are one, and that knowledge must have practical
> consequences.
>
> (ibid.)

In the later part of his career, Tao continued to critique Dewey:

> Tao likened Dewey's notion of school and society to caging
> a bird, then adding dried twigs to recreate the natural world.
> Rather, society should provide live lessons for learning. An
> experimental Village Normal School was established by Tao out-
> side Nanjing, where he attempted to make the school a functional
> part of village life and alert rural teachers to peasants' problems
> and aspirations.
>
> (Cleverley, 1985: 51–2)[18]

> [It] was intended to train teachers for rural areas, [and] was
> unlike orthodox training institutes. Tao required students to
> farm small plots and perform all of the menial work in running
> the school. He proposed that "one who cannot plant vegetables
> is not a student, and one who cannot cook cannot graduate." The
> curriculum thus sought to combine "teaching–learning–doing"
> into a unified process.
>
> (Rawski, 1979: 168)

Clearly this was seen as altogether too dangerous by the political authorities in the area (the Kuomintang) and the school was closed in 1930.
But Tao went on to develop experimental educational programs working
with urban populations. In 1932 "he established a 'work-study' system
among factory workers in a suburb of Shanghai... designed to help the
masses help themselves" (ibid.: 170). This approach also involved using
literate school children to teach illiterate adults. Literacy programs in
China by this time were capable of foreshadowing subsequent traditions
and made use of what we might now call authentic materials: "newspa-
pers, posters, and children's books, even books written by the students
themselves were acceptable if the peasants found them interesting. In
a night school for illiterate adults, students supplied their own reading
matter" (ibid.).

Educational traditions of the European continent

In reflecting on Western traditions, I should not oversimplify. Dewey's
ideas reached Britain via the Hadow Report (Board of Education, 1931,
para. 75): "The curriculum is to be thought of in terms of activity and
experience rather than knowledge to be acquired and facts to be stored."
But in that country, Dewey's ideas were apparently rapidly diluted
toward developmentalism alone (rather than challenge, exploration, and
inquiry). And indeed, other broader differences within Europe were and
are still to be found. For many EFL specialists I have encountered outside Europe, Western education is (in their conceptualization) largely
progressive, and being specialists in English, these teachers tend to think
of the English-speaking countries as exponents of "the" Western tradition. But the United States and the UK obviously do not exhaust the
European educational traditions. They do tend to dominate discussions
of English teaching, unfortunately, although they are themselves insu-
lar; they are not interested in teaching traditions from other countries
in the present era. However, throughout Europe and elsewhere, French
influence was strong in the 18th century, and German influence was
strong during the 19th century (including on the educational systems
of some Asian countries, notably Japan[19]). These influences extended
through to the 20th century. In addition, while many East Asian countries remain centers of comparative failure in English acquisition, many
developed European countries have been so successful in learning English
that their conservatives despair, talking of cultural imperialism; the
Académie Française notoriously fails to stem the tide of English influence on the French language, and countries such as Norway or Sweden
are vaguely perceived as having some sort of magic formula that can
explain their incredible success in learning English (e.g., Barnes, 1989).
So some notes concerning these alternative traditions, both in general and

in any manifestations of S/FL instruction we can discern, would seem to be justified.[20]

Overall, this is partly the domain of "comparative education." Within this substantial body of work, there have been a number of recent comparative studies which point to the differing cultural models of teaching (e.g., Anderson-Levitt, 2002; Broadfoot et al., 2000; Clarke, 2003; Reynolds & Farrell, 1996; Stevenson & Stigler, 1992; Tobin, Wu, & Davidson, 1989; *inter alia*). I will draw particularly on Alexander's (2000) prominent, prize-winning, multi-country study of elementary education to highlight just a couple of points of prominence, where all is *not* uniform across "Western" (in this case, European) educational systems.

One of the most obvious points of difference concerns centralization. The French system has managed to combine a strongly centralized structure with respect for the individual teacher, who can use any justifiable methods providing the results are positive (Alexander, 2000). This is in contrast to the older Anglo-American tradition that has carried through to TESOL, in which the teacher is legitimately expected to be a curriculum expert, capable of designing syllabi and materials; a position that is quite impossible for most TEFL specialists in state systems, but particularly those outside most of the West.

Then there is the matter of relationship of centrally mandated curricula to research. Alexander's respondents suggest that the Russian system, which draws on both French and German influences, is informed by an indigenous tradition of research, which regular teachers find plausible and acceptable:

> The "older tradition"...was claimed by interviewees in the Ministry and the Russian Academy of Education to be traceable back to Jan Komensky or Comenius (1592–1670). The line of descent probably goes via A. H. Francke (1663–1727), who developed and disseminated Comenius's principles of universal education and graded instructional sequences and opened schools run according to these principles in Halle. These celebrated establishments laid the basis for German secondary education, including the *gymnasium* and its attendant pedagogy, a model that Russia took over. However, Comenius influenced so many later educational figures that his ideas are as likely to have traveled from seventeenth-century Moravia to twentieth-century Russia by several routes. During the 1950s, for example, he was credited in communist Eastern Europe with having been the first person to campaign for a "unified school system from primary school up to the highest standard...[in which] all children are

given a general education without any discrimination of sex, social origin or property" [Sadler, 1966: 34].

(Alexander, 2000: 310)

Again drawing on Alexander's comparative study of primary education, a distinction between individualistic and other classrooms, is noteworthy:

> The centre of gravity for the lessons in Russia, India and [France] was the class, while in England, and even more in [the United States], it was the group and the individual. . . . Second, individual pupil talk of a very public and structured kind was a much more prominent activity in Russia and France. . . . Lessons typically required pupils to . . . talk to the class as a whole . . . [and] explain what they were doing . . . seatwork was just one activity among many. In England, in contrast, pupils . . . read silently or quietly to the teacher, they talked with each other rather than to the class as a whole . . . if they moved around it was . . . [not] to expose themselves to public scrutiny or challenge.

(ibid.: 354–5)

Alexander comments that in the Russian classrooms, in particular, tasks involved oral discourse, challenge, required student explanation to the whole class (and the teacher), and thus allowed whole classes to learn through the success or partial failure of students accessible to other students. A similar international pattern emerges concerning assessment:

> In Russia, while teachers were no less judgmental, they also made considerable use of self-assessment and peer-assessment, encouraging pupils to comment on their own and each others' answers, and indeed – because pupils were often encouraged to think aloud while tackling a problem – on each others' thinking processes too. . . . In many of the Russian primary classrooms pupils scored their own performance (on a scale of 0–5) by displaying numbers and discs, and collectively classes were invited to register their agreement or disagreement with answers and explanations.

(ibid.: 375)[21]

Shifting now to S/FL pedagogy, it is possible to some extent to identify differing European historical traditions as well. Van Essen notes that in France, the Direct Method was first established by ministerial decree for the whole of the country in 1902; but then, in the 1920s,

> was abolished as abruptly as it had been introduced. . . . France then entered upon a period of foreign-language instruction based

Values, Philosophies, and Beliefs in TESOL

> upon the precepts of Henri Delacroix (1925)...[involving] the alternate use of the native and the foreign language during the lesson at elementary level...translation of words was avoided by giving explanations in the foreign language. To make absolutely sure learners understood what they were reading, the mother tongue was used. At the more advanced level...some attention was also paid to cultural studies. These were very much an intellectual affair.
>
> (van Essen 2000: 272–3)

For applied linguists, the story starts here...

In EFL-related discussions over the last 20 or 30 years, a repeated theme is whether or not ideas about ESOL pedagogy that emanate from the perspectives of individuals closely associated with Britain and North America ("BANA"; Holliday 1994a, 1994b, 2005) can be productively utilized outside Western cultures. One reason for an answer in the negative is that non-Western cultures have "traditional" school systems, whose emphases cannot support the progressive elements within what the S/FL field calls "communicative" approaches. Whether or not this is true, the idea that non-Western cultures have had uniformly timeless and unchanging education systems is not borne out by the historical record. Not only are there indigenous aspects of these systems that do not completely conform to Western expectations of "tradition" (cf. Shin & Crookes, 2005a, 2005b), the history of contact and active uptake of certain traditions articulated by Western educational specialists is diverse.

More or less contemporaneous with the powerful East–West contacts I have sketched in the previous subsection, the beginnings of other East–West contacts more visible to the weak historical memory of our field had also occurred. The first inklings of "applied linguistics," as the would-be scientific discipline that went on to inform S/FL teaching, crystallized out of the Reform Movement at the tail end of the 19th century in, among other forms, Jespersen's *How to Teach a Foreign Language* (1904). The "top end" of ES/FL had spread internationally in the form of the conversation school, and non-Western countries were beginning to seek the expertise of BANA specialists. For example, Howatt (1984) provides details of the attempts of the Japanese Ministry of Education to improve EFL through the long sojourn of the influential Harold Palmer, who ran the Institute for Research on English Teaching in Tokyo from 1922 to 1936.

68

Most modern inheritances

I do not want to provide a quick history of the remainder of the 20th century "Methods." But ELT specialists who attach themselves conceptually to some kind of communicative approach (or indeed, those who are opposed to it) need to ask where it came from and what comes along with it. Clearly, for some specialists, communicative approaches are modern instantiations of an originally Pestalozzian natural approach. Recently, U.S. specialists Krashen and Terrell (1983; Terrell, 1982) have made no bones about their direct connection to this line. Their ideas about pedagogy are strengthened by reference to theories concerning the natural developmental stages in the growth of syntactic competence in the S/FL learner. The connection is also clear concerning the relationship between natural pedagogies and Rousseauian (subsequently Piagetian) stage theories of child development.

There is perhaps an additional point to be made about the inheritances on the British CLT side. Communicative Language Teaching is often thought of as driven by major changes in the analysis of language that allowed a functional, rather than structural, syllabus to be devised (the influence of Halliday being seen as particularly strong[22]). This may be correct with respect to the syllabus, but what about the material that is the exponent or manifestation of the syllabus, the means by which the content of the communicative course is learned? The 1960s were a period of suddenly increased immigration into English-speaking countries. In the UK,

> [a]n important step was taken in 1966 with the decision to set up a materials development project at the University of Leeds Institute of Education to design and pilot a programme of English for immigrant primary school children. Later, the project . . . was extended to cover children of secondary school age. The resulting materials, called *Scope* . . . pioneered new ideas in the integration of language teaching with the broader purpose of educational development and foreshadowed many of the activity-based techniques later associated with the communicative approach. The same could also be said of a second . . . project intended to help immigrant children with their use of English called *Concept 7–9*.
>
> *Scope* broke new ground in English language teaching by bringing together the EFL tradition of the linguistically organized syllabus . . . and the primary school tradition of activity methods which required the children to use the new language co-operatively to make . . . charts, models of various kinds, and so on . . . tying the language work closely into activities and small projects with an educational value in their own right, as well as

taking into account the children's needs for English both in and out of school.

(Howatt, 1984: 221, 275)

Like other analysts of communicative approaches, Howatt (pp. 279–80) distinguishes between a "weak" and a "strong" communicative approach. The former, he asserts, "has become more or less standard practice" since the mid-1970s, and simply involves direct instruction and practice in language which has a communicative orientation. The strong version, it is generally accepted, proposes that learning through use (with little or no need for direct instruction) is the actual dominant process in SLA. And it was this that was manifested in the early British ESL projects:

> One of the first examples of a "using to learn" strategy was pioneered in the project at Birmingham referred to earlier called *Concept 7–9* (1972). The [project] team, directed by John Sinclair, took the ... view that it was not the [immigrant] children's knowledge of English that was "restricted" but rather their experience of using it to explore the more abstract concepts and relationships required in school learning. The outcome was a "kit" of problem solving tasks ... which demanded the ideational use of English to communicate information about notions. ... The full weight of communication should fall on the precise use of information-carrying language for which the children would have to develop workable strategies.[23]

(ibid.: 279)

What it seems we have here is a fruitful contacting of streams. The activity-centered curriculum of the British primary school was an inheritance (mainly) from Dewey, except that it had taken greater heed of a developmental perspective, such that following a decline in the Progressive Movement, it was sought as a source for renewed inspiration by U.S. primary experts (even if it was "filtered and somewhat romanticized" (Alexander, 2000: 311)). It had also deviated from the mechanization of 19th-century traditions.

> At the end of the nineteenth century ... primary teacher trainers looked instead [of to Herbart] to Rousseau, Pestalozzi and Froebel. Subsequently, Montessori's principles of "scientific pedagogy" and her view of the classroom as a "prepared learning environment" provided inspiration for the growing early years movement. ... Secondary teaching developed ... closer to mainstream European lines, emphasizing the timetable, lesson structure, the logical imperatives of the subject taught, and the expository task of the teacher. From the 1930s onward,

and especially during the period 1965–90, English primary teaching...emphasized temporal and spatial fluidity, the psychological imperatives of development, the uniqueness of the individual, the child's active agency in his or her learning, the holistic nature of knowledge and the teacher's task as facilitator.

(Alexander, 2000: 313)

In any case, it had clearly maintained and developed an activity-based curriculum. In Howatt's account, Sinclair's team was enabled by this to place a communicative focus on language, informed by a Firth / Halliday perspective on language and the "strong" acquisition perspective on SLA, into a curricular container that already existed and was already set up for tasks.

Concluding remark

Institutions, philosophies, reformers, traditions...As I look at what has been written about past periods of practice in this area, I see repeated cycles of innovation, institutionalization, erasure, and return. The movement of ideas in and out of the mainstream seems particularly striking. In the 1890s (if Howatt is right) mainstream education could not accommodate the "natural" methods of Sauveur et al. In the 1790s, even the schools of revolutionary France would not accommodate the ideas of Rousseau. Yet later on, such ideas were taken into state school systems in various countries where they were accommodated for a while, before (according to some of our accounts) being stifled under the institutional constraints or changes in the political winds. And then, in some cases, we find that they are not extinguished completely and flourish in protected environments, whence they return when conditions are favorable again.

I also notice an apparent "thinning" or "thickening" of these streams of practice, related to questions concerning how conceptually well-grounded were the language teachers in those times. When a language teacher used Comenius's books, was he also committing himself to Comenius's views on the desirability of mass education? Possibly few of Berlitz's teachers (even those otherwise enlightened ones, like Wilfred Owen and James Joyce) knew they were using a line of practice that descended from Pestalozzi. On the other hand, did they perhaps nevertheless take it as "natural" that children, or adults, could learn a second language through "conversation"? If so, they may have been buying into a philosophical conception of the child such as that of Locke's, or a generally "developmental" view of learning in which the activities of the learner in dialogue with a teacher lead to the learner constructing meaning out of its absence.

But why was it, on the other hand, that perspectives such as those of Pestalozzi, Herbart, and so on, became fossilized almost immediately after they were systematized by a second generation, or taken up by the state? We cannot know, of course, whether the teachers who used the ideas of these specialists had philosophies of S/FL teaching that were fully congruent with the central views of Herbart, Pestalozzi, and others with their moral implications. One might wonder, as well, whether these teachers and their views were to some extent formed by their use of these materials. Similarly, do today's conversation school teachers, or for that matter, the 21st century's innovative teachers of EFL in high schools in, say, China,[24] realize they are working out (still, again) the ideas of reformers of the 19th century, who in turn were reworking innovative efforts of the 18th century and earlier? Does it matter, for their own practice, and for the continuation and development of the tradition they are working in?

Discussion questions

1. In what senses might it be reasonable to describe European philosophy before the 1400s as "anti-humanist"? What are some of the ways that humanism might manifest itself in language education? Do these things occur much in current language-teaching contexts you are familiar with?

2. What were some of the better values of the era of the French Revolution that were manifested in educational developments, including those of language teaching, in the 18th century and thereafter? In what respects were they different from those of Rousseau? Do any of these ideas hold up today?

3. Do you think that conversation schools these days are, in important respects, different from those of Berlitz in the 19th century? Give details.

4. Herbart was a psychologist, yet he said that pedagogy depends on ethics to provide the aims of education. Does this correspond with what you know of psychology, or of educational psychology? Do you think any language teaching you may have done might have corresponded (perhaps unknowingly) to Herbart's instructional principles? If so, what are the implications of that?

Notes to Chapter 3

[1] Pennycook (2000) notes that the small corpus of book-length treatments of the history of S/FL teaching is explicitly focused only on European perspectives.

[2] These dates are very much conventional, and subject to scholarly debate.

[3] His stay in England (1641–2) was curtailed because of the Civil War (1642–5).

[4] Protestants like Comenius, unlike Catholics, wanted the Bible to be available in vernacular languages, not just in Latin; and they wanted it read, studied, and discussed. Hence, the need for a widespread non-Latin literacy.

[5] Though perhaps with a precursor in Montaigne (Koops, 2003); he also seems to have been a precursor for the entire Enlightenment, according to Toulmin (1990)!

[6] Smith's language is similar to Jefferson's: "In free countries, where the safety of government depends very much upon the favourable judgment which the people may form of its conduct, it must surely be of the highest importance that they should not be disposed to judge rashly or capriciously concerning it" (p. 788).

[7] "where Oxford and Cambridge...enjoyed a secure freedom from government... while generally decaying" (Palmer, 1985: 38).

[8] "I know of no safe depository of the ultimate powers of the society but the people themselves. [We must] inform their discretion by education," he wrote. This was to be through "a system of general instruction which shall reach every description of our citizens, from the richest to the poorest" (cited in Battistoni, 1985: 70; see also Shannon, 2001); presumably this would not have applied to slaves.

[9] Most obviously in his treatment of the education of girls (cf., Martin, 1981).

[10] But see Pennycook (1989) whose account of 14th-century trading-oriented language teaching suggests that such students and such practical communication-oriented forms of language teaching have always existed.

[11] I should not, perhaps, leave the story of the private language school there. There has continued to be an unsung interface between the best such schools, their teachers, and the mainstream of TESOL. For example, van Essen (2000: 271) refers to Harold Palmer as having been "shaped...as a language pedagogue" by "the lessons he taught to adult learners at Berlitz schools in Belgium." Palmer went on to develop what van Essen calls a "first attempt" at a notional / functional syllabus (Palmer, 1927) as well as being judged (by Howatt) as the single person most responsible for making ELT / TESOL into a profession.

[12] Since a general concern of the present work is to highlight the rapid and early transfer of educational ideas across borders, let me refer to this method from the point of view of a study of France. At the onset of the restoration of the French monarchy (after the Revolution and after Napoleon), "In 1815 liberals set up the *Société pour l'Instruction Elémentaire* to propagate basic instruction for the poor using the monitorial method of Joseph Lancaster, whose school in Borough Road, Southwark [London] had been visited by a French deputation in 1814.... One of the most enthusiastic advocates of *l'enseignement mutuel* [French term for monitorial method] was the Duc de la Rochefoucauld, who had fled to England during the Revolution, and whose translation of Lancaster...(1803) was widely distributed in France...[B]y 1820 there were 1500 monitorial schools, mainly concentrated in the industrial cities" (Alexander, 2000: 56).

[13] Alexander (2000: 57) provides intriguing detail about how the pendulum swings in pedagogy moved in opposite directions in France and England during the same period, while each country separately thought it was "modernizing" its education.

[14] Prussian educational philosopher Fichte (1808, cited in Spring, 1975) commented, "The State which introduced universally the national education proposed by us, from the moment a new generation of youths had passed through it, would need no special army at all, but would have in them an army such as no age has yet seen."

Obedience and silence were what Prussian children were schooled in, said Tolstoy (1967: 12).

15 See Spring (2006) for a detailed account of the spread of the Progressive Movement between West and East.

16 In this, they were also emulating European nations behind the curve. Prussia modernized its education system in 1810, along French lines, following its defeat by Napoleon.

17 More recently, Woodside (1992, 1994) has noted that this process of reform was justified through Chinese scholars making a case for reform based on idealized versions of past education in China; a strategy that can be used in other cases (cf. Shin & Crookes, 2005a).

18 Tao's ideas led on to, for example, the use of students as instructors in peer literacy informal education. Thøgersen (2002: 101) paraphrases one report (Zhu, 1936) as showing the benefit that as a result, students "were forced to become more independent and active... [and] the professional tricks of the teachers would also be demystified, and the traditional hierarchical relationship between student and teacher would be shaken." Others in this group include Liang Shuming (Alitto, 1986), who drew on Mencius and Wang Yangming. He recommended, rather than lectures, "the discourse (*jiangxue*) model, in which a closely knit group of students together with a teacher formed a collective that was in charge of its own daily life and moral development" (Thøgersen, 2002: 93).

19 "Japan's application of German ideas in its school system was... extensive.... A series of school regulations promulgated in 1886 was inspired by German models. One of the regulations established a national Imperial University.... Renamed the University of Tokyo after World War II, this institution... was not only modeled after the German university but was also staffed with many German professors. During the Meiji period (1868–1912), the vast majority of students sent abroad by the government went to Germany, while German teachers hired by the government greatly outnumbered other foreign teachers" (Kobayashi, 1964: 22–3).

20 It is even the case that cultural traditions of teaching are backed up with different disciplinary distinctions. North Europe uses the term *didaktik* to refer to a conceptual and disciplinary area lying somewhere between pedagogy and curriculum, and at a lower level than education. This is primarily German in origin, and can refer to a general science of teaching (Kroksmark, 1995).

21 "Western commentators... equate Russian pedagogy with Soviet autocracy and ignore the fact that its distinctiveness owes as much to roots that it has in common with the pedagogies of central Europe as to Soviet additions. It is true that in this European tradition the teacher's authority is unquestioned; but it is equally true that this authority can be exercised in different ways" (Alexander, 2000: 521).

22 His personal account of his life in linguistics is of interest here: Halliday (2002).

23 Howatt's footnote (p. 291) on this kit remarks that it contains "what are probably the earliest examples of the 'information-gap' activities which became popular a number of years later."

24 See Lin & Luk (2002: 101–102) who do recognize such traditions in that location, and urge that we "attempt to understand the history of the present, and the socio-historical and political embeddedness of present-day educational canons."

4 Isms and systems

Introduction

In this chapter, instead of organizing the material by diachronic time sequence, I first use two synchronic analytic schemes commonly applied to systems of philosophy. A conventional manner of proceeding for philosophers of education is to identify some major systems, or positions, in philosophy, review their contents, and then consider how they may or may not apply to the practices or concepts of teachers. As is also well-recognized, this is not an entirely satisfactory expository maneuver, because many philosophers, including philosophers of education, have not attempted to develop comprehensive systems, and most teachers probably do not attempt to manifest a philosophy of teaching conceptualized in system-based terms. There is also not a direct translation from system to classroom practice. Indeed, as Ozmon and Craver (1999: 11) point out, "the current mood in philosophy of education is generally toward understanding issues in specific contexts, rather than a return to the idea that the individual, society, and education can be understood in an overriding system of thought." But again, the material with which I am grappling in this work is not particularly transparent or straightforward, so multiple passes through it, from different perspectives, are called for.

Systems of philosophy, or fundamental positions in philosophy,[1] can be seen in terms of three or four major domains that philosophies usually take a stand on.[2] These are metaphysics, epistemology, and axiology; to which, since we are now formally dealing with philosophies of education, or philosophies applied to education, we may add a fourth domain, education itself.[3] These areas can be glossed as, respectively, the nature of reality (or, what things are), the nature of knowledge (or, what can be known), the nature of values, and the nature of teaching and schooling. This metalevel analysis can be applied across systems of philosophy, so we have two potential ways to proceed. We can look at, for example, metaphysics, and having defined or illustrated it in general, go on to ask what the position in that category was for each of some systems.[4] Or we can take the systems in turn, and ask what each one has to say on metaphysics, on epistemology, and so on. Since, as I have already mentioned, the "systems" are not always fully systematic, I will use the former of these two procedures to bring the categories themselves into focus and give a sense of the questions that are implied by each of these broad domains of philosophical thought. I will then proceed to the (somewhat systematic) systems.

In the last part of the chapter, I will reverse direction and, following an earlier study of language curricula and their philosophies (Clark, 1987), attempt to show connections between language-teaching traditions and both movements and the elements of philosophical systems. (The caveats I noted in Chapter 1 still apply.)

Metacategories or a metasystem

To repeat then – since the 19th century, expositions of philosophies have drawn on a small, overarching set of categories. Since they are placed above systems, we can refer to them as metacategories, and they constitute a metasystem: The core three are metaphysics, epistemology, and axiology.

Metaphysics

This term has often been used pejoratively. If you have a very strong focus on the empirical and material, you may believe that any attempt to consider things that are less tangible is a waste of time; and you may apply to any such thought or effort the term "metaphysical," in a derogatory manner. This was the way analytic and logical positivist philosophy, in its heyday, regarded all other philosophy past or present, for example. However, all scientific theories have a metaphysics (Harré, 1985). That is to say, they take a position on the nature of the things to which they are referring and the meaning of their basic concepts.[5] In general, metaphysics is the study of the most abstract, and potentially universal, conceptions.

It is widely accepted that four main components of metaphysics can be identified: cosmology, theology, ontology, and (fitting less comfortably) anthropological perspectives on metaphysics (e.g., Knight, 1982). Let us briefly take them in turn. I think most readers will initially find these components positioned far from concerns with teaching, although ontology (or, the matter of what is), will in due course be seen to play into questions about the nature of language, or of the individual, which are a bit closer to our focus here.

Even though we are necessarily in an abstract realm, cosmology is particularly abstract. Questions in this area include how the universe came about and developed. However, we can also ask whether it has a purpose, at which point we are close to "What is the meaning of life?," which can inform questions like, "Why am I/why do I want to be a teacher?."

Theology is the component of the theory of religion that concerns itself with questions such as whether there is one god, no god, or many; what the attributes of such an entity might be; and what the relation(s) of humans to such entities are or could be. Just to illustrate one aspect of this – it may be of interest to know that there are at least six different preliminary responses to the first question just mentioned: Atheists would identify "no god," pantheists that "all is god," and of course while monotheists identify only one, polytheists identify many gods. A further distinction comes between deists who believe in gods, or a god, which has no interest in humans, and theists, for whom a personal deity (or deities) is a credo (Knight, 1982). Language teachers who have a spiritual position on their practice may find that their values will guide them toward an exploration of the theology of their religion as it plays out in educational contexts.[6]

Ontology is the study of what exists, and deals with questions such as "What do we mean when we say something exists?," "Is the thing or things that exist singular and material, or, say, dual, being composed of matter and mind?," "What are key features of reality?" – to which one possible answer is "change," another "stability."

Finally, many philosophical questions, particularly metaphysical ones, have received different answers in different cultures. So it is valuable to look across cultures as we pose such questions. In that sense, an anthropological perspective within metaphysics is possible and useful.

Epistemology

On the face of it, this category is "closer to home," because it is the domain of philosophy that concerns itself with the nature of knowledge; it develops, for example, theories of truth, and concerns itself with whether, how, and to what extent, we can be said to know something. Other key aspects of knowledge that regularly come up, particularly when, as teachers, we are considering the basis for our actions, include questions, such as whether truth is relative or absolute, the role of subjectivity in generating knowledge, or, to put it another way, the possibility that there could be truths that exist independent of humans.

We can also consider the sources of knowledge. In traditional societies, revelation is one source. In scholastic periods, authority is another. Reason is one source that happily seems to coexist with empiricism (the position stipulating that it is the senses that are the prime source for knowledge). Intuition is a source of knowledge that has its adherents, though they tend not to be those comfortable with reason or the senses as primary sources.

Finally, a crucial subarea here concerns the validity or dependability of knowledge. Even if we do not wish to say simply that something is true, we may wish to advance it as a plausible, warranted assertion. But how do we get to feel comfortable about a statement of that kind? Well, it may hold together with other statements or positions that seem to be true. In that case, we are advancing a coherentist theory of truth. Or, very commonly in the present era, we may simply assert that a statement is consistent with the facts; this remark in turn depends upon the plausibility of a correspondence theory of truth. Comparatively recently developed, a pragmatic theory of truth holds that a statement is warranted, in this respect, if it leads to workable, useful, and satisfactory correspondences. Note that these two sentences imply that this subarea can be conceptualized as relation to "theories of truth." Language teachers who wish to consult empirical research for input into their developing philosophies of teaching may have to grapple with the possibility that researchers are operating on different theories of truth when they present their findings.

Axiology

The third and final category of this conventional metasystem is perhaps the least familiar term, although it covers material essential to an authentic life, namely values; it also concerns itself with what is beautiful or of value in other ways. Thus it has two main sections: ethics and aesthetics.

Ethics, particularly in the sense of "an ethics," refers to a system or systems of morals. By extension, it also means the philosophical study of morality; the terms "ethics" and "morals" are often used interchangeably. Issues in the philosophical investigation of ethics include probing the possibility of absolute values, and of particular interest lately, how to address the problems caused by value systems that appear to be radically incommensurable across cultures. The interface of ethics and teaching does not necessarily imply the curricular area of moral education; that topic is certainly not under direct consideration in this work. The field of ethics however should be of interest to teachers because we often have to make difficult moral judgments, for which we need the assistance of ethical systems, and in respect of which we need to be clear which ethical systems are in play or are available to us.

Aesthetics can ask questions, such as "What is beautiful?" and "What should I like?" As such, although it clearly does and is originally intended to relate to what we might call the arts, in fact, it apparently can apply more widely. Lately it has been applied to aspects of professional practice in education by Cherryholmes (1999).

78

Systems or philosophical "-isms"

Now I will turn to a short system-level exposition. It is important to recognize that most if not all of the systems, or "schools," that I am going to summarize in the immediately following sections can be found from the earliest times, and regardless of geographical or cultural location.[7]

Idealism

Idealism, as that term is commonly understood, has associations with religion. That is, many religions (or traditions within specific religions), having committed to beliefs in an afterlife, or in noncorporeal and other-worldly beings, and so on, take a view of the physical world that renders it secondary in terms of importance and in terms of actual substantiality. What *is* real, or most real, then, becomes something nonmaterial, or spiritual. However, idealism is by no means exclusively connected with religion, and has also always been a strong tradition in philosophy. In European philosophical traditions, the concept of an ideal form, upon which all partial material forms are based, has been an influential idea since Plato. In East Asian philosophical traditions, besides appearing in some (though not all) Buddhist philosophies, it is particularly associated with the work of the famous neo-Confucian statesman Wang Yang-Ming. During the period of the European Enlightenment, it was a position to be found in the work of Descartes and Kant. In the hands of Descartes, for example, the mind has a certain reality that is distinct from the world that is produced for us by the senses, and the mind's reality is somehow prior, or superior, even. Because of this distrust of the empirical, the epistemology associated with idealism relies on consistency and coherence (not to mention intuition) to determine what is true or valid. In its subsequent European development, in the work of Hegel, idealism moved further away from religious philosophy, perhaps to some extent becoming a substitute for it. Hegel's conception of a world spirit, or a force in history, allows one to illustrate what ethical behavior is for the idealist: It is acting in accordance with this absolute.

With the decline, comparatively speaking, of religion in Europe, so idealism as a philosophy, too, has declined to a fair measure. It is surprising to learn, in the materialist, scientistic world of the early 21st century, that during much of the 19th and early 20th century, idealism outside of religion was the dominant trend in Western philosophy and education. This was due to the influence of Hegel, and his various followers elsewhere, including in the English-speaking world, such as Green[8] (in England) and Royce and even Emerson (in the United States). Some of these philosophers had a strong reform orientation in connection with education (Gordon & White, 1979). The work and key

79

concepts of Hegel continued to be developed in Germany and France but disappeared from the mainstream of Anglo-American philosophy, which took a completely different turn (toward empiricism and realism). This is one reason why, when there was a substantial return to contact between these lines of thought about a hundred years later, Anglo-American philosophy found it difficult to digest the transformations of Hegelian ideas as they appeared in developments from Nietzsche to Foucault, or indeed even earlier in their manifestations within the work of Marx.

Realism

The metaphysics of realism is simple and in a clear sense opposite to that of idealism. It is the position that nothing exists which is not in some sense tangible, real, and of this world. Now it is true that religions as conventionally understood, and thus idealism, were very prominent in the early history of human civilization, but at the same time there is a lack of appreciation of the diversity of philosophical opinion in early non-Western civilizations. So it is important to point out that materialist positions can be found in the early history of China (e.g., Hsun Tsu/Xun Zi) and India (the Cakravartin school of philosophy that led into Jainism and Buddhism), not to mention Greece (Leucippus and Democritus, 5th century BCE). Just to take the first of these as an example of realism in ancient philosophical thought – Xun Zi (fl. 298–238 BC) was one of several major thinkers who followed Confucius (two others often mentioned in the same group being Mencius and Mo Tsu). His ideas "marked the last stage in the development of the Confucian school during the Warring States Period [and] epitomized the materialistic ideologies of the pre-Qin time" (He et al., 1991: 62). He recognized the movement of the sun and moon, the passing of the seasons, and all such events, as natural and without a spiritual dimension, and having no relation to humankind.

Although I have associated idealism with certain broad aspects of religion, there certainly have been religious realists, who would assert that the material world exists on its own terms. So what, if anything, is particularly important for us (as teachers) about the realist position? Perhaps it is that, as an implication of the nature of material things and of human beings as understood within realism, the possibility of knowing "things" is great. That is, many realist philosophers would agree that the material world can be known in a more-or-less complete way. This leads to a favoring of rational thought, possibly empirical enquiry, and potentially a foundationalist position on knowledge: that things (and perhaps even values) can be known absolutely and completely.

It is difficult to set down these two positions (idealism and realism) briefly and do justice to them; great diversity is possible under a single philosophical label. The two simple characterizations both stand in opposition to a third one more characteristic of modern times, namely pragmatism.

Pragmatism

This is regularly identified as a recent development of 19th- and 20th-century American philosophers, notably Peirce, and potentially James and Dewey. However, there were Europeans and Asians who were exploring the same domain of ideas at this time.[9] For that matter, the school has its classical antecedents in Heraclitus (who agreed with them about the constancy of change) and the Sophists (who agreed with most pragmatists on the impossibility of knowing absolute reality).

Before getting into the details of this school of thought, let us quickly take up two common uses of the root "pragmatic." In S/FL studies, we are familiar with the area known as "pragmatics," which is the study of how utterances are used in practice, in contexts. Insofar as this derives from the idea of the practical application of a linguistic utterance being its actual meaning, it is close to the source of the philosophical position known as pragmatism, though most studies of SL pragmatics have nothing much to do with philosophical pragmatism. The second sense of the term is indeed its commonsense meaning of being practical based on what happens; but it was also used philosophically, notably by Kant, "to distinguish between rules and standards based on experience, and those above or beyond experience" (Marler, 1975: 377; McHoul, 1996).

The initial formulations of modern pragmatism were developed by Peirce (1839–1914), in his 1878 article "How to make our ideas clear," though this early effort was largely ignored for the next 20 years until James and then Dewey took up and developed its implications. What Peirce, and those who followed him, wanted, was to diminish or eliminate the separation of matter and mind; Peirce claimed that "Our idea of anything *is* our idea of its sensible effects" (1878: 293). Thus, what we do is not separate from what we think; having an idea, or knowing something, has results in the real world that are not actually distinct from what is apparently merely mental.

William James's development of Peirce's ideas (and his popularization of them) included an attack on abstract ideas of truth. In his view,

> [t]ruth is not an absolute and immutable; rather, it is made in actual, real-life events. Truth does not belong to an idea as some property adhering to it, for it is found in acting on ideas, in the consequences of ideas. Truth is not always objective and verifiable; it is also found in concrete individuality. . . .

> In the life of an individual, experiences occur that have mean-
> ing and truth to that individual but that cannot necessarily be
> verified objectively to someone else... [T]his... is what James
> called "radical empiricism." In effect, he held that truth is insep-
> arable from experience; to get at truth, we must study experience
> itself, not some immutable, otherworldly Absolute, extraneous
> to experience... James called on thinkers to concentrate on
> experience in lieu of essences, abstractions, and universals.
>
> (Ozmon & Craver, 1999: 136–7)

In turn, James's work was further developed and made widely accessible
by Dewey. Dewey had an exceptionally long life and career as both an
active philosopher and as an extremely influential educator. As many
commentators on Dewey have pointed out, he was of his times as well
as contributing to their development. He was, for example, one of the
first modern philosophers to be heavily influenced by the implications of
evolution and the ideas of Darwin; he was also one who took to heart
the concepts of social progress that were popular at the end of the 19th
century and continued through the optimistic phases of the 20th century.

Dewey was originally a follower of Hegel, and thus an idealist, but he
became dissatisfied both with this position and its apparent alternative, a
strictly realist or materialist view. Dewey continually tried to unify these
two positions; like Peirce, he thought many problems had been caused
by philosophers separating out a primordial unity into one thing (ideas,
the mind) or another (reality):

> For Dewey, experience is not just an isolated happenstance; it
> has depth and reaches into nature. Experience and nature are not
> two different things separated from each other; rather experience
> itself is of nature. Experience could, in the reflective sense, be
> divided into the experiencing being and the experienced things,
> but in the primary sense of the word, experience is of nature.
> People do not experience "experience" but the world in which
> they live, a world of things, ideas, hopes, fears, and aspirations –
> all rooted in nature.
>
> (ibid.: 138)

Dewey's perspective is strongly action-oriented and problem-solving:

> Dewey holds that genuine thought begins with a "problematic
> situation," a block or hitch in the ongoing stream of experience.
> In encountering these blocks, consciousness is brought to focus
> and one is made more acutely aware of the situation. In dealing
> with these real problems, Dewey argued, creative intelligence is
> capable of development. Whereas traditional philosophies take
> problematic situations and attempt to fit them to a preexisting

set of abstractions, Dewey urged that each situation be looked on as unique and dealt with experimentally by investigating the probable consequences of behaving in particular ways.

(ibid.: 138)

Thus his ideas clearly link up with the exploratory and problem-solving approach to professional practice that goes under the heading of action research (cf. Dewey, 1910). Sometimes this aspect of his work led him to prefer the terms "instrumentalism" and "experimentalism" to describe his position. He believed that people could improve their lives through sustained thought and action guided by such analysis; this drove his desire to unify social action and an investigative or experimental form of education.

An issue that is of general concern to us as teachers is the relationship of individuals to one another, and of the individual to the social world. One common metaphor that we use to understand this is highly atomistic. But are we really separate, hard-edged, bouncing off one another like ball bearings? Or would the metaphor of a network serve us better? Or even something with fewer edges and points, like an ocean? Many philosophers have addressed this matter and their positions have implications for science and professional practice, as well as for personal (teaching) philosophies. Ozmon and Craver comment that Dewey's treatment of "individuality in the social world" led to controversy, perhaps because of the complexity of his ideas, or the way he tries to keep two apparently distinct positions in play at the same time:

> Rather than accepting the extremes of subjectivity or objectivity, Dewey tried to show that experience is first and primarily gross and macroscopic and that distinctions of subjectivity (or individuality) and objectivity (or the social and physical environment) come out of experience. In short, the one is not necessarily more real than the other because Dewey viewed subject and object or the individual and society in precarious balance, a transactional relationship. Of course, individuality can be submerged or lost by rigid institutional restrictions, and sociality can be denied by a rampant individualism of the economic laissez-faire variety . . .
>
> Dewey thought that modern industrial society had submerged both individuality and sociality. Because of the confusion of modern society, he argued, the school should be an institution where both the individual and the social capabilities of children can be nurtured. The way to achieve this is through democratic living. Individuality is important because it is the source of novelty and change in human affairs. Dewey defines individuality as the interplay of personal choice and freedoms with objective conditions. To the extent that personal choice is intelligently

made, then, individuals exercise even greater control over their personal destinies and the objective world surrounding them. . . .

Sociality refers to a milieu or medium conducive to individual development. In Dewey's mind, genuine individuality could not exist without humane democratic and educative social conditions, consequently the category of the social is the inclusive philosophic idea because it is the means by which the distinctly human is achieved. Therefore, individuality and sociality cannot be divorced.

(Ozmon & Craver, 1999: 140–41)

These are rather subtle analyses, and they were also quite influential. To some extent, I believe, the ideas have been absorbed into the conventional wisdom of liberal democratic societies, and to the extent that much modern schooling has progressive tendencies or inheritances, the Deweyan perspective on matters such as knowledge and the role of school in democracies is often present in the background.

Educational-philosophical movements and language-teaching traditions

For some specialists in the philosophy of education, there are a range of positions, or classifications, that have implications for teaching but which are in some way not fully fledged or valid philosophies. They have been described as "graphic terms . . . distinctive to education" that are "simply ways of grouping philosophical orientations" (Strain, 1971: 13). They can also be identified as historical movements rather than systems. Four such positions that are often identified are progressivism, reconstructionism, perennialism, and essentialism. Embodying values and manifesting themselves in education systems, they also strongly interact with political positions, and, at another, simpler analytic level, can thus be seen as manifestations of liberal or conservative positions on a variety of socioeducational and philosophical topics, and which can be found at most times and in most developed cultures (Dupuis, 1966; I draw on Simpson, 1995, for the following review).

Attempting to interpret the entirety of educational practice through the lens of a specific philosophical system is problematic, as many authors have commented. However, the interpretive and expositional problem can be mitigated to some extent by focusing on the curriculum alone. And indeed, if the curriculum is conceptualized as something prior to practice, and if we recognize that in state systems of education it has usually been designed and promulgated by "higher authorities" who indeed may well have been in close touch with official values, or for that matter driven by quite conscious principles and aspirations, then we might expect the curriculum to explicitly manifest the kind of theoretical positions taken in philosophical systems.

Some attempts have been made to apply these "graphic terms" to aspects of, or movements in, second and foreign language teaching. Clark (1987) investigated the conceptual and philosophical positions implied in foreign language teaching, and did this by means of analyses of FL curricula of the 20th century. The systems he identified as useful for analysis of FL curricula were "classical humanism," "reconstructionism," and "progressivism," presumably following the well-established analytical scheme in philosophy of education just mentioned.

Progressivism, reconstructionism, perennialism, and essentialism

To some extent, the development, labeling, or identification of reconstructionism, perennialism, and essentialism are a response to the prominence of progressivism, so let us address that term first.

Progressivism

Progressivism was the position associated with a broad movement for social improvement through the means of modern science as it appeared during the first two or three decades of the 20th century, particularly in the United States. It had a variety of manifestations and was not limited to education. As I have already mentioned, it was often associated with the name of John Dewey. At one level, perhaps, it was a manifestation of pragmatic philosophy, but as many commentators have pointed out, Dewey was often critical of the movement. It had a strong commitment to democratic values and encouraged teachers to act and teach out of such a position. Schools were to prepare their students for an active civic life in which they would actively participate in society at an international level. School had the goal of preparing sophisticated and morally astute students. As a position or orientation, this includes different strands of historically situated thought. First, the "child-centered movement of early progressive education" or "naturalism," with its emphasis on "the natural development of children" (Strain, 1971: 13) – which we have already met in the work of Rousseau and his followers. But also, "second, the social-centered movement" which was "critical of its predecessor's permissiveness and sought to construct a better world by controlling human experience" through science and the scientific method (ibid.). This has also been described as the "hard" wing of the progressive movement, and it is from this, allied to the testing practices of early behaviorists like

85

Thorndike, that we get the inclination to stream and separate by ability or intelligence (or scores on tests that claim to measure such things as if independent of culture or home background; cf. White, 2006).

A number of concepts and methods that were developed by Dewey and the progressives (though not necessarily original with them) have passed into common practice in the education systems of many countries and are also drawn upon by language-teaching specialists:

> Pragmatists are adherents of action-oriented education; therefore, they would suggest an activity-oriented approach to curriculum, so students would learn not only that they can relate various kinds of knowledge and use them to attack a problem but also that they can act on them as well. . . .
>
> Because pragmatists are concerned with teaching children how to solve problems, they believe that real-life situations encourage problem-solving ability in a practical setting. . . .
>
> Pragmatist educators advocate meeting the needs and interests of the child. . . .
>
> One approach suggested by such pragmatist educators as Kilpatrick is the "project approach" to learning. This is a systematization of the general approach that Dewey used at the Laboratory School. . . .
>
> In many respects, the pragmatist curriculum is a process as much as a distinct body of knowledge. . . . Pragmatist curriculum is composed of both process and content, but it is not fixed or an end in itself.
>
> (Ozmon & Craver, 1999: 154–8)

In Clark's (1987) analysis of this movement, he associates the label "progressive" with Rousseau and Piaget, with Rogers (the founder of the area of humanistic psychology) and among language-teaching figures, with Krashen (not to mention Prabhu).[10] He emphasizes the "process-oriented" aspects of the progressive curriculum. In the literature of our field, an emphasis on the curriculum as process, or "process syllabi" (Candlin, 1984) implies some form of negotiated syllabus, considerable faith in the learner's own abilities to determine needs and, for that matter, to learn (perhaps unconsciously) through use (rather than study) of the target language. With its emphasis on the learner, this is a rather asocial, nonpolitical perspective on some of the radical developments in education from the 1960s. This particular form of progressivism is highly child- or student-centered, in line with Rousseau, and concerns itself more with the internal than the external aspects of "progress," there following Carl Rogers (e.g., 1969) and the humanistic psychology of the 1950s and 1960s more than other sociopolitical manifestations of that or other eras.

Reconstructionism

Although progressivism seemed very radical at some point, there were those for whom it was not radical enough. These educators (e.g., Counts, 1932) called for education that would completely reconstruct society, rather than merely evaluate and improve it in a meliorist manner. In a way they, and reconstructionism, seem to have been the forerunners of what we could now call critical pedagogy (except for the latter's emphasis on learner-direction of the curricula).

There are some intriguing tensions in and between progressivism and reconstructionism. First, in hindsight, how progress was conceived at the turn of the 19th to 20th centuries was a little ambiguous. On the one hand was a strongly democratic, egalitarian current; in this, social and political developments were going to make the world a better place for ordinary people. This trend tended to be antiaristocratic and anti-clerical, and potentially politically radical. On the other hand, though not at the time clearly distinguishable perhaps, was an equally anti-traditionalist position in which science, medicine, and rational expert approaches to government, social policy, and business, were going to lead to an era of wealth and resources for all; the "hard wing" of progressivism just mentioned, and presumably the wing least comfortable with reconstructionism.

For the FL analyst Clark, reconstructionism surfaces in our field during the post-World War II era, in the efforts of the Council of Europe to design curricula that would go along with the reconstruction of Europe in that period. ES/FL teachers, and teachers of other languages, may be familiar with notional/functional syllabi or curricula as one of a number of options within the communicative tradition, but may not be familiar with the social and political forces associated with their initial inspiration and uptake. The first widely influential notional/functional syllabi were developed through a large international project; the intent was to develop a foreign language qualification or standard (a "unit/credit scheme") that would be internationally recognized across the main European nations (see e.g., van Ek & Alexander, 1975). "The aim of the work...is to encourage the development of understanding, cooperation and mobility among Europeans by improving and broadening the learning of modern languages by all sections of the population" (ibid., unpaginated prefatory material). The thrust of this kind of curriculum was international communication for travel, tourism, and employment-related purposes; target groups included migratory workers, that is, the disadvantaged as well as the advantaged learner; and the associated pedagogical goals were very much focused on the communication of meaning.

Indeed, clearly the long-running political efforts to permanently eliminate the threat of another major war in Europe by moving to the integration of the nations of Europe could very much be seen as reconstruction; this was a term used in the post–World War II era. Since broadly communicative curriculum structures have become widespread, they may not now be seen as Clark saw them, that is, as manifesting reconstructionist ambitions. At the same time, this type of curriculum has some of the scientistic, rationalistic traditions of the second kind of reconstructionism just mentioned, in that it stresses objectives. That is, it is closely connected to developments of "rational" syllabus design (following Tyler, 1949: based on assessment of needs and clearly specified, measurable objectives), as determined by experts.

Essentialism

Essentialism is the "back to basics" position that encourages a supposedly simple and direct focus, in schools, on those things that children "need": basic skills of literacy or oracy. "It emphasizes the primacy of knowledge" (Strain, 1971: 12). The term was first coined by Demiashkevich in the 1930s, to signify a position that was opposed to that of progressivism (see Demiashkevich, 1935). In the developed world, it is also directly justified by the supposed needs of commerce, industry, or employment – the things that schools should teach are those things that will enable school students to get a job. In this it certainly connects with a very visible tradition in school that has manifested itself vigorously since the late 19th century. It is interesting to discover that not all attitudes to school in the West have been utilitarian. In fact, in the Anglo-American tradition, prior to that time, that is, during most of the 19th century and earlier, a more elevated tradition dominated. This was closely linked with the classics movement. It is why the great bulk of the 19th-century curriculum involved extended contact with the classical works of Latin and Greek literature, at the expense of supposedly more useful "modern" languages (e.g., French), let alone vocational subjects such as accounting, or more modern subject matter, such as the physical sciences. This tradition was only abandoned under the pressure of "men of business" toward the end of the 19th century. Along with developments in management and business (Fordism, Taylorism), we see the decline of the "classical" curriculum and the rise of a strong vocational dimension in schools (Kliebard, 1999; Sola, 1973, 1974).

Perennialism

Perennialism could be seen as a label for a very widely established tradition in education across all times and cultures. I would suggest that, if a culture is not in a time of revolutionary change, then school will be seen (rightly or wrongly) as a place in which the "best" values of the culture are transmitted. In turn, a conservative perspective is quite likely to see those values as timeless, or perennial. From a philosophical systems point of view, this position draws on both realist and idealist positions, and has a humanist emphasis. It is likely to draw from history, literature, and religion, and from classic texts.

For Clark (1987), the classical humanist tradition in modern education is an offshoot and development of the classics movement of the 19th century (in the West). But any curricular or pedagogical tradition that places strong authority in ancient texts, and sets up school practices with the intent that students engage with foreign languages so as to derive meaning and values from those texts, could be seen as classical. They will also be "humanist" if a religious element is weak, or if it is explicitly deferred in favor of human (rather than other-worldly) values. Thus I suppose that long periods in Chinese and Islamic education would have been, or still are, exhibiting characteristics similar to those of the classics movement. Once the language of those religious texts becomes archaic, or if we consider countries in which those are foreign languages, then we are likely to find a classical FL tradition. It is noteworthy that the techniques Clark finds as most likely to be associated with this tradition are probably more or less the same regardless of the specific cultural contexts in which classical FL studies appear. As Clark writes,

> The methodology favored lays considerable stress on conscious study and deliberate learning, on understanding the particular rules or principles underlying the particular knowledge elements to be learnt, and on conscious reapplications of them in new contexts. The teacher presents data designed to highlight a particular rule.... The best-known approach to the foreign language curriculum to which classical humanism has given rise is the grammar–translation method.
>
> (1987: 7–8)

And it requires very little effort to turn up reports of their use as applied to a variety of languages in a range of different cultures and times: e.g., French in 19th-century England (Kern, 2000), or Chinese in Japan during most of its history (*yakudoku*; Gorsuch, 1998; Hino, 1988; *kambun kundoku*; Wakabayashi, 2005) not to mention, of course, regrettably, English at the present time in many countries.

Concluding remark

This chapter has provided two system-based overviews representing conventional understandings of the domain of philosophy of education: (1) the components of any complete philosophical system, and (2) a brief listing of three major "schools" of philosophy. The major schools of philosophy necessarily stand at quite some distance from educational practice and do not directly imply specific unitary sets of practices. I reviewed them partly to establish the meaning of some important technical terms; and also to introduce the philosopher of education (Dewey) whose work and whose school (pragmatism) has a more substantial though unacknowledged influence on some aspects of recent language teaching than might have been expected. The idea of a small set of major philosophies of schooling is obviously an oversimplification of complex material, and I am not trying to suggest at all that teachers fall into one (or any) of some "official" set of categories. However, Clark did show how this simple structure from the philosophy of education has been used to interpret broader and less explicit sets of positions visible particularly within the curriculum literature of our own field. I assert that within, or below, such curricular positions and broad philosophical concepts can be found more fundamental assumptions that deserve to be explored by reflective language teachers developing their philosophies of teaching.

Discussion questions

1. Do grammatical structures exist? Does a notion or a function have reality?
2. Do you know anything absolutely, or do you know things through your experience of them? As a language teacher, what are some things you know about language learning and teaching (and how did you come to know them)?
3. Are you an individual or a member of society? How did you come to be so?
4. Okay, you don't get asked this question very often, so it's about time: What is the meaning of life? Does the fact that you are (or intend to be) a language teacher have any connection with your answer? (See also Chapter 5 on this.)

Notes to Chapter 4

[1] Or even "thought patterns," as Strain (1971: 12) calls them.
[2] The division of philosophy into three or four main domains, as implied here, is historically concurrent with the rise of philosophy as a modern academic discipline, which is to say, the 19th century. Dubray (1909: 506) notes that "the term epistemology is of recent origin" and attributes Ferrier's "Institutes of Metaphysics: The Theory of Knowing and Being" (1854) as a prominent early use of the term.

3 Some specify "logic" as a major component, also.

4 An older, extreme position attempted to derive systems from principles at the level of metaphysics, epistemology, etc. This expository strategy was criticized for forcing matters, reification, and so on (e.g., McMurrin, 1968).

5 For example, Einstein's space–time theory includes the metaphysical position that the concept of "absolute space" is meaningless. In Einstein's view, a space is only meaningful relative to another; hence his work is referred to as "relativity" theory.

6 For some Catholics, for instance, a "preferential option for the poor" is the outcome of a particular theological tradition that has clear educational implications; this theological line may be disputed by others within the same religious tradition.

7 I am not sure, however, if they are timeless. Strain (1971) was convinced that there were exactly nine systems that were in play in "modern" education; some of the same candidates appear in many different expositions though in more recent treatments the list is less fixed.

8 From whom Dewey derived his initial major contact with Hegel: Gordon & White (1979).

9 E.g., Schiller, Balfour, and Vaihinger (see Marler, 1975: 377) in Europe, as well as Hu Shih, in China. And "as early as 1908," at least 13 different varieties had been identified (Lovejoy, 1908); present-day (neo)-pragmatism is equally diverse (Gimmler, 2004).

10 This would appear to be a rather different understanding than that of the "progressive school" of the United States in the 1920s to 1940s.

5 Two recent philosophical movements, language teaching, and the way the world is going (perhaps)

Introduction

In this chapter, I return somewhat to a historical organization, getting up to the present and briefly reviewing two "schools" or viewpoints, which have recently provided ways of thinking about important ideas that dispute the status quo or that reflect a claimed change in the world. It is a fundamental tenet of philosophical method that all assumptions are subject to question. Perhaps one could say, in the current state of the world, that the "status quo" has strongly Anglo-American aspects to it (even beyond the matter of English as a world language). Thus it might be understandable that some of the challenges to the philosophical status quo have come from elsewhere – and are named as such, under the heading "continental philosophy." Although I will point out the limitations of the term, it can get us started on some interesting areas whose developments and applications have been, or are, playing out in some parts of our field.

One thing about studying philosophy, whether as a basis for one's own philosophy of teaching or for any other reason, is that it does develop one's sense of perspective. Many of the issues under consideration have been the subject of extensive discussion off and on for thousands of years, and across all the civilizations and cultures of East and West, "developed" North and latterly "poor" South. Not only has there been no final resolution of these various matters, but a remarkable number of differences of opinion often develop within what one might otherwise think were singular or unitary positions. For example, refer back to a philosophical position introduced (simplistically) in the previous chapter: realism. This is a term around which there was some debate in the research end of our field a few years ago. Yet there are a very large number of different types of realism.[1] Discussions in our field that merely refer to realism (or, say, its presumed opposite, relativism), without identifying the variety in question, are thus usually identifiable as naïve or uninformed, immediately – though this may be excusable in textbook presentations, as opposed to works written for supposed specialists. Few philosophical positions can be captured in a single label, and most have a multitude of quite diverse, even mutually contradictory variants. Debate that makes use of unqualified versions of such terms is likely to be unproductive.

It is also intriguing to discover how ideas themselves have fashions; ideas can vanish from sight for long periods of time, and then return, as good as new and indeed be viewed by many (lacking historical memory) as if they *were* new. This sort of thing is, in a sense, exacerbated by the tendency for cultures to be carriers of sets of ideas; perhaps, in a way, like continents carry particular animal species. When there are land bridges, the ideas (and animals) interbreed; when the bridges are submerged, separation and speciation takes place, and eventually what was the same comes to seem rather different. And in regard to these different positions, if one wants to understand an intellectual position, one often has to try to find out *against what* it has been established (or is being advocated). It is difficult to understand a conversation when one comes into it part way through. It is even more difficult, perhaps, to understand an argument under the same circumstances. Why are the speakers so fired up?, one wonders. Why do certain terms apparently carry so much significance? And in other cases, one finds, on probing, that one is listening to a mediator, a third party trying to bring two sides together.

Although the positions we will engage with in this chapter are in this sense timeless, they are also recent (or recently resurgent) developments in the world of ideas. Thus they are not part of common sense, and are consequently unfamiliar. However, they play into discussions of long-standing topics in many areas that will be of use in the development of a philosophy of S/FL teaching, so we need to be aware of how the landscape of ideas has changed.

The first section addresses the original separation of paths between Anglo-American and continental traditions in philosophy. This enables me to go over a somewhat influential alternative philosophy that some-times appears in educational contexts: existentialism. My account then passes back into an area familiar to language teachers, namely structural-ism. This school was the parent of more challenging recent manifesta-tions of continental traditions (still involving the word "structuralism") that have been involved in discussions of language, in questions of what we can achieve, as language teachers, and of what we can know, or base our teaching on. It thus should be taken, among other things, as a metacomment on the chapter that follows (Chapter 6), which draws on a more mainstream approach to epistemology.

The nonempiricists

Let us recall that not much more than 400 years ago, in Europe, Christianity was quite all-pervasive.[2] Also at this time, however, after being absent from the Western world of ideas for some considerable time (though preserved and developed in the Islamic world), many pre-Christian philosophical traditions had begun to resurface. Many were accommodated with varying degrees of ease, but some seemed particularly challenging, or led to striking developments.

One noteworthy resurfacing, in the 16th century, was of the ideas of the skeptics, a school of thought, which was part of the later Greek and Roman tradition. This, along with the challenges posed by early European science, called into question Christian faith as a way of understanding the world. Some began to wish to put their trust only in what could directly be perceived: the empirical world. Doubt of this kind was to the benefit of political authorities who felt too constrained by the power of the Christian Catholic church. It was against this sort of challenge that Descartes, in France, began his own test of faith through a process of doubt, in the hope of eventually being able to defend Christian faith against all forms of skepticism (e.g., 1640/1998). Descartes is less well-known now as a defender of faith; ironically, he is known as someone who advanced an extreme form of rationalism. Despite Descartes's efforts, faith continued to be questioned by philosophers, and as the Enlightenment continued, the influential philosopher Hume, in Scotland, advanced an extremely doubting position (e.g., 1748/1999). One famous response to these two sides of an argument came from Kant (e.g., 1781/1990), who tried to unify the insights of Descartes, a Frenchman, with the strengths, as he saw them, of the Anglo-Scottish tradition of Hume and Locke. This he did by proposing certain innate cognitive structures but at the same time emphasizing the role of the senses in developing our understanding based on them.[3]

In the philosophical developments that continued this discussion, some of those who defended faith in a nonreal world developed philosophical systems that favored the mind and the ideal, but diluted the religious component. These were the idealists, associated with the foundation of new universities in northern Germany (such as Jena), above all Hegel. As ever, it is worth mentioning the political dimension to this movement. These small universities had a specific role to train the priests of the areas, and accordingly were funded by the local rulers with particular ideological objectives. That they produced not only clerics but also philosophers is interesting, and we can half expect the philosophical doctrines in question to have some political responsibilities to the professors' paymasters.

Around this time, about the early 1800s, an important parting of the ways begins. On the one hand, we have the German idealists' persistent and continuing interest in the internal life of the mind – of things beyond the tangible, and a concern for consciousness itself. On the other hand, offshore of the continent of Europe, British philosophers developed their concern with the immediate matters produced by the senses.

I am simplifying, of course; ideas (and people) did crisscross the oceans. As mentioned earlier, there were British and American idealists, as well as continental ones. But distance, different languages, and the difficulty of both sets of ideas made misunderstanding and mutual disinterest likely. And in due course, not only were there cultural differences, there were also political differences to contend with. The dominant British traditions were the developments of the empiricists, in the work of J. S. Mill, for example; this was also closely associated with the ideas of representative democracy (e.g., Mill, 1859/1975). On the other hand, Hegel was the doyen of German idealists, with a concern for historical trends as a manifestation in this world of things otherwise distant, and with a statist orientation. His student Marx maintained the interest in history while substituting a strongly materialist position for the idealism. Others in Europe, notably Nietzsche, continued a tradition of stylistically innovative (if difficult) writing and trenchant social critique. In the 1950s, the term "continental philosophy" came to be used as shorthand for a variety of philosophical positions taken mainly by European philosophers, as opposed to British or American philosophers, since the 19th century (Glendenning, 1999). Clearly it is a rather parochial term, since philosophy is on the one hand an international endeavor, and then, if we must divide it, there is Western and Eastern philosophy; by the time we have carved out a certain (continental European) portion of Western philosophy we have, on the face of it, a rather small part. Or, you might say, what about Greek philosophy? Is that not also from the continent of Europe? In the matter under consideration, a geographical term is being used to actually refer to the thinkers of a particular historical period and with a particular historical inheritance within the history of ideas. So why persist in the term? Well, it is convenient; and the distinctiveness of the tradition also persists. Even in the latter half of the 20th century, at a time when we might have thought that separation by language or geography was diminishing, the area still proved capable of producing initiatives in the world of ideas that were regarded as shocking, incomprehensible, and indeed a threat to civilization as we know it, by mainstream philosophers, researchers, and eventually by some S/FL specialists. Thus if we are to be current, to say the least, we should have some familiarity with this apparently inexhaustible stream of challenging ideas. But, you may say, you have no interest in being fashionable. What has this to do with language teaching? Well, one strand of this thought is manifested in a particular set of curricular orientations in education generally (and in language teaching) in the 1960s that still resonates; and a later strand of this thought provides a current challenge to the supposed research bases for language teaching. Both thus could play into a language teacher's philosophy of teaching.

Traditions of continental philosophy

Idealisms naturally lead to a concern with consciousness. That is, a turning away from the "real" world would presumably suggest consideration of the interior world. If this seems plausible, then the concerns of German idealists such as Hegel, with "spirit" (or *Geist*), can lead naturally to developments of techniques and concepts that focus on consciousness. Notable among these was phenomenology; closely related is hermeneutics; and drawing on the perspectives of both came (by the mid-20th century) the tradition of existentialism. This philosophical approach, or school, had some implications for education, even if its most famous or central exponents did not address themselves to educational matters to the extent that Dewey, for example, did. After the decline of the Progressive Movement (by the 1940s), those who wished to articulate alternative, nonmainstream positions in education reached for the concepts that this alternative conceptual movement had to offer. Since existentialism was an outgrowth of phenomenology (and to some extent hermeneutics), let me very briefly try to define these before turning to existentialism itself.

Phenomenology is a descriptive science concerned with the objects and structures of consciousness. (The term was coined by one of Kant's correspondents and popularized by Kant himself.) It can be seen as deriving from Descartes's "method of doubt," and was drawn on by Hegel, but is particularly associated with Husserl (born in Moravia, Czechoslovakia, but working in Germany), who flourished during the 1920s and 1930s, and his student Heidegger. Above all, it attempts to identify the persisting features of subjectivity (or consciousness). Heidegger continued the willingness of other German scholars to develop philosophical systems of enormous complexity and great stylistic impenetrability, and thus contributed to the myth of "continental philosophy."

"Whereas phenomenology seeks an ordered description of the objects of consciousness, hermeneutics concentrates on the interpretation and meaning of conscious experience over time" (Ozmon & Craver, 1999: 257). Sometimes confused with phenomenology, this has been described as a philosophical search for meaning, rejecting both foundationalism and nihilism, and accepting contingency and historicity. Hermeneutics was originally associated with the interpretation of texts, but the approach came to be applied to the events of life and of consciousness as well. The term "hermeneutic spiral" is applied to this kind of interpretive understanding; coming to understand is more like getting acquainted with a person than like following a demonstration. Possessing a strong engagement with language itself, this is a way of practicing philosophy that should be of interest to second language teachers. The two individuals most associated with this development of the language aspects of consciousness have been Gadamer and Ricoeur. To the latter is sometimes attributed the "linguistic turn" – the movement toward exploring the extent to which "everything" is language or text.

Existentialism

In the period immediately after the end of World War II, the existentialist movement burst onto the scene of the world of ideas in the classic manner – rapidly taken up, even if only partially understood; iconoclastic, denounced in the popular press, associated with the young and the "hip"; and initially published mainly in a language other than English – this itself clearly constituting an insult to the dominant powers of the "free world" at that time! Even worse, though the movement was not explicitly political, some of its leading figures turned out to have left-wing sympathies. The best-known of these, of course, was Jean-Paul Sartre, who had studied Husserl and Heidegger in Germany before World War II. In the period of turbulent cultural and intellectual change that immediately followed the war, between about 1945 and 1965, existentialism was an important intellectual component.

Existentialism is a theorizing of the individual and individual consciousness. (Though it is not concerned with the analysis of human subjectivity, and our consciousness, into some lower levels of structure the way that cognitive psychology is.) It rejects the idea of a preformed human nature, and emphasizes the freedom of human beings, a freedom to make themselves through planning, reflecting, choosing, and acting.[4] Existence involves conscious awareness of our human condition, including death, and responsibility for the sort of person we have become. If those are the basic concepts, existentialism actually would seem particularly appropriate to the idea of a philosophy of teaching as quite constitutive of oneself as the person (and teacher) one would like to be; in constructing a philosophy of teaching we are to some degree setting up ideals we will try to steer by and thus we are trying to construct ourselves. If we cannot, indeed, make and remake ourselves, the concept of a philosophy of teaching would seem to be less relevant to professional practice.

One major distinction among existentialist philosophers is between those who worked with ideas of religion and those who were agnostic or atheist. Religious existentialists (Buber, Kierkegaard, Tillich) emphasize the relation of individuals to God directly rather than through systems. Tillich emphasized the human need for an "ultimate concern" without which life would have no meaning. By contrast, nonreligious existentialists, e.g., Sartre, refer to "optimistic toughness,"[5] which seems to imply a willingness of individuals to get on with human life with all its limitations, and without complaint. In this position, what humans do is what becomes human nature. Both groups emphasize the "absurdity" of human life, referring to the absence of a rational plan from God (or any other external authority) concerning human life. Recognition of this situation, however, causes anguish (the famous existential *"angst"*). Existentialists suggest that we either accept that there is no meaning to life, or get out there and make one (a perspective quite useful for those seeking "the meaning of life"; cf. Baumeister, 1991; Lurie, 2006).

Sartre is the paradigmatic existentialist philosopher. In discussing his views (as expressed in his *Being and Nothingness*, 1956) as potentially useful for a teacher developing a philosophy of teaching, Ozmon and Craver observe that:

> Sartre's point of view is very austere ... Yet, it would be an error to take this notion too far. Sartre stated that "existence precedes essence" and meant that if we are indeed without meaning when we are born, then we can fashion our own meaning in the world in any way we see fit. According to Sartre, if there is no ... First Cause ... then there is nothing to prevent us from becoming whatever we desire because there is no predetermined self or essence.
>
> The same can be said for physical reality and science because Sartre saw science as a human creation, no better or no worse in and of itself than any other creation. Thus, when we step back and view ourselves as we really are, we see that *nothing* determines us to do anything; all the absolutes, rules, and restrictions are simply the puny and absurd creations of humans. If there are not primal restrictions, then there is no determinism. Everything is possible. Humanity is absolutely free; as Sartre put it ... "Man is condemned to be free."
>
> (1999: 250–51)

Existentialist ideas were taken up and digested for educators in the English-speaking world (by, for example, Kneller, 1958; Morris, 1966; and the dates are indicative of the time of greatest popularity of this philosophy). From that time on they have provided philosophical resources for nonmainstream teaching. Referring to practical implications of this line, Ozmon and Craver explain:

> The first thing that most existentialists want is a change in our attitude about education. Instead of seeing it as something

a student is filled with, measured against, or fitted into, the existentialist suggests that we first look at students as individuals and that we allow them to take a positive role in the shaping of their own education and life.... Existentialists urge that schools and other institutions be free places where students are encouraged to do things because they want to do them....

Existentialists would like to see an end to the manipulation of the student with teachers controlling students along predetermined behavioral paths. Existentialists would like the children to choose their own paths from the options available to them. Schools often contain uniform materials, curricula, and teaching, and although educators have talked quite a bit about promoting individuality in education, most programs and teaching methods have tended to become more alike. Existentialists argue for diversity in education not only in curriculum but also in the ways things are taught.

(1999: 263)

Some observers have argued that existentialist ideas diffused rapidly into Western cultures in the late 1950s and were carried on into the social and educational revolutions of the 1960s. A couple of directions offered themselves. One was toward the trend of social criticism that was associated also with personal development (the women's movement would be one such). For as one existentialist educational philosopher, Maxine Greene, has observed, freedom does not come from a system; people are not free unless they make themselves so. The individual is not alone, however; in Greene's view, we need others to help us in the struggle to be free and redefine ourselves in creating our life. This position can be (and was) a starting point for discussions of pluralism and identity.[6] In addition, ideas from this philosophical movement, notably "the focus on becoming and particularly the recognition of human will, creativity, and freedom" (Neumann, 2003: 16–17), fed into humanistic psychology, which in turn influenced some of the so-called "alternative approaches" in language teaching that flourished temporarily around this time:

From the perspective of humanistic psychology, the individual's ultimate goal is self-actualization, self-realization, or the full functioning of potentialities and capabilities.... This requires a focus on the growth potential of the learner, which in turn calls for "student-centered" approaches to teaching and curricula.

(Neumann, 2003: 16–17)

Related language-teaching traditions

There is a small group of language-teaching traditions, admittedly not particularly substantial on the ground though appearing regularly in discussions of Methods in our field, that to a greater or lesser extent did derive some of their definitional ideas from existentialism or its close American cousin, humanistic psychology.[7] These Methods are often referred to as "humanistic" (by e.g., Stevick, 1990) though whether all of them are is disputable.[8] The Method most centrally related to existentialist ideas and humanistic psychology is counseling–learning (Curran, 1961), also referred to as confluent education (Galyean, 1976a and 1976b, 1977; Rardin, 1982), a term that captures the confluence of humanistic psychology with existentialism.

The early ideas of Curran concerning language teaching drew from humanistic psychology and focused on addressing the language learner's anxiety, which in turn arose from the difficulties the beginning learner has expressing him or herself as who they are in their first language. The link to the well-known concept of existential *angst* is not totally direct; nevertheless, anxiety is taken as a likely central feature of the initial phases of second language learning in this tradition, and then the teacher–student relationship is structured using insights from counseling to address this.

Another term that occurs repeatedly in this tradition and has clear links to existentialism, is the "whole person." An emphasis on the individual as embodied[9] was typical of existentialism, as was the emphasis on the individual having real needs for meaning (and now, not at some time in the future). Counseling–learning came to the fore in the days of the Audiolingual Method, a time when the learner as having specific needs, and an affective life, was not typically understood or responded to by mainstream language-learning materials and techniques. If the learner is conceived of as a behaving organism, or merely a cognitive system, no account is taken of the learner as a person with real needs to express emotions as well as engage in thinking, an individual with a body as well as a mind.

Galyean's simple pedagogically oriented discussion (1977) put the emphasis on the teacher's selecting material and teaching points that allow the manifestation of students' individual needs and ability to express themselves as individuals. This does *not* refer to job-related "needs," but rather to a sense of how an individual is doing at the level of "lifestyle" (an admittedly dated concept that was once new). She emphasized "interpersonal sharing" and "self-awareness" as "cornerstones of humanistic teaching" (1977: 148). Student goals, and the "meaning–needs" theory identified with humanistic psychology are also referred to. In the latter, "Meaning arises from an individual's urge to seek fulfillment for basic needs, and attitudes, perceptions, and behaviors are shaped by these needs, then all learning is viewed as essentially self enhancing" (p. 150). Galyean and others in this tradition allied themselves with the U.S. perspective on communicative teaching of Savignon (see 1972); they shared a needs perspective with the UK tradition in applied linguistics of this time but clearly separate from its later vocational orientation. In a slightly more developed presentation, Galyean (1979) identified "three philosophical underpinnings" as the foundations for her perspective: behaviorism (*sic*), existentialism, and humanism. The first of these (*contra* Curran, obviously) she believed was necessary to support imitation and repetition of structures. More interestingly, "existentialism, with its emphasis on experiential learning as the root of all other modes of learning, provides teachers with suggestions for 'here and now' situational activities for real life learning" (p. 122). And humanism is equally important for this tradition, as we have already noted. In this case it "views all learning as learning about oneself" because "individuals are essentially motivated by the natural drive for self-understanding and realization" (ibid.).

Existentialism's emphasis on the individual came as a distinctly different, new concern to educators of the 1950s and early 1960s. Particularly those brought up in a Deweyan approach had tended to emphasize societal and group concerns. Elsewhere, the world was just recovering from emphases on the state, and nationalism was probably the major driving force for education. So a focus on the individual (that seemed unwarranted to the survivors of World War II) was indeed one of the things that existentialism was stereotyped for. "Doing your own thing" was initially a loaded phrase used to describe a perception of illegitimate self-centeredness that began to appear in the youth culture of the 1960s.[10] However, as we have had since then not only the "me-decade" of the 1980s, but also the acceptance of "learner-centered education" both in language teaching and elsewhere, this focus is quite accepted now. But as Rardin's remarks make clear, at the time this was something of a new departure:

> What does it mean to call myself a humanistic educator? It means that I respect an inner capacity – an integrating principle – in each learner to gain insights and make choices appropriate to his / her own learning process. Interwoven with this is an appreciation of the uniqueness of each learner. I constantly work against the notion that I have a "group" in front of me. I have, in fact, twenty-five or thirty individuals in class, each of whom will be relating to the learning process and tasks in his/her own ways.
>
> (1982: 62)

I think, then, that this is a case where what were originally quite challenging new ideas have been substantially integrated into mainstream culture as a whole. Nevertheless, the teacher who wishes to develop a clear philosophy of teaching may wish to consider what, indeed, is their conception of the person. Insofar as a language teacher conceives a student as having an emotional engagement with learning and the language, they are operating with concepts from humanistic psychology. To some extent when they consider the individual learner as having specific needs and a strong desire to make meaning of what they are learning, so as to make choices concerning their life, then again they are in line with the existentialist view of the person and of the student.

Structuralism and reactions to it: Post-structuralist ideas about language and consciousness

I move now to a second, more recent "continental" challenge. In order to provide what I hope is a useful perspective on fairly recent developments in the world of ideas that are relevant to language teachers, I need to back up to the very beginning of the 20th century to pick up the trail. In this case, we are dealing initially not with the mind, or being, but with language. Philosophical interest in language has never been purely instrumental, in the sense of only being interested in an object that we humans use. Off and on over many eras and cultures, language has been seen as having far more power. It has been seen as a window into the mind, the soul, or the individual, and as having control over the world (Formigart, 2004). A prominent intellectual movement of the 20th century picked up ideas originally developed with reference to language and used them to organize thought about other fundamental philosophical ideas. This movement was structuralism.

Because of their backgrounds in linguistics, many language teachers will be familiar with the name of Saussure, de facto one of the founders of structuralism. Toward the end of his life, this linguist was lecturing on topics whose development and publication he did not complete. After his death, the material was written up by his students from lecture notes, as Saussure's *Cours linguistique* (1916/1959). The work delivered its key message – that language was an arbitrary system of distinctions – into the hungry bubbling cauldron of ideas that was the early decades of the 20th century. This deposit turned out to be very fruitful, spawning not only schools of linguistics and further conceptions of language but also interacting with the interest in consciousness that the idealists had recently made prominent. On the one hand, this interest in structure, particularly in the sense of *underlying* structure, when transmuted through an emphasis on behavior in the American mid-century, produced a kind of theoretical linguistics that most S/FL teachers are somewhat familiar with (even though they may not use it to teach with).[11] But on the other hand (and this has been the more marginalized tradition, until recently), it spawned a line of development in continental European thought that persisted in inquiring into the ways language was involved, underlyingly, in the development, construction, repression, of people themselves (e.g., Levi-Strauss, 1963).

On the one hand, this line of thought generates a very decontextualized understanding of language. Structure seems inevitably to be what is left, like a skeleton, when the context (or meat, or life) is removed. But on the other hand, some who made use of these ideas (as the 1960s moved into the 1970s) saw the all-pervasiveness of structure as having power, or strong implications, concerning thought, and concepts, within society. Through inquiring into the interface between language and various societal forms, they developed a highly implicated understanding of language, as impossible without a social dimension: language as action or function, rather than entity;[12] language as discourse processes, literacy and oracy, as opposed to language as subject–verb agreement or computer program.

Before we move on to the later responses to structuralism, let me point to one side, rather than forward. As ever, it turns out that at the same time as one system of ideas was new, fresh, and energetic, another which might displace it already coexisted with it, though on the margins or at a distance. A simple way to characterize the different conceptualizations of language just alluded to is formal versus functional. And almost as early in the 20th century as Saussure, but in a separate area not well-connected to the mainstream of European ideas (provincial Russia under Stalin), the functional understanding of language, in the person of Mikhail Bakhtin, was also present:

> Language is unitary... only as an abstract grammatical system of normative forms, taken in isolation from the concrete, ideological conceptualizations that fill it, and in isolation from the uninterrupted process of historical becoming that is a characteristic of all living language. Actual social life and historical becoming create... a multitude of bounded verbal-ideological and social belief systems...
>
> (1935/1981: 288, cited in Lee, 1992)

More or less implied in the last sentence of that quote is another angle on language as functional, which has also become more influential of late. One philosopher of language puts it this way:

103

> The point is that language is as practical as it is theoretical, that utterances are acts as well as descriptions. Even more important, rhetoric and theoretical discourse are themselves actions. Utterances are at least partly . . . speech or utterance acts, and as such acts inhabit public milieux of power relations and political efficacies. Even this account falls short, for legislation, discourse, analysis, all the forms of representational "writing," regarded as the production of texts rather than utterances, also exhibit and inhabit power relations and have political force. In this respect, there is no discourse that is not uttered in a social and political, though also an individual, milieu.
>
> (Ross, 1994: 76)

Here Ross is moving through two phases of our recent understandings of language. The idea that utterances are acts has been very influential and indeed beneficial for S/FL teachers: Speech act theory (discussed briefly in the following chapter) has fed successfully into the functional versions of L2 teaching. Going beyond this account of language that "falls short," Ross alludes to language and especially writing that has "political force." Here we have the idea that forms of language are not entirely separable from action in a sociopolitical context. It is akin to a move from viewing language "as a relatively homogenous language-object, to a view of language as a heterogeneous set of discursive practices" (Lee, 1992: 134). And it encompasses the position that these discursive or discourse processes have both constructive and destructive force in society and on individuals. This view has been a powerful transformative upsurge in the last 40 years of thought about language.

The emphasis on language as inextricably involved in social processes (thus, language as discourse), is an idea strongly associated with the French post-structuralist Michel Foucault. One could chose a date like 1970 to mark the emergence of these ideas, when Foucault gave his inaugural lecture at the Collège de France on some aspects of discourse, which included a reference to its active force as its "heavy and threatening materiality" (Foucault, 1970/1993, cited in Wodak, 1996: 24). So it is around this time that structuralism begins, in some areas at least, to give way to post-structuralism. What does post-structuralism (and its associated term postmodernism) have, if anything, to offer the philosophy of language teaching specialist?

To some extent, the viewing of language as active is a reaction to its dissection under structuralism, and thus it is natural to place it under the heading post-structuralism (the second manifestation of "continental philosophy" with which this chapter is concerned). This area of thought, often referred to by the term postmodernism – though there are some important differences between it and post-structuralism – manifested itself eventually in a very similar way to the existentialist movement mentioned earlier.[13] Equally propelled by a concern with consciousness and an interest in "the subject" (or the person), this movement is seen as emerging from France about 20 years after existentialism. It too, intriguingly, called forth exactly the same response that existentialism received: incomprehension, shock, opposition, and/or rapid uptake coupled with only partial understanding.

From my point of view, the important thing about Foucault is that his work encourages one to question the "truths" produced by academic disciplines.[14] His work does this by following the tradition of the academic field known as the "history of ideas" (e.g., Canguilhem, 1988). Much of Foucault's work, and of those who followed his lead, involves the documenting, in some detail, of how ideas in society that we now take as givens (commonsense concepts, mainstream ideas) at one time did not exist, and subsequently and gradually were produced and entered mainstream discourse, often through the interactions of political needs and pressures with the actions of specialists and scientific disciplines.[15]

This position has been taken up[16] by some critical ELT specialists. For example, Pennycook provides an exposition of related material and refers (quoting McHoul & Luke, 1989) to this position as one major understanding of discourse:

> A continental European (predominantly French) approach, by contrast, tends to theorize discourses from the very beginning as "socio-historically specific systems of knowledge and thought."
>
> (1994: 127)

Focusing on the work of the individual of interest here, Pennycook continues:

> A key part of Foucault's work...is his analysis of how various knowledges and disciplines – medical, psychological, psychoanalytical, penitential, sexual, and so on – normalize social institutions and practices in society. Central to this attempt to write histories of how human beings are made subjects (the subject, "individual," or "man," are produced, not pre-given categories) is the notion of discourse, for "it is in discourse," he suggests, "that power and knowledge are joined together" (Foucault, 1980: 100).
>
> (ibid.)

Foucault's insistence that knowledge and power are inseparable does not mean that no knowledge can be arrived at, though it does perhaps mean that no knowledge is absolutely "pure," or absolutely general. In any case, it is a position that need not be held entirely separate from more mainstream positions such as that of Popper, for whom scientific knowledge is always strictly tentative, or Dewey, with his emphasis on warranted assertion, as truth being no more than what works for now. Foucault himself emphasized "local knowledge." As a specialist in prison reform, based on his historical knowledge of the development of penal institutions, he did not shrink from publicly advocating certain measures for which he believed there was good empirical evidence. But this position was generally consistent with the famous remark of another postmodernist, Lyotard, concerning "incredulity toward meta-narratives" (1979/1984: xxiv–xxv). That is, knowing the means by which ideas were produced and became part of culture might lead one to question the likelihood that any single explanation would suffice for all times and places.

Doubts about the utility of Foucault's work have focused on another aspect of his studies. He was interested not only in knowledge as produced by discourses, but also how it (arguably) produced "subjects." The ambiguity in both French and English here is such that we can talk about subject matter as well as people using the same noun. Insofar as and to the extent that the disciplines of society produce the subject, so the less is that subject the Kantian autonomous rational knower/agent.[17] Foucault's ideas imply a constituted subject and perhaps one with multiple or shifting identities, challenging Descartes and Sartre. This concept, provocatively referred to as the "death of the subject," has been seen as threatening the agency of any actors challenging the status quo, and is the reason that some of those interested in social change have been quite negative about this line within post-structuralist theorizing. So this kind of "continental philosophy" is initially antithetical to an earlier set of continental philosophers and social theoreticians, such as Marx, Bakunin, or Proudhon.[18] (The development of these viewpoints for language teaching is deferred to Chapter 9.)

Let me highlight one more shift, or tension, here. Once we (teachers of language using the work of theorists of language) focus on language as act rather than structure, it is natural to attend to the embodied forms of language enacted: Language becomes manifest as literacy and oracy. Indeed, while language may have abstract structure, it needs literacy and oracy to manifest in the real world; without them, how can it have agency? Similarly, language teachers have been well aware that when they were not teaching "grammar," they were teaching either the old "four skills" of listening, speaking, reading, and writing; or, if we take a more integrated perspective, the social practices of literacy and oracy. Thus students of the acquisition of second languages increasingly focus on the acquisition not just of structure, but on the acquisition of the socially (and politically) situated second or foreign language literacies with their associated degrees of agency.

Modernism and reactions to it: Postmodern ideas about society and change

Throughout this work so far I have emphasized the importance of seeing ideas in their historical contexts. Post-structuralism and existentialism are certainly responses to specific historical circumstances; some post-structuralists also responded to what they saw as the distinctly different social conditions of the late 20th century by trying to theorize them as involving a break, or rupture, with what had preceded them in the world of ideas. Specialists in these areas abstract from the conditions, ideas, and values of modern (as opposed to traditional) societies and refer broadly to "modernity." Some, particularly scholars associated with the developments of continental philosophy, advanced the possibility that we are now in an emerging condition called "postmodernity."[19] If the term is developed as a descriptor concerning social conditions, it indicates, in particular, conditions of nonhomogeneity. Populations are not static, but move freely or under constraint around the world. The vast and often illegal migrations from South to North would be indicative of this; the fact that there are undocumented Pakistani migrants in Japan,[20] villages in Italy populated by workers from Mali and Senegal,[21] vast upsurges of individuals from Central and South America in North America, East Asians in Canada and Australia; and so on. Associated with this has been a willingness of social theorists to point out the extent to which the homogeneity of cultures was never more than an effect of description; there were always marginal groups, it is just that we are much more aware of them now than we were before. Continuing the emphasis on nonhomogeneity, at the level of the individual, theories of personal identity have advanced the view that people are not necessarily fixed themselves; multicultural individuals (our consumer group, if we are language teachers) often could be thought of as having "multiple identities" (a term that would have been thought to indicate a pathology in much of the 20th century). This can also operate at the level of gender, as well as culture, and the binaries of race (inherited from the structuralists) are called into question also.

Many would not agree that conditions in the world, or in developed countries, have in fact radically changed from those of "modernity." Particularly reacting to the loose, unhelpfully broad and often pejorative use of the term postmodernism, some analysts prefer to confine it to its original area of reference, namely art and architecture, and when describing society and social changes instead refer to "late capitalism," or even "fast capitalism" (Agger, 1989). For this line of thinking, the decline of the Second World (the former communist bloc), the lowering of tariff barriers (freer movement of capital), and migration reflecting the increasing impoverishment of the Third World (freer movement of labor), are the conditions of "globalization," in which an earlier trend (internationalization) has been to some extent hijacked by forces associated with international business (or what used to be called "finance capital").

In getting caught up with movements in the world of ideas, I think it is important that language teachers, particularly English teachers, who are heavily involved in facilitating the movement of individuals across cultural and linguistic borders, locate themselves with reference to some of the ideas associated with globalization, and possibly postmodernism as well.[22]

Concluding remark

Certainly the "continental" traditions I have briefly alluded to in this chapter are not comprehensive systematizing initiatives. As ever, besides their substantive contributions, they are also responses to previous positions; so some, under the heading of postmodernism, are actually attempting to rebut some flying the flag of existentialism. As the first flush of enthusiasm (or horror) passes, there is also a rapid move, particularly by those who disapproved of the movements in the first place, to declare them "dead"; but in some instances what has actually happened is that the primary concerns of these fields of ideas have been taken up and integrated into ongoing discussions of long standing; often without resolving contradictions. This has been the case, in my opinion, for existentialism's idea of the self-created self. It has very much been the case for the conceptions of knowledge and discourse enunciated by post-structuralism.

The relationship between language, the individual, and the world ought to be of great concern to language teachers. Thus we ought to concern ourselves with the full range of options that specialists suggest are possible, while not dismissing our own judgment, or our own ability to theorize from practice. The continental tradition in philosophy has taken the creation of the individual as a central concern, rather than taking the individual as given. The most recent versions of it engage with language as a very active form of social practice and present a challenge to the idea of language as mere structure, claiming instead that it, along with power, is making us and what we know, rather than any other way around. Space does not permit me the time to review the details in sufficient depth for a persuasive case to be made one way or the other, but I do not think a philosophy of teaching can respectably be made without an engagement with these recent arguments that have troubled some taken-for-granted positions.

108

Discussion questions

1. Would you agree that the idea that we should develop ourselves to the fullest is more or less accepted in mainstream culture? If so, is this an example of how mainstream culture has swallowed a key concept of existentialism and/or humanistic psychology? How is self-actualization (the corresponding concept within humanistic psychology, perhaps) to be achieved? Can language teaching facilitate this? Under what conditions?

2. Do you feel a drive, or a need, to make sense of your life? Can you do so through a process of self-creation or re-creation? Under what conditions could you, as a language teacher, reflect such concerns in your orientation to your work?

3. What are some of the differences between viewing language as a relatively homogenous object and viewing it as a heterogeneous set of discursive practices (and what are the associated implications for language teachers)? From what philosophical traditions do those differences in perspective arise?

4. To what extent (if at all) are you the result of discourse processes rather than self-created? How about your students?

Notes to Chapter 5

1. Naïve realism, commonsense realism, hypothetical realism, critical realism, metaphysical realism, internal realism, and possibly more. Besides the naïve one, the rest are associated with various scholars; respectively Wittgenstein, D. T. Campbell, Roy Bhaskar, with Hilary Putnam claiming *both* the last two, at different times (on Putnam's realism, see Stoutland, 2002).

2. And indeed continued to be so in the world of ideas for a very long time: "Before 1860, the president of every major American college was a clergyman; every professor of philosophy, similarly, had a guarantee of moral rectitude through a ministerial degree" (Martin, 2002: 29).

3. Kant's innate ideas seem to have manifested subsequently in our field in Jespersen's set of categories (Jespersen, 1924) and yet again in the "notions" of the notional / functional school (see Howatt, 1984: 280).

4. Sartre's explanation of why we are free is summarized by Ozmon and Craver as follows: "Sartre investigates consciousness (being-for-itself) and the objects of consciousness (being-in-itself). Consciousness, or being-for-itself, is the reflection and negation of the objective world. It is as if human consciousness tries to be its objects, as in the case of the self-conscious person who, in playing a role, literally tries to be the other person ... Consciousness, or individuality, cannot really be what it is not. Being-for-itself always transcends, negates, or goes beyond being-in-itself. This means that human consciousness or individuality is free. In a sense, it could be said that consciousness deals with the meaning of things and not with raw objectivity or things-in-themselves"(1999: 250).

5 This expression was originally used by Sartre in the 1946 publication of a lecture given the previous year, *The humanism of existentialism*. Subsequently, it appeared in English (Sartre, 1957).

6 Perhaps her most classic work, from the time when existentialism was quite dominant, is Greene (1973), but see Greene (1995) for a recent helpful review pertinent to this work.

7 "The ... symposium on existential psychology ... at the 1959 [American Psychological Association] meeting ... cemented the final identification of Rogers, Maslow, May, and Allport with an American brand of existential psychology. It was only in the mid-1960s that this homegrown existentialism was labeled humanistic psychology" (DeCarvalho, 1991: 64).

8 From personal experience, the Silent Way seems pretty inhuman (cf. Brumfit, 1982).

9 In contradistinction to the Cartesian tradition, and that of its descendant, cognitive psychology, in which the individual is reduced to a mind, divorced from race, gender, class, or historical context.

10 Though associated with the hippy movement, it may well have been inherited from the beats / beatniks, who had stronger connections with popular existentialism. Readers over the age of 60 are welcome to write in and correct me on this point. But remember, as John Lennon said, if you can remember the 60s, you weren't really there (man).

11 I.e., Bloomfieldian structural linguistics, and its descendants, Chomskyan theories of language.

12 This does seem to be a pragmatic conception of language, and thus reflects a philosophical tradition crucial for educators.

13 This term is particularly problematic. Just as Marx said he was not a Marxist, Foucault claimed not to know the meaning of the term postmodernism.

14 There were and are a number of other major thinkers who regularly appear under the heading "post-structural" but I do not intend to discuss them here. It is worth saying, however, that as a group their views are quite nonunitary, and that they engaged in vigorous polemic against each other.

15 E.g., Foucault (1978); see also Shapin (1994).

16 Within ELT, Foucault's ideas have been most strongly taken up by the testing community (in the area of "critical language testing"). McNamara (2001, 2003) notes that it is through tests that ELT most obviously "disciplines" its participants, so this is a particularly likely location for the deployment of Foucault's ideas.

17 Marshall (1995: 24) comments, "According to Foucault the arts of government, or governmentality, ... or reasons of state, have touched us all, so that we are not the free autonomous individuals and choosers of individual projects that the liberal framework, and liberal education ..., would make us out to be."

18 The matter is by no means settled. Foucault's views on the matter changed throughout his oeuvre, and recent discussions have highlighted his concern with resistance, which naturally implies some degree of agency (e.g., Deacon, 2003). Foucault commented to this effect toward the end of his life: "If there are relations of power throughout every social field it is because there is freedom everywhere" (1987: 124); "People ... are much freer than they feel" (1988: 10).

19 E.g., Harvey (1990); and for our field, Johnston (1999) advances the claim that English language teaching internationally exemplifies a response to postmodern conditions.

[20] What are Pakistanis doing in Japan? (*The News International* [Pakistan], May 2001; retrieved October 24, 2007, from http://pakavenue.com/overseas/news_updates/news_updates_007.htm)

[21] "Italy's 'little' Senegal" (BBC report, April 19, 2004; retrieved October 24, 2007, from http://news.bbc.co.uk/2/hi/africa/3622953.stm)

[22] This is an extremely broad subtopic whose literature is expanding rapidly; space does not permit more than an opening of the topic here. For a book-length treatment in our field, see Block & Cameron (2002).

6 Epistemology and the S/FL teacher

Introduction

As briefly sketched in Chapter 4, epistemology is the domain of philosophy that investigates knowing. It asks, "What does it mean to know?" or "What is knowledge?"; thus it concerns "theories of knowledge" and "theories of truth." As language teachers, this domain of philosophy can help us have an informed perspective on important aspects of our practice, which after all, does concern knowledge. First, we have knowledge of our subject matter, and after some study and practice, our students also come to have knowledge of a second or foreign language (usually!). Clearly, a thorough understanding of the nature of knowledge of language (and of its learning) ought to be helpful to our efforts. Second, we ourselves have knowledge of teaching. Finally, and closely related to this, our professional practice is itself supposed to be informed by knowledge; the supposed "knowledge base" of the profession – part of our professional beliefs. Here again, theories of knowledge should come to bear. My tentative formulation of the connection can be put more trenchantly:

> At the core of any ... educational enterprise lies a philosophical attitude towards knowledge and the process of its acquisition. On the surface, the terms "curriculum" and "instruction" take precedence in the discussion of schooling; but at a deeper level, epistemology truly holds the key to the learning process in a specific cultural milieu. How a person knows an object and what objects are worth knowing remain the essential questions in an examination of education.
>
> (Stanton, 1990: 68)

We can expand our preliminary understanding of the topic by referring to Scheffler (1978), an educationally oriented review of epistemology. Scheffler identifies the question, "What is knowledge?" as the primary focus of epistemology, but specifies four other related questions:

> The evaluative question: "What knowledge is most reliable or important? ... [which] asks for a classification of sorts of knowing. ... The genetic question: "How does knowledge arise?"

To answer this question is to give an account of the processes or mechanisms by which knowledge develops; it is, typically, to provide some model of the mind that may render learning processes intelligible. Fourthly, there is the methodological question: "How ought the search for knowledge be conducted?" ... Fifthly ... the pedagogical question: "How is knowledge best taught?"

(1978: 5)

Besides the matter of knowledge itself, I will spend some time on sorts of *knowing*, an important area for us, as well as on the "genetic" question, equally important. On this genetic point: Perhaps some knowledge arises innately, but other knowledge presumably comes about through learning. Thus theories of learning, inherently important for the teacher, come in here. As White says,

That area of philosophy known as epistemology has been concerned with questions of how knowledge is acquired and the distinction between knowledge and belief. Epistemology is not concerned with empirical questions about how we learn, but with providing a framework in which such questions can be answered. Questions about how we learn are closely related to these epistemological preoccupations and rest on them to a large extent. The scientific enterprise of learning theory rests on a variety of related epistemological positions and cannot be understood except in terms of them.

(1998: 3–4)

This somewhat neglected area of the philosophy of learning will be taken up quite briefly further on in this chapter.[1] The next of Scheffler's questions concerns research but is posed in the context of education and teaching, and a first response would be to ask, "Which kind of knowledge do you have in mind?" This leads to concerns addressing both (a) the philosophy of scientific research methods, and (b) the status of teacher knowledge and professional knowledge vis-à-vis scientific knowledge. The former, even when restrained only to the S/FL research field, is a large and contentious literature, a survey of which would not be relevant to the goals of the present work. The latter, however, is important in considering how teachers' knowledge is developed and must be reviewed to some extent. Scheffler's last question is one for teachers (rather than the present work) themselves to answer, partly by reference to their philosophy of teaching (or to be incorporated into it).

The first major part of this chapter (the immediately following subsections) bears most on our own knowledge, as teachers, of our field and of our subject matter, and also on that suggested to us by researchers. It is this sort of knowledge, conceived of as primarily propositional, that is mostly explored by current epistemology. After reviewing this area, I will then move to consider knowledge of language and then in turn to teachers' knowledge.

Knowledge

As with a number of philosophical areas, there seems to be a relatively small set of classical positions in epistemology, which have probably coexisted as long as humans have been philosophizing. In addition, there is one area that perhaps was truly overlooked before and has achieved greater prominence lately. But let us begin with the classical orthodoxy.

If we start at what the West seems to think is the beginning of philosophy (the Greeks, again), then from our present-day viewpoint, specialists will claim that for these philosophers, two views contended. One, perhaps the dominant view of the period, was that of Plato: that knowledge is knowledge of preexisting, elsewhere existing truths; and one comes by knowledge mainly through the exercise of one's rational judgment. These truths are propositional: They take the form "I know that P," where P is a proposition, such as "A triangle has three sides." For Scheffler and many others, this is the prime example of the "rationalistic" tradition of knowledge:

> For the rationalistic tradition, mathematics is the model science. Mathematical truths are general and necessary, and may be established by deductive chains linking them with self-evident basic truths. Demonstration forges the chains, intuition discloses the basic truths.
>
> (1978: 2)

Observation, by contrast, is not needed; nor is there any role for the interpretive perspective of the human individual. A second view of knowledge is also to be found in the same productive context of ancient Greece: This alternative position (associated generally with the Sophists), is indicated by the famous phrase of Protagoras, "man [the human being] is the measure of all things," that is, through human interpretation and experience comes knowledge.[2]

If we fade out the role of interpretation in this position, we end up with the view that human knowledge arises from our perceptions of the exterior world. This position is called empiricism. It too was to be found in early Western philosophizing, notably in the work of Aristotle. With the revival of pre-Christian philosophy during the Renaissance, it came to be closely associated with some of the philosophers who coexisted with

114

the beginnings of modern Western science, notably Locke and Hume (the "British empiricists"). As Scheffler says,

> In the empiricistic tradition, natural science is taken as the basic model. Natural phenomena are revealed by experience; they are not disclosed by intuition...the relationships among elementary phenomena...cannot be inferred by logic...they are natural associations tentatively projected as generalizations...The mind...is a *tabula rasa*...at birth, and it is dependent upon experience both for the content of its elementary ideas and for their interrelationships.
>
> (1978: 3)

A third tradition, which does not have such an ancient heritage, perhaps, is one we have already encountered: the pragmatic line.

> The pragmatic view [of knowledge] stresses the experimental character of empirical science, putting great emphasis upon the active phases of experimentation.... Experimentation involves active transformation of the environment, in a manner dictated by leading ideas put forward in response to problems and directed toward the resolution of these problems.... In Dewey's [1916/1961: 139] words, the process is one of *trying and undergoing* – trying an idea in practice, and learning from the consequences undergone as a result of such trial.
>
> (ibid.: 4)

Finally, yet one more long-standing ancient tradition of relevance here is skepticism, a tradition justifying degrees of doubt in some or all of the main philosophical domains: epistemological, ontological, and metaphysical. We know of skepticism as an old philosophical position appearing in Eastern (e.g., Nagarjuna, *fl.* 150–200 CE) as well as Western philosophy (e.g., Pyrrho, 360–270 BCE). The written works of Pyrrho (who had contact with Indian philosophers) were completely lost, but through the later account by the Roman Sextus Empiricus we have some idea of them. A key central aspect might be said to be a simple distrust of human faculties, or an awareness of their limitations. Whether there is or is not a real world, Pyrrho would probably have said that as human beings our ability to know it completely and absolutely is quite limited. This position in epistemology is said to be "antifoundational." No truths are self-evident, and things cannot be known absolutely. It was partly because of the revival of skepticism in Europe in the early Enlightenment period that science was able to make progress, so the position has an honorable history; though in extreme forms, it was and still is considered dangerous. Much of the work of Descartes was a response to it; one reason the recent developments in the world of ideas discussed in the second half of the previous chapter have been attacked emotionally is because they are seen as a resurgence of extreme skepticism.

Theories of truth; truth and associated concepts

Knowledge and truth closely interact. One view is that truth exists separately from knowers, and knowledge is that subset of truths known by humans. This perspective tends to call for a "correspondence theory of truth" – that is, an understanding of truth as correspondence to the facts.[3] Correspondence theories of truth are not the only kind of theories of truth, and at the present juncture in the world of ideas, many specialists would prefer one major alternative – a coherence theory of truth (or knowledge); this may be needed simply because many "facts" are not in themselves checkable. Other problems that have been raised concerning correspondence theories of truth are the weakness of observation statements in the past tense, that language often does not point to facts, but to other language; and finally, that apparent objects and states of affairs often depend on the theories and language we use.

Having caught up with developments in the world of ideas (in Chapter 5), we will not be surprised to learn that, as Noddings (1995: 105) puts it, "Many philosophers today have suggested we abandon the traditional questions of epistemology. For them, truth is described 'locally' or as a function of power or as an artifact of language . . . " They question the extent to which true statements can point to things "outside language," though they assert that "it is still possible to speak of truth-telling and lying" within specific contexts. This position coexists happily with concepts such as "justified true belief," a formulation that is intended to stand in for truth, but recognizes the human limits of truth-creation and perception. It refers to knowledge that is neither perception, nor opinion, nor true opinion by itself, without justification; and justified true belief involves recourse to knowledge. A belief is "a proposition that is accepted as true by the individual holding the belief" (Green, 1971: 104). One person's belief, unfortunately, is not always another person's knowledge.

Some current theories of knowledge; and of its acquisition

Theories of knowledge can be divided, at one level, into foundationalist and antifoundationalist theories; the latter have more recently come into a primary position. Foundationalists feel the need to base their truth claims on some indubitable or self-justified beliefs. Rationalists say it can be done, and refer to some truths they hold to be "self-evident." Empiricists, our familiar other camp here, fall back on empirical observation. (But of course we always can ask ourselves whether we can trust the evidence of our senses.) "Most philosophers today have given up the search for absolute truth... but thinkers... rely heavily on a combination of observation statements and self-evident truths of reason to back their claims to knowledge" (Noddings, 1995: 102).

I will briefly draw attention to the positions associated with three individuals: Dewey, Popper, and Piaget. The first of these has implications particularly for teachers' knowledge, the second for scientific knowledge, and the third for learners' knowledge and for learning.

Dewey and Popper

I have mentioned on numerous occasions so far the influence of Dewey in the philosophy of education. Dewey's epistemology, like most of his work, reflects his interest in unifying dichotomies opened up by the two major philosophical schools of his time, idealism and empiricism. The first assumes that knowledge is of ideal forms; the latter that it is of the real world, to which we are assumed to have more or less direct access. Dewey felt that we have to take seriously our status as human beings in the real world, and indeed as beings subject to evolution. Thus, for him, knowledge is only obtained through our action on the world, and in some sense subject to survival constraints:

> Emphasis on the reciprocity of theory and praxis, knowledge and action, facts and values, follows from [a] post-Darwinian understanding of human experience, including cognition, as a developmental, historically contingent process.
>
> (Siegfried, 1995: 730)

Dewey's position also suggests a way to cut through the common theory–practice division: Theoretical knowledge is that which is arrived at through practical inquiry (usually by teachers) when reflected upon and tested in practice. Language teachers should engage in praxis – that is, theoretically motivated practice.[4]

Within science, the very mainstream work of Karl Popper (e.g., 1963) established an antifoundational theory of knowledge as the default position. During the mid-20th century, Popper was a critic of the logical positivist movement, and set in place the position, which is currently widely agreed upon, that while normal methods of science can plausibly establish the falsity of general statements, they cannot establish the truth of such statements. Science thus ends up with its effective working theory of truth being not foundationalist in nature. Instead, a historical account of how knowledge has been arrived at is to be used to justify it.[5]

With this as the background, scientific knowledge is clearly (a) arrived at through social processes, and (b) acceptable if agreed to by a particular set of hearers (the community of investigators in a particular field or discipline, for example), and through a public process. Popper's epistemology was similar to that of Dewey. Hutcheon notes:

> Popper did not formally acknowledge that he was building on Pragmatism. However, he claimed the originator of that philosophy, Charles Peirce, as his intellectual hero, and a close reading of Popper's work indicates that he had only one major disagreement with his hero's ideas. This had to do with the crucial "test for truth" on which every philosophy must take a definitive stand. The Pragmatists had declared that the test of verisimilitude is what "works" to permit dependable expectations of results. In other words, a proposition expressing a regularity in human experience has a tentative "truth claim" to the extent that it is instrumental in allowing us to control the consequences of our acting on the basis of it. . . . [But] Popper also believed that the Pragmatists were being inconsistent in defining their criterion in terms of verifiability. David Hume had already demonstrated that verification is not possible by the test of experience. The only thing that can be accomplished conclusively by the empirical process of science, concluded Popper, is falsification!
>
> (1995: n. p.)

Piaget, genetic epistemology, and current philosophy of learning

The work of Piaget is a useful entry point for a discussion of philosophy of learning (as part of the context of epistemology). Piaget is best known to most teachers as a theorist and researcher of child development, a developmental psychologist. However, he referred to himself as a genetic epistemologist. He was interested, that is, in the genesis of knowing. His empirical work supported his extensive stage theories of knowledge and have been particularly influential in first and second language acquisition theory. Piaget's epistemology is a form of constructivism, and derives substantially from Kant, who rejected both the innate ideas of rationalism and the position of the early empiricists (the "blank slate" view of Locke). Kant's opinion was that we can never know the world in itself, only the world as it is constructed. Piaget developed Kant's position by saying that Kant was wrong in thinking of these structures as static and given. Like rationalists, Piaget assumed mechanisms of mind that make knowledge possible, but like empiricists, he required that organisms test their knowledge against the world of sensory experience (thus to some extent his is a nonfoundational epistemology). Piaget's cognitive structures are in principle nonobservable, though explanation of various phenomena is facilitated by positing their existence. Developments of Piaget's position are very widespread now in education; the position that knowledge is constructed by learners and is not the result of passive reception now has produced several varieties of "constructivism."

Thus, we can talk about weak as well as strong constructivism. If all learning is active, even rote learning must involve some form of construction, and a recognition of this would be weak constructivism. Then, much learning takes place in social interaction rather than just working with objects or alone (as in Piaget's clinical experiments) and this takes us to the variant established by Vygotsky – social constructivism. If we say "all knowledge is mediated by our cognitive structures and theories," we can go on to say that those structures are social and historical in nature; if we add the possibility that these are almost always accompanied by real-world cultural artifacts, which play a crucial role in learning, we are then in the realm of "activity theory" (which has the unpleasantly long alternative title of sociocultural-historical theory; see e.g., Thorne, 2004). Finally, radical constructivism emphasizes the way that "coming to know is an adaptive process that organizes one's experiential world" rather than discovers a preexisting world (Matthews, 1993: 305, cited in Noddings, 1995: 117). Most of these varieties of constructivism have had influence on second and foreign language teachers' understandings of how students learn. First language acquisition stage theories, which closely followed on Piagetian stage theory work, also influenced early SLA theory with their emphasis on clear and predictable sequences of acquisition uninfluenced by instruction or empirical input (Brown, 1973; Burt, Dulay, & Krashen, 1982). The emphasis on interpersonal interaction in task settings in early SLA naturally led to a closer look at the social dimensions of interaction, so the constructivism of sociocultural theory followed on in due course. And the critical turn that has begun also finds a natural partner in the emphasis on the historical and cultural conditions for learning implied by activity theory (Thorne, 2005). All these varieties of constructivism seem to comfortably accompany an active, student-centered, task-based pedagogy, which has come to be the default setting (though capable of being interpreted both broadly and loosely) in much current SL thinking about pedagogy and curriculum.

Let us be skeptical again...

In most recent developments of epistemology, we find reference to the "naturalization" of epistemology – the coming together of philosophical and empirical studies of knowledge. Social epistemology (as its name suggests) emphasizes studying the way knowledge arises from and is supported by social forces and practices. A critical spin on this is visible in positions that assert that knowledge in general (or in the abstract) can not be studied because of its inseparability from power. Recent years have also seen the development of "standpoint epistemologists," of which feminist epistemology is the best known. This position argues that the inner view is more authentic, above objectivity; bias is unavoidable, but the only way to avoid pernicious bias is to include the views of all interested parties in accounts and arguments, rather than attempt to screen them out.

All this looks a bit optimistic from a postmodern position because of the authority it gives to a constituting subject. As we saw earlier, a prominent stance in the present world of ideas is to have some doubts about the free-standing, unsupported nature of the self. In this view, there are a lot of associations, content, undertones, and hidden assumptions that have already been constructed for us in the language we use (and the associated discourse processes), to the extent that we do not ourselves freely construct the reality we are part of. This somewhat skeptical position is concisely summarized by Ryder as follows:

> The issue can be considered in terms of four key propositions that map out the family resemblances of many of the philosophical traditions that have prevailed during the past several centuries. The first two express a modernist point of view, while the second two embody a postmodernist angle of vision:
>
> – Natural phenomena have objectively determinate traits.
> – The traits of natural phenomena are knowable.
> [as opposed to]
> – The process of inquiry is necessarily conditioned and perspectival.
> – Human interaction with the rest of nature, cognitive or otherwise, is active and creative.
>
> (2003: 64)

Knowledge of language and of second or foreign languages

It may come as a pleasant surprise to the language teacher that there *is* one area of epistemology that s/he is already something of an expert in – of course – that which concerns languages. Most teachers of languages are quite familiar with the always-continuing debate concerning what knowledge of language really is; that is, answers to the question, "What does it mean to know a language, or an L2?" (but see Mitchell & Hooper, 1991).

Most of us, as specialists in this area, having heard that knowledge is generally conceptualized as propositional, would recognize that we have a different position to articulate. The present era in applied linguistics and Second Language Studies seems to accept that knowledge of a language is particularly, in Ryle's (1949) term, *knowing how*. That is to say, knowing a set of facts about an L2 – knowing, that is, a set of propositions concerning the language – is anywhere from completely useless to only partially useful in enabling a language learner to actually communicate in the language. This sort of position, in which the L2 is seen as primarily a skill, and the knowledge or knowing in question is then "know-how," is quite familiar to us. As a consequence, we may not have realized that from a philosophical point of view, we are indebted to the epistemological work of Gilbert Ryle, a British philosopher of the immediate post–World War II era.

Ryle's work was intended as a critique of certain aspects of the theory of mind which supposed that intelligent performance required a preexisting intellectual mastery of rules or conditions. In a well-known passage, Ryle is quite dismissive of the idea that,

> [t]he chef must recite his recipes to himself before he can cook according to them; the hero must lend his inner ear to some appropriate moral imperative before swimming out to save the drowning man; the chess-player must run over in his head all the relevant rules and tactical maxims of the game before he can make correct and skilful moves. To do something thinking what one is doing is, according to this legend, always to do two things: namely to consider certain appropriate propositions, or prescriptions, and to put into practice what these propositions or prescriptions enjoin. It is to do a bit of theory and then to do a bit of practice.
>
> (1949: 29, and see also p. 38)

Ryle was an "ordinary language" philosopher who was exploring the many dimensions of knowing, and who had a particular complaint about the tendency to overlook what he saw as a significantly distinct aspect of knowing. It is a distinction that has proved important for our field, and it is good to have our practice-based understanding supported by philosophical inquiry into the distinction. Note, of course, that the existence of this kind of knowledge, or knowing, does not eliminate from consideration the more traditional "knowing that." But it does help us if we feel that we are being told that merely knowing the rules of a language is sufficient.

Incidentally, some L2 specialists would say, however, that knowing a language is not merely having "know-how" that pertains to the construction of grammatically correct sentences. It also involves knowledge that enables those sentences to function effectively when communicating within another culture. In which case, knowledge of language has to be encased within knowledge of a (second) culture.

In our field, Ryle's two terms were to some extent replaced by the terms "declarative knowledge" and "procedural knowledge," to be found initially in the cognitive psychology of skill, and subsequently appearing in the SL literature (Johnson, 1998; McDonough, 1981) and studies of teacher knowledge (see below). Elsewhere, there was a growth of interest in knowing, rather than just knowledge. This may be seen as part of a larger move by some philosophers (perhaps starting with Wittgenstein) to view any entity that could be seen as social as being constituted by the activity of those beings whose concern with it render it somewhat social. A core manifestation of this is work on "practices." May (2001: 8) defines a practice as "a regularity (or regularities) of behavior, usually goal-directed, that is socially normatively governed" (see also Schatzki, 1996).[6]

Thus just as language can be seen as having structure, but also as socially created and manifested, as individual but also social in nature, so can knowledge. Knowledge can be seen as *knowing*, and as a social practice rather than something individual. This is equivalent, in epistemology, to moving from an individualist, foundationalist epistemology to one which is social and antifoundationalist. Among those identified as initiating this move (in the mid-20th century) are Kuhn (e.g., 1962) and Gadamer (1960/1975). The former is more accessible, and I will simply remind the reader that his work (with its concept of paradigm shift) was a breakthrough in identifying the social bases of scientific knowledge. For Gadamer I rely on May's summary:

> The German thinker Hans-Georg Gadamer, a student of the famous (and infamous) philosopher Martin Heidegger, published his major work, *Truth and Method,* in 1960, just two years before Kuhn's *The Structure of Scientific Revolutions.* In this book, Gadamer laid out his own view of the philosophical approach known as *hermeneutics*, which might broadly be defined as the theory of interpretation. Gadamer's view was that it is a mistake to think of knowledge (knowing-that, but also knowing-how) as something that occurs outside the traditions in which we are brought up and through which we are taught to see the world. Instead, we should see knowledge as something that occurs in our interaction with the world by means of these traditions.
>
> What Gadamer struggled against – and what Descartes and Hegel were struggling *for* – was the idea that there could be a pure standpoint, untainted by our traditions and our prejudices, from which any knowings-that could be had. Descartes and Hegel

sought cosmic assurance that some kind of knowledge could form a foundation of certainty that would anchor the project of understanding ourselves and the world, a knowledge that would avoid the uncertainties that arise from our limited ability to understand the world through daily interaction. Gadamer denied that there was any such kind of pure knowledge. He argued forcefully that in order for there to be knowledge there had to be language, and that language always occurs in the context of traditions in which viewpoints develop, social relations form, and individual lives unfold. . . .

When Gadamer talks about understanding occurring within a tradition, one of the ways in which to take this talk . . . is to recognize that he is talking about knowing-that (and, in Gadamer's case, we can probably throw in knowing-how as well) and telling us how it arises in the context of our historically situated, socially normatively driven, goal-directed behavioral regularities. In short, our practices.

(2001: 79–81)

This is really quite important for us as teachers. It puts us much less at the mercy of the expert or the researcher; it emphasizes the importance of our own locally situated, locally developed knowledge, and it also suggests the possibility that knowledge tends to be "interested," that is again, reflects the views and standpoints of those who create it. Again, I believe this is why it is important for a teacher developing a philosophy of teaching to be aware of the existence of a range of "theories of truth"; the dominant theories have not always been to our advantage and the mere understanding that there can be more than one such theory is itself emancipating.[7]

In due course, the understanding of knowledge as a social practice has joined with lines of influence deriving from sociocultural theory and activity theory and has become more prominent in mainstream social science and in studies of language learning and teaching.[8] For teachers in what are supposed to be "learning organizations" (Senge, 1995; Senge et al., 2000) – that is, schools – an interpretation made of this perspective by organizational theorists and knowledge utilization researchers ought to be useful. Orlikowski refers to this position as

a perspective on knowing in practice which highlights the essential role of human action in knowing how to get things done in complex organizational work. The perspective suggests that knowing is not a static, embedded capability or stable disposition of actors, but rather an ongoing social accomplishment, constituted and reconstituted as actors engage the world in practice.

(2002: 249)

123

Thus teachers' knowledge (to foreshadow the next section) is not necessarily the knowledge of an individual teacher, but rather the knowing practices manifested by groups of teachers in social organizations under better or worse conditions.

Professional knowledge

Let me begin this section with a naïve question – why should language teachers have, or claim to have, knowledge anyway? Temporarily setting aside what might be meant by the term knowledge, most teachers would presumably agree that we have to have some sort of knowledge in order to do our job properly. But it would be both legitimate and to our advantage to dignify the knowledge in question a bit further, or indeed to honestly lay claim to quite considerable amounts of knowledge in a variety of relevant areas. Because we, as teachers, are part of a profession, it would be normal to lay claim to "professional knowledge." And turning it around, perhaps second and foreign language teachers, and particularly teachers of English, should indeed really emphasize our knowledge, since it seems we are not always recognized as professionals. Thus in this section I go on from a general discussion of knowledge to a pair of related subdomains: professional knowledge and then teachers' knowledge. Saying what one knows might plausibly be important in a philosophy of teaching; identifying oneself as a professional, too, might be important in that context, because it suggests a set of values, or aspirations.

Professions defined, or theorized

Our field has clearly used the term professional quite a lot. Since we include among ourselves both teachers and academics, and possibly translators and interpreters upon occasion, it has certainly been convenient to have a term for the membership which is not just "teachers" – the other general term being "practitioners." But more than that – individuals in TESOL have regularly called for the increased professionalization of the field (see e.g., Pennington; 1992, Staczek, 1987; Wright, 1988); and elsewhere in FL education (e.g., Schrier, 1993). In some cases this has been simply a way of saying, "Let's not have so many part-time and casual hires"; it has also been a way of pushing for more graduate degrees and fewer backpackers.[9] Professional standards, however defined, have been called for.

When one digs into terms that appear to make up the way our world is, it is often surprising at first to discover that they have a history. From the beginning of the present work I have emphasized the importance of historicizing our work and recognizing that ideas have a sociocultural location and are the creation of women and men. Not surprisingly, the term profession has a history and is a contested site (Bennett & Hokenstad, 1973). One of the earliest discussions (Flexner, 1915) states that "a profession (1) is based on intellectual activity, (2) requires from its members the possession of a considerable amount of knowledge and learning, (3) has definite and practical purposes, (4) has certain techniques which can be communicated, (5) has an effective self-organization, [and] (6) is motivated by a desire to work for the welfare of society" (Bennett & Hokenstad, 1973: 24).[10] In more recent discussions, many of those original ideas are preserved. For example, according to Middlehurst and Kennie (1997), some key characteristics are "expectations of individual autonomy, expertise, and intrinsic motivation for self-actualization through worthwhile work." This strand of work also, at some point in the optimistic, scientist 20th century, picked up a sense of progress in many fields of work being associated with the term "professionalization." Hence Wilensky's (1964) article, entitled "The professionalization of everybody."

From the 1960s on, dissent from the positive conceptions of profession implied above began to be articulated. Etzioni (1969) provided analyses of what he called "the semi-professions." These are generally taken to include school teaching, nursing, and social work. Some propounding this understanding of these fields say that they are never likely to gain full professional status. One of the main differences between the semiprofessions and the professions, and this is an acute problem with S/FL teaching even more than with other subject area domains of education, is control over entry into a field of work. The language-teaching "profession" in particular has even less control over entry than nursing or social work; and we do not "police" (as the term is) ourselves for violation of standards of professional conduct.

Also from the 1960s on, if not earlier, more radical critiques of all major professions developed, in which "professional aspirations are seen as ... detrimental to humanistic and/or egalitarian goals" (Bennett & Hokenstad, 1973: 259; e.g., Goodman, 1956, 1962; Illych, 1970; Newman & Oliver, 1967; see also Ginsburg, e.g., 1988). The difference between these two perspectives on professionalism has been summarized as follows:

> Traditional models have tended to treat attributes such as the knowledge base as structurally given, relatively static, and non-ideological. They were seen as social facts, not claims, viewed as in the mutual interest of client, professional, and

society, not as self-serving. Similarly, professions were seen as homogenous and cohesive communities.... Critics, on the other hand, have emphasized political process and outcome rather than intrinsic attributes. They have seen professions as occupations which achieve occupational control by credentialing and licensing.... From this perspective, knowledge and expertise are not ... neutral scientific elements ... but political resources in the battle for power and status, constructed and advanced by occupations and segments within occupations to forward collective aims.

(Hoffman, 1989: 3)

Some of this critique has surfaced in TESOL-related discussions of professionalism. Johnston's (1997) study of Polish EFL teachers alludes to the destructive critique of the concept lately articulated by Burbules and Densmore (1991), Popkewitz (1994), and Welker (1992). Thus perhaps this is an area that one actually has to make a decision about, as a teacher of English in international contexts – is one to regard oneself as a professional, or not? If one does have status and possibly favorable working conditions, is that because one is a professional, or is it the result of supply and demand and international politics?

Knowledge(s) are a key characteristic of professions

Let us explore this knowledge aspect of professions as an aspect of our work. A prominent analyst of the professions for the last 30 years, Freidson, refers to "the use of a circumscribed body of knowledge and skills" (2001: 18), as "one of the two most general ideas underlying professionalism" (p. 17; see also Freidson, 1970). Professionals, Freidson observes, make use of "discretionary specialization.... [which] requires the employment of a body of knowledge that is gained by special training" (p. 24). It is precisely for that reason that we claim (and other professions similarly claim) that not just anyone should or could do what we do, and that we have therefore professional discretion and abilities for which we should be given some recognition and not subjected to bureaucratic control when we are engaged in our work.

However, there are problems with the way "knowledge" in professional contexts is conceptualized. Our field has had plenty of discussions of the difficulties of applying the supposed "scientific" knowledge of SL learning and teaching to the actual realities of the classroom, by the actual classroom practitioners. Those difficulties have often been attributed to the form in which such knowledge has been generated and propounded, along with the working conditions of those supposed to make use of it; and at the same time the devaluing of the actual knowledge of practice that practitioners themselves have. There are, however, other problems.

First, a unitary conception of knowledge in professional contexts is inadequate. Freidson comments,

> Skill may ... be kept analytically separate from the substantive knowledge connected with the task itself ... Skill is itself a kind of knowledge, namely, of the techniques for using or applying substantive knowledge ... It is facilitative in character.... Some of the skills required for applying knowledge to the performance of a task are formal in character, codified in texts, or otherwise described clearly and systematically in the course of training for work. Other skills, however, are tacit – unverbalized, perhaps even unverbalizable, but in any case not part of a formal corpus of codified technique.
>
> (2001: 25)

Another useful distinction of Freidsons's is between "everyday" and "formal" knowledge. The former is that which is acquired through normal socialization and is needed to perform "the everyday tasks of daily life" (p. 28). But distinguishable from that is "formal knowledge," which has also been called "public codified knowledge" (Myers & Simpson, 1998: 77). This is "institutionalized into and by what Foucault (1979) called 'disciplines' and Holzner (1968: 68–70) 'epistemic communities'" (Freidson, 2001: 29). Describing this area, Freidson comments: "These are of course inevitably rooted in everyday knowledge but are organized in institutions set apart from everyday life.... The formal knowledge of particular disciplines is taught to those aspiring to enter specialized occupations with professional standing. Much of it is abstract and general in character, however, and cannot be applied directly to the problems of work. For actually performing work, formal knowledge may be needed in some cases, but so also are specialized knowledge and skill of a more concrete nature, and of course, everyday knowledge" (2001: 29). Myers & Simpson (1998: 78) comment on this, too, remarking that "academic disciplines are usually formulated by researchers and scholars ... in ways that fit their purpose, rather than by practical users of the ideas ... when teachers use a particular set of ideas for professional purposes, they cannot simply select them without reconfiguring them ... (Eraut, 1994)." These "take on meaning only as they are acquired by teachers and transformed by them into forms that become part of those teachers' individual professional knowledge, competencies, and value systems" (ibid.).

Others (e.g., Kennedy, 1999) would distinguish a third kind of knowledge, "expertise," in this, again with a highly contextual character.

127

Similarly, Cochran-Smith and Lytle (1999) refer to knowledge-for-practice (formal knowledge), knowledge-in-practice (the embedded, contextual variety already mentioned under several headings), and knowledge-of-practice, which last has a strong teacher-research character.

The two more concrete, less disciplinary forms of knowledge are valuable, indeed essential for practice; unfortunately they are deprecated and devalued by knowledge-creation practices and personnel central to an uncritical concept of a profession.

Conditions for the creation of formal knowledge

It is this formal knowledge, not all of which is conscious, and not all of which is disembodied or separate from specific situations, that is inherent in what Freidson calls the "ideal-typical professions": "The ideal-typical position of professionalism is founded on the official belief that the knowledge and skill of a particular specialization requires a foundation in abstract concepts and formal learning and necessitates the exercise of discretion." He goes on, incidentally, to remark that, "When so recognized a number of distinctive institutional consequences follow" (Freidson, 2001: 30), the most obvious of which, of course, is a profession's monopolistic control over its own work.

Formal knowledge is the kind of knowledge that academic specialists in TESOL (like myself) have mainly concerned themselves with. Besides concerns about its applicability, clearly the critical turn also would question this form of knowledge on other grounds. In the 1980s and 1990s, some attention to this topic in our field came as a reflection of its popularity in mainstream educational scholarship, as follows.

One strategy used to argue for increased discretionary powers, or at least to push back against deskilling efforts, has involved attempts to delineate the knowledge in question. In the last 20 years or so, serious efforts have been made to define and delineate the supposed "knowledge base for teaching" (Galluzzo, 1999; e.g., Shulman, 1987). Even though the idea of the possibility of identification of a definitive knowledge base was immediately disputed (Ayers, 1988; Henderson, 1988), starting from this initiative, publishers such as Pergamon increasingly began to turn out encyclopedia-sized tomes that present this knowledge, reflecting the interest the field was showing in fostering professionalization, it appears. Reynolds (1989), in the introduction to one such heavy item, states "this book seeks to demonstrate that teaching does have a distinctive knowledge base, that the knowledge is expressed in articulated understandings, skills, and judgments which are professional in character and which distinguish more productive teachers from less productive ones" (p. ix). Desirable as the concept of a "knowledge base

128

for teaching" might appear – and it is often appealed to, in our field as in others – specifying such an entity appears more difficult than it looks. Munby et al. refer us to Donmoyer's (1996) critique of the concept, saying:

> For Donmoyer, the enterprise of building a knowledge base is naïve because it overlooks the political character of knowledge, so he reviews arguments linking knowledge and politics and then offers four rebuttals.
>
> (Munby et al. 2001: 884)

As Galluzo (1999) points out (see also Jenlink, 2001), this project has faltered. Clearly, at the present time, some parts of our field and education in general have caught up with those critical and skeptical developments to which I alluded in Chapter 5 (those of Foucault, at least). As Freidson says,

> All work presupposes knowledge, that it is the practice of knowledge, and that the social and economic organization of practice plays a critical role in determining both what knowledge can be employed in work and how that knowledge can be exercised.
>
> (2001: 27)

Here we come up against the blunt fact that the working conditions of teachers do not afford them the opportunity or encouragement to create formal knowledge. In addition, it is important for TESOL-ers to recognize, as we increasingly do, that a lot of the creators of formal knowledge for our field come from specific national, class, race, and gender backgrounds, which may show up in the forms this knowledge takes.

Continuing this process of dissecting our professional use of knowledge in doing our work, Freidson goes on to focus on this "specialized knowledge and skill of a more concrete nature" (2001: 29) that is nevertheless needed for us to discharge our professional duties adequately. He draws on the work of Scribner on "practical thinking," which is "thinking that is embedded in the larger purposive activities of daily life and that functions to achieve the goals of those activities. . . . So conceived – embedded and instrumental – practical thinking stands in contrast to the type of thinking involved in the performance of isolated mental tasks undertaken as ends in themselves (Scribner, 1986: 15)." Freidson continues that "Much of the knowledge and skill this thinking employs is developed and learned situationally, on the job, as information about the tasks to be performed and as skills to be employed in performing them" (2001: 31). The almost inextricable association of skill and thinking with knowledge is important for this discussion.

Teachers' knowledge

Teachers' knowledge could be considered a subordinate category of professional knowledge.[11] Those who have investigated it have certainly drawn from more general discussions, such as that of Schön (1983).[12] What teachers in general know, and what forms that knowledge might take, has been the subject of considerable inquiry, but only recently. Perhaps this line of investigation only began to be seen as inherently interesting once the idea took hold that teachers' knowledge might not be identical in form (let alone content) to the way knowledge had hitherto been conceived. In a prominent review, specialists in this area Munby, Russell, and Martin state that:

> The category "teachers' knowledge" is new in the last 20 years, and the nature and development of that knowledge is only beginning to be understood by the present generation of researchers in teaching and teacher education.
>
> (2001: 877)

As usual, research in the area dealing specifically with language teachers has appeared later and in a much smaller quantity.

Among those prominent in more or less the first phase of work in this area were Elbaz (1983), Munby (e.g., 1986), and Connelly and Clandinin (1984). Elbaz identified five domains of teachers' personal practical knowledge. She also made use of a three-level framework for organizing this, involving rules of practice, practical principles, and images. Munby drew on Schön's epistemology of practice and focused on teachers' knowledge as expressed in metaphors used in framing and solving classroom dilemmas. Connelly and Clandinin looked at teachers' knowledge in terms of images and narratives. But a little later, and perhaps not particularly building on this work, came the very popular and widely used work of Shulman (1987), concerning teachers' knowledge. Shulman divided the area into content knowledge, general pedagogical knowledge, curriculum knowledge, pedagogical content knowledge, knowledge of learners, of educational contexts, and of educational ends, purposes, and values. This work was associated with efforts to clarify and develop the so-called knowledge base for teaching, part of a drive to both professionalize teaching and develop standards for teacher assessment.

An interesting alternative conception (Donmoyer, 1996) of what professionals do in connection with knowledge recognizes that they do have knowledge, but they use it in "practical reasoning" (a term that harks back to Aristotle) and case-related argument and analysis, "careful consideration of means, ends, alternatives, relevant information, and deliberate choosing" (p. 112). For Munby and colleagues, the concepts of practical reasoning and practical argument, as further developed by Fenstermacher and associates (Fenstermacher, 1994; Fenstermacher & Richardson, 1993), constitute a bridge between propositional versions of knowledge, and teachers' possibly nonpropositional knowledge-based practice. Carter is a prime exponent of the nonpropositional position:

> Teachers' knowledge is not highly abstract and propositional. Nor can it be formulated into a set of specific skills or preset answers to specific problems. Rather it is experiential, procedural [Leinhardt, Young, & Merriman, 1995], situational, and particularistic.
>
> (1990: 307)

An approach to categorizing teachers' knowledge that is somewhat congruent with this is that of Myers and Simpson (1998). They make use of a tripartite analysis: practice-based professional teacher knowledge is divided into technical knowledge, practical or craft knowledge, and tacit knowledge.

Myers and Simpson exemplify technical knowledge as "knowing that having clear and well-organized classroom routines and firm behavior management strategies contribute to the smooth operation of classes; knowing that student attention during recitation lessons can be maintained better by raising questions for the whole class before calling on a specific student" (1998: 82). Clearly one could find a statement of that kind in a book, but the point here is that it is more likely to be developed through practice, and possibly is quite often developed solely through practice, reflection on practice, or direct transmission from other practitioners. Myers and Simpson remark that "it can also be transmitted in the form of principles of practice and can evolve into codified professional knowledge" (ibid).

Practical or craft knowledge is the knowing-how aspect of knowledge: the ability to do, rather than know about, something. "Some people think of it as being learned only by individual teachers from their personal practice . . . and as being specific to the situations in which it is learned. . . . It is not often thought of as something that can be passed from teacher to teacher. Instead, it is seen as something that individual teachers do but not something they write about or formulate into generally useful statements for other teachers to study" (Myers & Simpson, 1998: 83). Whether this is correct or not seems disputed. This might perhaps be expected to be fairly nonpropositional.

Tacit knowledge, a long-standing conception of professional knowledge that appears in this mini-taxonomy, is something that by definition is hard to articulate and presumably difficult to transmit. It is basically knowledge that we possess without knowing that we know it (and is most often associated with Polanyi, e.g., 1964). It is a concept that was further developed by Schön in his explorations of professional practice. These days it seems that it is central to concepts of reflective practice, much of which involve raising tacit knowledge to consciousness.

The processual, or dynamic, and potentially interpersonal aspects of this approach to knowledge creation, and this approach to conceptions of knowledge for our profession, are important. It is one reason why the idea that young teachers, students in the profession, can, over the course of a couple of years of graduate or postgraduate work, somehow acquire through study at a university that which they need to know to discharge their professional duties subsequently, is clearly wrong. This goes along with the greatly increased recognition of the local and contextualized nature of almost all knowledge of the human world. Rather than having a body of knowledge, teachers need to know how to make knowledge, or get knowledge, or integrate with others in the use and application of knowledge.

Concluding remark

Let me recap the thread of argument that has run through this chapter. Clearly, as teachers we are supposed to have knowledge. As language teachers we should presumably know something about the nature of knowledge of language and of second and foreign languages and cultures. What we find, when we explore the area of philosophy in which such concepts should be located, is that we can come to an understanding of the area, as well as a recognition that the dominant conceptions of knowledge may not be entirely adequate for our needs. As sophisticated reflective practitioners and language teachers, we are entitled to have a questioning attitude to the way the concept of knowledge itself has previously been presented. But we do need to have a meta-understanding of what it means to know language.

In a brief discussion of the nature of learning, I have placed labels on several prominent positions. A philosophy of language teaching must be able to say something about one's understanding of the nature of L2 learning; this is a rapidly diversifying area within applied linguistics (and the remarks here merely point in a direction that teachers will need to explore as their careers continue).

As well-qualified language teachers, we should have an overarching understanding of the nature of scientific knowledge, and we are entitled to have a questioning attitude to it and to what passes for knowledge in our field. Knowledge is closely tied up with the idea of being a professional; in developing a philosophy of our work (surely something equally associated with the idea of having high standards to guide our practice) we should have probed the concept of "professional" itself. This we have done, and if my discussion is plausible, it is found that the concept has both strengths and at the same time definite weaknesses, and is quite differentiated, rather than unitary.

Teachers' knowledge is a domain of inquiry that has developed in recent years; this should be of importance to us and again it turns out that it is both a useful corrective to an undue dominance of scientific knowledge within professional practice, and at the same time has its own limitations, and is very much still a work "under construction."

When (in professional development workshops) I ask language teachers bluntly to "write down what you know," they find it hard to comply. The extent of the domains in which we feel we have knowledge is large, but organizing it, putting it down on paper or expressing our knowledge aloud seems difficult. Much of what we have doesn't necessarily feel like knowledge as that term is commonly understood. I hope this survey of a complicated area has provided some suggestions as to why a task such as the one I have just mentioned turns out to be much more complex than it looks. Nevertheless, to the extent it is possible, I do think we *should* develop a comprehensive understanding of our knowledge as language teachers.

Discussion questions

1. How theoretically grounded is your practice as a teacher? Can you theorize your practice? (Try to make some statements concerning what you know, as a language teacher, that you have come to believe as a result of trying things out in practice and determining their success or failure.) Do you have a pragmatist epistemology with regard to your professional knowledge?

2. Presumably a philosophy of teaching needs a philosophy of learning (which I am not treating in great detail here). Do you feel you are getting, or have gotten enough on this topic, from elsewhere in your professional development experiences, professional reading, or coursework?

3. Is it really true to say that all varieties of constructivism "comfortably" accompany a task-based pedagogy in language teaching? Would they "accompany" other curriculum theories as well?

4. If you are teaching, consider your department, program, or yourself together with your fellow teachers. Can you think of examples or cases in which your professional knowledge is jointly, rather than separately, manifested (that is, has an "emergent" quality)? Relate this to the ideas of Gadamer and/or the concept of socially distributed knowledge.

5. As a language teacher, do you have whatever status you have because of your professional knowledge, or primarily for other reasons? What part of your knowledge is "everyday," and what part is "formal"? Are you a member of an "epistemic community"? Do you presently contribute to the growth of formal knowledge in our field? How about in the future? If not, why not? How useful is this conception of knowledge for language teachers? What other conceptions would you favor, in addition/instead?

Notes to Chapter 6

1 There are almost no book-length treatments of this topic, except Winch (1998). What is constituted by the philosophy of learning is a sustained conceptual analysis and comparative study of the assumptions and intellectual inheritances of theories of learning. This domain of philosophizing is manifested, within applied linguistics, when theories of SLA are compared (e.g., Mitchell & Myles, 2004), but such works do not usually go deep enough into the philosophical positions implied by such theories, nor extend broadly across the domain of learning in human life.

2 As quoted by Sextus Empiricus (trans. Bury, 1961: vol. 2, p. 33, *Against the logicians*, book 1, section 60). The work has an alternate title: *Against the mathematicians* (book 7).

3 This sort of synopsis of a standard issue in philosophy appears in many places; here I am drawing on Noddings's (1995) exposition.

4 Pennycook develops this point very well in the only account we have of a language-teaching practicum conducted from a critical point of view, which he calls a "praxicum" (Pennycook, 2004).

5 *Historical* is used here in the sense that a short history of the investigative procedures used is related. This is technically known as an "externalist" theory of truth.

6 The concept of practices is not intended to be a single-factor reductive explainer, but rather directs attention at a particular level of analysis, says May (2001: 192). "If you want to know how religion works and what it has to do with who we are, you have to look at religious practices.... If you want to know what families are all about, you have to look at familial practices.... Don't opt for a perspective that's too large – society as a whole, knowledge as a whole, the cosmos as a whole. Instead, look at the various points at which people intersect with their societies and the norms afloat in those societies: look at their practices. The perspective of practices does not give us an object to look at so much as it gives us a way of looking at a network of objects."

7 Lest this sound too radical, note that Gadamer's perspectives were generally conservative: looking backward toward tradition.

8 As found in the work of Cole, Engeström, Lave, Wenger, and Hutchins (discussed in Thorne, 2005).

9 At least some part of the field uses this pejorative term to denote young native-speaker travelers who visit EFL countries for tourism and while sojourning, engage in English teaching, often without much or any training.

10 Others involved in this apparently long drawn out program of analysis were Carr-Saunders, 1928; Hughes, 1958; Moore, 1970; Parsons, 1937; and Wilensky, 1964.

11 A variety of terms have been used to refer to this knowledge, including "Situated knowledge (Leinhardt, 1988), event-structured knowledge (Carter & Doyle, 1987),

personal practical knowledge (Connelly & Clandinin, 1985; Elbaz, 1983), images (Calderhead, 1988 . . .), and knowing-in-action (Schön, 1983) . . . metaphors (Munby, 1986), voice (Richert, 1992), and craft knowledge (Grimmett & MacKinnon, 1992)" (Munby, Russell, & Martin, 2001: 887).

12 Schön's work, for example, has been seminal for concepts of reflective teaching, but his original work concerned the knowledge and practice of professionals such as architects. (Indeed, their conditions of work allow for the verbalization of knowledge in action much more easily than do teachers', which results perhaps in some subsequent difficulties in fully using his ideas for thinking about teachers' knowledge.)

7 Ethics and morals

Introduction

Ethics, the philosophical study of morals and morality, was mentioned earlier (Chapter 5) as part of one major component ("axiology") that would appear in a philosophical system. I now return to this major area and examine it in more detail. For any teacher, the ethical aspect of practice is important; when speaking generally, however, language educators I have talked to and worked with seem inclined to subsume much of this under a general allegiance to "professionalism"; thus you or I might say that it would be wrong to do something because it would be "unprofessional." Presumably, a professional teacher acts, by definition, ethically (notwithstanding the problems with the term professional, discussed in the previous chapter). But what does it mean to act ethically, and how does this interface between ethics and professionalism come about, and what does it mean for us as second and foreign language specialists?

Until very recently, little attention has been given in the literature of S/FL teaching to matters of ethics.[1] Early treatments in our field (of a practical rather than theoretical nature) come from those concerned with administration (with the areas of testing and research methods close behind). For example, Stoynoff (1993) identified three main areas within which ethical dilemmas are likely to occur for ESL program administrators: (1) access to information and right to privacy; (2) personal and professional integrity; and (3) professional standards and practices. Under (1), the dilemmas are likely to come from conflicts between legal and ethical considerations. Under (2), the problems may come from conflicting priorities concerning fiscal versus academic responsibilities; or in the area of advertising one's program (truth in advertising versus actually getting students to come); or use of recruitment agents. Under (3), there are tensions between the highest professional standards (implying, for example, full-time positions for all teachers) and what a program can afford. Usefully for the present work, Stoynoff (1993: 5) recommends "clarifying significant values and principles before an ethical dilemma emerges.... Preparing a personal philosophy statement is one way of accomplishing this." He also recommends referring to a professional code of ethics statement, though this cannot replace one's own personal reflections. The early lack of attention to the topic has changed, and more recently, our area has responded to a general upsurge of interest in the topic (across many aspects of society), and a handful of book-length treatments have appeared (Hafernik, Messerschmitt, & Vandrick, 2002; Johnston, 2003[2]). In addition, literature in our field, which asks about the overall desirability of our work (most obviously, Phillipson, 1992, and the many studies that have followed it), implies an ethical standard applicable to English language teaching as a whole.

In the following discussion I will approach the topic first from a mainstream philosophical perspective. I will then address some of its applied education-oriented aspects and the matter of professional ethics. I conclude the review by going over some of the specifically ESL-oriented material presented by Hafernik and associates (2002).

A quick history of ethics

Classical ethics[3]

Early views in both East and West present ethics as primarily systems or sets of virtues embodied in individuals. Many Western overviews of ethics begin their account with Aristotle, whose views were drawn from real life and set down in his *Nichomachean Ethics*. Aristotle's basic position was that we become virtuous by behaving virtuously. The Confucian tradition is similarly a "virtue ethics," and is very much concerned with developing the good person.[4] To some extent this suggests that if we have the virtue of, for example, patience, we will behave patiently. Perhaps at one level this is a satisfactory position to start from, particularly if one is concerned mainly with individual behavior, but it provides little basis for considering our actions in their contexts, of existing cultures or societies. If we think that something is wrong, or some unethical act occurs because society is wrong or because structural forces impinge on individuals and cause them to act wrongly, a purely individualist analysis may be insufficient.

Aristotelian ethics arose out of a specific (Greek) society and is sometimes held to primarily reflect the mores of that society. Critics emphasize the relativism of an ethics thus developed and structured. What is good in one society may be bad (or irrelevant) in another. In addition, there may be no way to adjudicate between one and another.

Another problem with a virtue ethic is (as Noddings, 1995, puts it) that it requires that we become virtuous through practicing specific virtues. (Aristotle assumed that the state would provide moral education to inculcate virtues in its citizens; however, he did not expect all to achieve excellence in this area.) Critics would argue that we are enabled to achieve virtue differentially because of our various different positions in society and access to resources. Thus the rich are more likely to be virtuous.[5] If there is a hierarchy of virtues, as Aristotle was willing to countenance, it may induce and maintain a hierarchy of status or privilege.[6]

Modern European ethics

Prior to the modern era, state and religion in Europe were very close and the individual's freedom of action was constrained. Under those circumstances, one can expect moral systems to emphasize "authority and deference to practice" (Noddings, 1995: 140). An ethic of "order, obedience, tradition, and acceptance" (ibid.: 141) held sway, with the intention of ordering life on earth, not improving it. In due course, however, group or individual agency came again to be emphasized in European thought, from the Enlightenment on. The developments in ethics that occurred during this time are referred to as either deontological[7] or consequentialist (the latter is also called teleological). The former emphasizes behaving ethically as behaving in accordance with one or more general rules; the latter sees ethical behavior as involving the weighing of consequences.

Deontological ethics

In ethics, according to Kant, we are responsible for our choices and they are moral if they are derived from absolute principles of duty. Kant proposed what he called a categorical imperative: "So act that the maxim of your will could always hold at the same time as a principle of a universal legislation" (Kant, 1788/2002: 30). Noddings (1995: 141) paraphrases this as, "so act that you can logically will that your decision be made law; ... act in a way that you can without contradiction insist that all others in similar situations should also act." Kant's perspective gives particular attention to human rationality, autonomy, and individualism. His approach, notably through the use of the categorical imperative, pushes us to produce absolute ethical principles in connection with which the consequences of an act are irrelevant. Following the procedural aspects of ethics, we are encouraged to do what is right, setting aside the contextual or ends aspect of ethics, or of ethical action.

Kant's work in this area was a very important contribution to the European Enlightenment, which overall resulted in the Western tradition in ethics becoming less connected to Christianity.[8] It also was in a position to question tradition: Ethical systems or principles, originally derived from the morality of a community, could (according to Kant's way of thinking and arguing) be subjected to a logical test (Noddings, 1995). Kant's view was that each person must make her or his own decisions about what is right and wrong, drawing primarily on a sense of duty. At the same time, though it involves individuals, it seems that

Kant's ethics can be applied to a community or a society; one can ask if the way society is organized is moral.

A range of criticisms have been made of the Kantian position, including again that it still privileges a culture, class, or gender-specific way of looking at the topic. Another criticism is that Kantian ethical agents are constrained *not* to do things that will interfere with the free agency of others, but are not required to perform *positive* acts to help others. These are referred to as "supererogatory" – above and beyond the call of duty. It is a negative ethics, telling us what not to do, not indicating what positive actions should be performed.

Utilitarian ethics

Developing in England at about the same time as the work of Kant, philosophers and social theorists known as utilitarians (Bentham, e.g., 1789/1961, and Mill, e.g., 1861/1998, are the two most famous names in this context) were also responding to some of the same social and cultural changes of that period, resulting in a desire to move away from the vision of any particular religion in deciding what was right action. The utilitarian vision of the good precedes determination of what is right, and for these thinkers, happiness, or utility, is the best thing for human beings. Having made that determination, they suggest we should maximize "utility" (the ratio of pleasure to pain), and seek the greatest good for the greatest number. This is a familiar concept, and many teachers will recall making decisions after some thought about what would be best for their class as a whole.

In addition, being founded upon a calculation applying across a set of individuals, this ethic is potentially more clearly a "comprehensive ethic," which "speaks both to individual behavior and the moral behavior of whole societies" (Noddings, 1995: 144). The views and theories of the utilitarians became fairly well-integrated with the development of the liberal-democratic state, so they may be familiar or taken for granted by many users of the present work. We are accustomed to arguments about social and educational policy being buttressed by phrases or sentiments concerning "what is good for the country/university/school etc. as a whole."

Pragmatist ethics

Although the three positions in ethics just sketched are and have been very influential, there is continuing debate and development in this area. Many current philosophers specialize in ethics, and others treat or develop it as part of a broader body of work. Dewey, as the preeminent philosopher of education and also one of the most prolific of

Values, Philosophies, and Beliefs in TESOL

the past century, would be an example here. Dewey's view of ethics can be described as "consequentialist" (and thus is in same camp as the utilitarians'), but it differs from the utilitarian position in saying that other goods at other times may be preferable to happiness, and suggesting that a single definition of happiness is unsatisfactory. Responsibility is emphasized – a moral agent must explore the range of possibilities and consider if s/he is willing to take responsibility for outcomes; others who are involved should be included in problem-solving procedures. Consistent with the overall pragmatist position, Dewey's line involves developing working rules and is opposed to the idea of some absolute foundation for morality.

Ethics in education

Pendulum swings

Given this brief sense of the domain of ethics, one might next ask, "How has this topic played out in schools?" If we go back two centuries, closer to the beginning of mass education in Europe, we find that structures for teacher preparation, not to mention schools and colleges themselves, were still closely connected to organized religion, and there were quite firm assumptions made that teachers and educational administrators should be "of good character." In that sense, perhaps the virtue ethics side of the domain dominated. Subsequently, economic and social developments early in the 20th century in many parts of the world were coupled with the rise of commerce and business. Thus in schools and curricula we may perceive an emphasis on efficiency in mere transmission of content (rather than the shaping of character or the development of the literate, liberally educated individual), and the growth of curricula oriented primarily to preparing students to perform tasks in business and industry (through addressing their "needs," narrowly specified in terms related to the performance of the activities of work as defined by the business owner or manager). By the mid-20th century, approaches to curriculum and practice that could be presented as "scientific" were highly valued, and the development in education of the new science of administration emphasized an "objective understanding of the phenomena without confusion between facts and values" (Beck & Murphy, 1994: 21). Language teaching has often had some concern with work-related communication, but this perspective seems to have been a particularly prominent contributor to developments in English language teaching during the 1970s and 1980s, with vocational perspectives developing into the area of English for Specific Purposes, and a concern for instrumental needs as driving curriculum design becoming widespread. Teaching language that was "needed," in the most efficient manner, was considered to be sufficient, and sufficiently ethical. However, in mainstream education (i.e., outside of the narrower world of language teaching), beginning right at the end of the 1980s, some specialists identified a renewed focus on the moral dimensions of schooling. Beck and Murphy (1994: 27) say that "this ethics agenda [was] an extension of critiques... [and] a condemnation of the way the inequities of wealth, power and status play out in schools" and of "increasing recognition of the moral foundations of teaching and of the value-laden dimensions of instruction and schooling."

Having observed that the topic has come back into prominence, let us now consider the topic as it relates to educational considerations (rather than philosophical systems). Beck and Murphy (1994: 2) say that "authors writing on this topic seem to think about ethics in one of two general ways. Many concentrate upon identifying... principles" used in making educational decisions. Others look more widely and try to get educators to identify their assumptions and beliefs about the world and in particular about education, as a basis for ethical decision making and action.[9]

Principles for decision making

In the first case, principles, or sets of values, can be broad or narrow; unfortunately it is not always clear upon what grounds a specific principle or value has been selected or is being advocated. For example, Crittenden (1984: 22) puts forward a broad list of values linked to supposed common needs and abilities of human beings, which for him include "love, loyalty, justice, honesty, courage, generosity, truth telling and promise keeping... [respect for] political authority, property, and family." Around the same period, the noted U.S. educational researcher Sergiovanni (1980) suggested we work with a narrower set: utility, transcendence, and justice. The first of these emphasizes the practical, trading off costs and benefits. The second relates to "the capacity of an alternative to increase the potential of society for achieving humanness in the pursuit of happiness" (1980: 4). The third relates to a just distribution of benefits. More recently, for our field, Edge (1996) has specified diversity, inquiry, cooperation, and respect.

At one level, it is presumably a matter of personal judgment which set of principles one finds personally compelling, or useful. However, if we are thinking only of state schools, it has been argued that teachers and educational administrators who are state employees are thereby "trustees of a public social good" (Beck & Murphy, 1994: 7). Such individuals must "allow themselves to be guided by certain tenets of public moral-ity" (ibid.), such as (according to Crittenden, 1984: 18) "justice, truth telling ... concern for others ... mutual help." These are transformed into "specific principles and procedures" by "the political and legal systems of the country" (ibid.: 21). So educators "in societies whose governments are committed to certain fundamental principles, such as justice, toler-ance, and respect for and fair treatment of all persons, can and should look to laws and public policies for ethical guidance" (Beck & Murphy, 1994: 7). I assume this means that those of us working in countries where this is not the case, or not entirely the case, must use our judgment as to whether or not we allow ourselves to be guided by the law. Or indeed, under some (difficult) circumstances a teacher might be guided by the spirit of the law, as manifested in principles such as justice, tolerance, and fairness, then note that the law as implemented failed to manifest such principles, and act accordingly. In line with this, besides the law or principles implied by it, one other obvious set of principles that we might turn to for guidance would be that embodied in any of the codes of ethics that have been developed by various parts of the teaching pro-fession. It is not clear to what extent, if at all, teachers consciously refer to any specific sets of principles in decision making. I am not saying that they do not; rather, I think it is an open horizon for empirical investiga-tion. However, the moment-to-moment nature of teaching does suggest a different perspective on ethics in teaching, to which I now turn.[10]

Ethics as informative

In the second of Beck and Murphy's conceptions, to act ethically, as a language educator, one would first have to have thought about such mat-ters as the fundamental purposes of schools as institutions, the role of language (or a foreign language) within them, and one's responsibilities as a moral agent. Thus ethics is a way of understanding purposes, roles, and institutions. The position that moral perceptions precede moral judg-ment (Blum, 1991, 1994) may help clarify this point. Unless a teacher sees a situation as, say, morally wrong, or an action as potentially uneth-ical, s/he is unlikely to apply any of the concepts I have been reviewing so far. So, if you take the view that "the poor are always with us," star-vation in the streets will not be perceived as needing a moral response. To turn it around, if we follow Hodgkinson (1991), who comments that educators (and he is thinking here particularly of school leaders) must be guided by more than "mere pragmatism, positivism, philistinism, and careerism" (p. 165), then, I suppose, ES/FL teachers must have an ethical perspective on their work that goes beyond mere efficiency. (This is the basic position that Johnston, 2003, urges.)

A related version views ethics as closely connected with or informing a critique of society and in due course, a political position. If you have applied your ethics to society as a whole, from a political standpoint, and found it wanting, then your ethics of social justice and compassion may play in to your work as a language teacher. A variety of curricular and pedagogical options then follow, many of which would be associated with the realm of critical pedagogy (see Chapter 9).

Finally, recent developments in ethical theory allow us to consider an ethics grounded in a commitment to persons: This is the position of feminist ethics, associated most notably with Noddings (e.g., 1984). Beck and Murphy (1994) summarize her position as "that schools must focus, first and foremost, on promoting the development, health, and happiness of individual human beings, and because persons are fundamentally relational, they must also focus on developing capacities for interpersonal caring" (p. 15).[11]

According to Noddings (1995: 187), starting from our situation in the world, caring for each other requires no justification; our sense of what should be done is said to arise directly from our experiences, present and past, as human beings who have been cared for; thus there is, potentially, a spontaneous natural understanding of what should be done for others. (Here Noddings's theory of human nature follows that of Hume, 1739/2000.) Noddings recognizes that actually carrying out the implications of an ethic of care may not always be something we want to do, but dismisses Kant's idea that we need a rule to guide us or get us started, asserting instead that we simply have to reflect on our memories of having been cared for or related to properly. However, in the most difficult situations, principles fail us, she says; she suggests that a carer can and should then turn to the cared-for for guidance. Noddings recognizes that the initial idea of care could be formulated as a principle, but because she is concerned to prevent the decontextualization of care she insists that "carers must rub elbows with the recipients of care" (ibid.: 188) and recognize cultural and personal differences, which result in different manifestations of care. The ethic of care is based in a relationship, which of course makes it potentially useful to teachers – care does not reside solely in the attitude or intentions of the carer. Both parties are constrained to care for each other (in a relationship), so if a selfish person makes demands on another, the latter is allowed to withdraw to maintain her capacity to care. If used in moral education, raising boys and girls to be competent carers and sensitive cared-fors should prevent exploitation. The Kantian line requires moral agents to be separately responsible for their own moral perfection; the Noddings line requires each of us to recognize our own frailty and bring out the best in each other.[12]

Professional ethics

One of the defining characteristics of professions is that they, or their practices, have an ethical character that goes beyond the needs and demands of everyday individual life. As teachers, then, we would expect to supplement our normal ways of making decisions about what we should do by reference also to professional codes of practice. I will first enter a caveat, however, about the outcome of this discussion. As Carr says,

> [O]ne should not regard problems of ethics and moral practice as resolvable in the manner of technical problems. A potential error here is to suppose that there are rationally neutral strategies of ethical analysis, of, perhaps Kohlbergian dilemma resolution or utilitarian calculation, which would allow us to return unequivocally positive or negative responses to given ethical questions, or decisively adopt one course of action over another in the teeth of moral conflict or dilemma.
>
> (2000: 208)

So in the end, one still has to make a decision, rather than opt, through a completely rational calculation, for what has to be done.[13]

In a previous work (Crookes, 2003) I referred to the fact that whereas a variety of national education associations had established codes of ethics, the major international organization for ES/FL teachers, TESOL, had not.[14] One possible explanation for this (apart from the overall neglect of this area until recently) is the role played by culture and social expectations in some ethics, notably the virtue ethics referred to earlier. For that matter, even though ethics concerns the space between individual freedom and the law,[15] since breaches of ethics can in the worst cases involve legal recourse, again a national orientation is quite likely. (One might turn to the law of the country one was living in for recourse; and this is more likely than an appeal to international law.) In this line of discussion, it is noteworthy that one of the first handful of book-length works in this area intended for teachers in our field – Hafernik, Messerschmitt, & Vandrick, 2002 – confines itself to the concerns of ESL teachers, not EFL teachers, and indeed is written solely with the U.S. postsecondary ESL educator in mind.[16] This review of practical issues orients itself initially to the (U.S.) National Education Association (NEA) Code of Ethics, but goes into greater detail concerning the work of another professional organization (besides TESOL) that is of relevance to ESL teachers in the United States, namely *NAFSA: Association of International Educators*. As Hafernik, Messerschmitt, and Vandrick point out:

In international education [in the United States] NAFSA...has taken the lead in addressing the issue of ethics. In the early 1980s, NAFSA began work on an Ethics Program and established a Committee on Ethical Practice. The NAFSA Ethics Program consists of a Code of Ethics, Principles for International Educational Exchange, and Procedures for Handling Ethics Related Complaints.

(2002: xii)

As the authors point out, NAFSA's publications in this area deal with ethics in recruitment, marketing, and assessment, but "few deal with ethics and the ESL classroom instructor" (ibid.). As Hafernik et al. (2002: xiii) say, their work is "not a theoretical treatment of ethics and social justice in ESL."[17] Instead, they proceed by presenting a series of scenarios that imply ethical problems; in particular, those that are dilemmatic because they offer no obvious solution. What they do not do is offer any explicit codes or theoretical systems that an ESL teacher could use in trying to solve their scenarios. In fact, through a rather general introductory discussion, they broadly refer to the social justice literature and critical language education (citing Wenden, 1995) as the source from which at least a fair measure of guidance could be taken by ESL teachers confronting ethical dilemmas.

Hafernik, Messerschmitt, and Vandrick's list of the sort of areas in which ethical problems confront post-secondary ESL teachers includes:

- faculty responsibilities
- classroom management, inappropriate comments and complaints
- testing assessment and evaluation
- cheating and plagiarism
- advising and personal relationships
- gift giving

(2002: xiii)

In regard to the first two areas, they believe, for example, that ESL teachers should model "civility, respect, and consideration" (p. 19) and require "active participation in class" (p. 18).[18] Thus they seem to take a culture-specific (and possibly homogenous) view of what is correct behavior, and want ESL teachers to understand their "ethical" responsibilities to inculcate this. However, they also write that "ESL professionals must acknowledge [cultural] differences [among students] and make sure that students are taught the dominant academic culture which so many of them eventually hope to enter.... There is always the danger of imposing one's culture on others.... Teachers must value their students' cultures and heritages, but at the same time realize that, whether by choice or

145

not, these students are now in a new culture and society. ESL instructors are in a good position to help them adjust" (p. 21). Likewise, in the area of classroom management Hafernik, Messerschmitt, and Vandrick comment that "faculty have the ethical obligation to treat students fairly and with respect," which includes "ensuring that the classroom is a safe environment, conducive to learning" (p. 25); they are concerned about students who behave "inappropriately," which includes "exhibiting poor study habits . . . being rude or inconsiderate . . . disruptive, abusive, and even violent" (ibid.). Perhaps the "culture" that the authors have in mind is a common expectation about behavior in U.S. postsecondary classrooms; since probably the cultural nonhomogeneity of other aspects of the "culture" in question would preclude such blanket statements.

Though confined to ESL contexts, the work of Hafernik and colleagues is valuable for a number of reasons, including that it develops the "ethics as informative" position for TESOL specialists. That is, it provides a sensitizing function, alerting us to certain aspects of our practice (conceived narrowly, albeit) that should be seen as coming under ethical scrutiny. This too is part of the agenda of one of the few specialized contributions to this area in our field. Johnston (2003) focuses attention on matters such as voice, silence, curriculum content, the selection of the variety of English to be taught, tensions between the teacher's responsibility to students versus that to the employing institution, and between one's own values as a teacher and students' cultural values, not to mention core moral features such as the teacher–student relationship; his objective is to open discussion on the very possibility that such issues are matters of moral concern in language teaching, a topic that is new in our field. As a result it is perhaps asking too much of these two field-specific discussions that they go on to say *how* language teachers should confront moral dilemmas and make decisions about them. Indeed, as yet such research in regard to teachers in general seems scarce. Points of departure include an emphasis on due process and careful information gathering and decision-making procedures (as sketched by Mattison, 2000, for social work), the systematic use of cases ("casuistry"; Freeman & Francis, 2006) as well as data-based accounts of actual (or simulated) decision-making processes (as in Klinker & Hackman's 2003 account of principals confronting ethical dilemmas). It is perhaps not surprising that this last study implies that many educators do indeed make such decisions on the basis of only partial understanding of ethical systems, relying heavily on intuition. Perhaps, as more information in this area accumulates, along with increased practice of teachers' developing philosophies of teaching, there will be less reliance on intuition and more dependence on understood sets of beliefs and associated good decision-making practice.

Concluding remark

My review of this area has briefly alluded to systems and views that could be tapped in more detail by the concerned language teacher. I think it is accepted that this is an area that had temporarily been thought of by many as a personal matter, but that has returned to wider social and educational attention in the last decade or two. Perhaps for that reason (of partial previous neglect), we are only just beginning to see attention to the topic within the literature of TESOL or ELT. Even in mainstream educational research, there seems little evidence yet about how teachers make the decisions that we do nevertheless make quite often, which seriously impinge on ethical areas or for which ethical guidance would seem to be necessary. In this important area for one's philosophy of teaching, resources focused on the language teacher are still somewhat slight and could in any case be no substitute for extended reflection and discussion.

Discussion questions

1. Do you have a moral perspective on your work that goes beyond mere efficiency?
2. Under what conditions would you be satisfied with turning to the laws of the country you are living in for a guide to the ethical behavior of teachers, and concerning what areas of practice?
3. Use Crittenden's, Sergiovanni's, and Edge's sets of values as stimuli (along with your own introspection) to help you construct a short list of values for yourself.
4. Think of an ethical dilemma you may have faced in your practice thus far as a language teacher. Bearing in mind the quote from Carr, how did you solve it? (*Did* you solve it?)

Notes to Chapter 7

1 The research fields connected with S/FL teaching have been more proactive, as both the British Association of Applied Linguistics (BAAL) and the research interest section of Teachers of English to Speakers of Other Languages (TESOL) had constructed and disseminated position statements earlier (BAAL, 1994, and Scott, 2000, respectively). Consequently, in a recent introduction to the field of applied linguistics, Davies (1999) was able to provide an introductory discussion of the topic; however, he approaches it from the point of view of a professional ethics oriented to research and the researcher, rather than that of the teaching applied linguist.

2 Also of note: Buzzelli & Johnston (2002); Johnston et al. (1998). For a sample code of ethics, see www.tesol-law.com/codeofethics.php.

3 This subsection draws on Noddings (1995).

4 Though I suppose a notable exception is the legalist school, whose adherents thought of human nature as fundamentally bad and were interested more in keeping its effects in check by law, rather than through the cultivation of good people.

5 Considering the lifestyles of the "rich and famous," this cannot possibly be correct!

6 There is also an empirical line of criticism concerning the ineffectiveness of the direct teaching of virtues, within "character education" (cf. Yu, 2004).

7 Etymologically, this term is derived from Greek roots denoting "duty" or "law."

8 This was ironic, as part of Kant's long-term goals in philosophizing was actually to show the limits of reason, so as to make room for and defend religious faith.

9 From their second perspective above, they move to look at how "ethics provides a perspective on educational purposes, roles, and practices...and the development of ethical leaders [through] cultivating certain fundamental ways of thinking and understanding." This line suggests that ethical educators view the world and their work in distinctive ways. Such individuals, they think, will "identify education's deepest and finest purposes"; "will understand education as a social enterprise...and will seek to uphold certain political values and ideas.... and make decisions and engage in actions that honor, respect, and support individuals" (Beck & Murphy, 1994: 3).

10 Little research seems to have been done on the ethical decision making of practicing teachers, which I imagine is not an easy matter to capture, since such decisions are often made on the fly, if of lesser importance, or require confidentiality and extended consultation, if of greater importance. The few studies of the decision making of administrators, counselors, and the like outnumber those of teachers in the ERIC database (e.g., Dempster et al., 2004). Lampe's (1994) study of student teachers suggests a move toward a lower level of moral development after two years of teaching, and toward decision making solely reflecting rules and the law rather than other considerations!

11 See White (2003) for a recent review, which locates Noddings's ideas more closely to our subject area and develops her ideas in some areas where they are subject to criticism.

12 By no means do all feminists accept this position. More radical feminists than Noddings find it unhelpful, for example, because its initial impetus may have had essentialist tones, and thus it may still cause women to be positioned (as ever was) as those responsible for care, while men are excused from it. M. Ramsay (1997: 209–220) is an interesting review which shows up some strengths as well as weaknesses, while indicating that an ethic of care is not so distinct from an ethic of justice as Noddings might think.

13 At this point, some would place us in the existentialist tradition, of choosing to create one's life, in some sense going beyond criteria (Wringe, 1988: 48ff).

14 There is, however, a mission statement, which includes some values (www.tesol.org/mbr/whatis.html).

15 This position is attributed to Moulton (1924).

16 Although the authors do claim that "parts of [their] book may be applicable to EFL or K–12 educational settings" (Hafernik, Messerschmitt, & Vandrick, 2002: xiii).

17 They pair social justice with ethics because they say, "What is social justice but an ethical relationship with and toward others?" (2002: 5).

18 A moral requirement for participation, transmitted by communicatively oriented ESL teachers, is noted and analyzed in Johnston et al. (1998).

8 Mainstream social and political philosophy and language education

Introduction

How society, government, and the state should be organized has been a concern of philosophers since the first records we have; many philosophers have commented on schools and educational systems because education in general, and the institutions of education also, seem to them vital for achieving good government, peace, equity, and many other qualities essential for developed human life.[1] Teachers too, naturally have perspectives on the characteristics and organization of the societies they live in. A teacher who is part of a state education system is clearly part of the political system. Also, in democratic countries, most teachers are (minor) political actors in their roles as citizens of the state. Teachers of language, particularly of English, and their students, may be mobile across political borders. Perhaps some of us who are bilingual or bi-cultural, or culturally hybrid individuals may increasingly think of ourselves as cosmopolitan, or as global citizens (cf. Nussbaum, 1997, 2002). Those of us who are actively part of our professional organizations may be, on a very small scale, international political actors.

Of course, one way or another, language teachers are also acted *upon* by the political system. So having a stance toward the political may well be part of a teacher's philosophy of teaching, and teachers may well draw upon political and social philosophy as they develop their positions. In addition, since classrooms are social systems that are to some extent governed by the teacher, there are certain concepts that teachers apply to their classrooms (or which students may expect them to apply) and that are likely to have sociopolitical dimensions. Teachers who reflect on what their students expect of them in this domain may find themselves wishing to experience the benefits of good governance, just as they try to implement this themselves in their classrooms. Finally, I believe it may be possible to see some aspects of recent language-teaching traditions as connecting with certain commonly accepted parts of social and political philosophy (particularly in the area of autonomy).

Definitions and the topics encompassed by this area

In beginning a discussion of political and social philosophy in the context of a philosophy of teaching, one must first deal with the word "politics" itself. There are several uses of the term, and perhaps a couple may induce negative responses in the reader. For many people, the first understandings of the term relate to the views espoused by particular political parties, or worse, the often odious practices engaged in by politicians. Those are not the senses I will be concerned with here.[2] In addition, a pejorative sense of the term is common in schools – one may hear a phrase, such as "That's just politics," to refer to the hiring or firing of a teacher. In this sense, it relates to the *arbitrary* use or command of power in a school and is more technically known as "clientelistic politics."

While we are rightly dismissive of clientelistic politics in our schools, we would probably like to see the appropriate, and appropriately controlled, use of power in them. I like to draw attention to a definition well-known in political science: that politics is concerned with who gets what, when, and how (Lasswell, 1936).[3] Political systems do indeed allocate resources, set priorities, and so on. Similarly, we recognize schools as places in which resources are allocated under conditions of scarcity, and thus political, and we would accordingly like an appropriate politics to be in place. The language classroom, too, is a place shot through with power, even when benign. In and through this, resource allocation takes place (where the resources include speaking turn, teacher attention or correction, emotional support, not to mention similar matters provided by peers, and so on). The payoffs in such an economy are believed to be important for language learning, of course. In saying that I am also recognizing that our efforts as language teachers can help our students to better jobs and better lives and indeed prepare them to participate in the political lives of their countries (or more widely). The latter aim is a well-established responsibility of state educational systems in democracies. Accordingly, if you accept the basic idea that underpins this chapter – that, one way or another, you as a teacher are engaged in a form of politics – then in the course of developing your philosophy of teaching you may wish to develop your understanding of political philosophy as it plays out with regard to language in schools, language-teaching traditions, and also with regard to the global aspects of English, which is the main international language and a tool, perhaps a force, in some aspects of international politics.

Having said a word or two about politics, let me consider definitions of political philosophy and the closely related domain of social philosophy. Historically a central part of philosophy, political philosophy is "that branch of philosophy which deals with political life, especially with the essence, origin and value of the state" (Runes, 1983: 257). Social philosophy is not clearly distinct from political philosophy, so I could have referred, in the title of this chapter, to sociopolitical philosophy instead of using two words. Flew (1984: 328) remarks that "originally it was applied to any general and comprehensive vision of how society is or ought to be.... More recently [it] has come to be used like 'political philosophy'... to mark out an area within philosophy as an academic discipline." Similarly, Narveson (1995: 747) notes: "social philosophy [is] broadly, the philosophy of society, including... political philosophy, most of what we now think of as ethics...." Narveson points out that, in a narrower sense, it is also "the part of moral philosophy that concerns social action and individual involvement with society in general" (ibid.). Much political philosophy is founded in critiques of the status quo, and in a sense that present social arrangements are morally wrong. Beck's (1979: 1) definition highlights this: "social philosophy... is a philosophic critique of social process with reference to the principles underlying social structure and functions." Many of the major philosophers we have already mentioned devoted part of their efforts to social philosophy. One approach to the topic is through the study of the "ideas and doctrines of thinkers in the history or tradition of political philosophy," and another is through "analyzing concepts prominent in the politics of a number of past and present societies." Both approaches to the area of political philosophy "consist in large part of discussions of authority, obligation, freedom, justice, and equality" (Flathman, 1973: v).

To avoid associating this chapter with party political conceptions of politics, I will approach the topic by following on directly from that of the previous one – from, that is, the arena of ethics.[4] Some of the critics of conventional ethical systems aimed their complaints at the apparent focus on the individual, in Kant's work and in that of the utilitarians, not to mention the internal orientation of some virtue ethics. They emphasized that potentially, ethical systems apply to societies as well as to individuals, and/or that an individual cannot develop ethical qualities or act ethically in isolation. Everyday parlance certainly does not hesitate to describe certain social practices, and sometimes entire subcultures, as unethical, and as Beck (1979) noted, philosophizing includes engaging in a normative or evaluative practice. Many philosophers have connected individual ethics with social ethics, and we can go all the way back to Plato for a powerful early example:

> Plato... articulated the idea of justice in terms of harmony and measure, and he believed that justice and law are the common spiritual substance of a society that bring and hold it together. He understood justice in terms of an adjustment that gives the

parts or factors forming a society their proper place.... While this conception of justice is a principle of social ethics that gives coherence to the community as a whole, it served Plato as an idea of individual ethics as well. In fact, Plato quite deliberately compared society and the individual, holding that both are made of parts or elements, that both demand meaningful unification, and that both ought to be ordered by reason in the light of the idea of justice.

(Beck, 1979: 23–4)

It seems, then, that there is a philosophical connection between exercising ethical judgment about one's own actions, those of other individuals, and about the social and political systems in which we participate as language educators.

Sociopolitical concepts in democracies

In technical terms, most (but by no means all) readers of this material are probably working in liberal states – that is, they are not working in absolute monarchies or dictatorships.[5] Given this point, to develop a sense of the sociopolitical aspects of our philosophy of teaching it is probably a good idea to review the characteristic qualities esteemed in liberal states, such as justice and equality. As teachers, perhaps we consciously or unconsciously try to manifest such qualities in our own work, and perhaps would also use them as criteria against which to judge the overall working of the education systems we are in, and possibly the polities we are in. Thus the focus of this chapter will be a group of concepts that apply to our own work as teachers, our own classrooms, and are at the same time manifested in our sociopolitical contexts, particularly in liberal democracies. Given that orientation, central sociopolitical concepts that can inform our practice as teachers and our orientation to the world, as intellectuals, derive from or were first extensively manifested in the philosophical works of the European Enlightenment, particularly in the work of Hobbes, Locke, Rousseau, Kant, Bentham, and Mill. These concepts include justice, equality, freedom, liberty, autonomy, and rights.

The inheritance in question is a particularly mixed one: The two main strands of liberal thought are, to say the least, in tension. The term "liberal" was first associated with those who favored limiting the power of the state (typically, of a monarch).[6] This has been described as European or conservative liberalism; it can be associated with the term "liberty." Close behind it, historically, was a second version of liberalism, associated with the term "equality" and the work of J. S. Mill. This leads on to "welfare liberalism" in the 20th century, a close companion to socialism. Despite the historical orientation of liberal traditions to "free markets," unfettered capitalism is not essential to liberalism (e.g., Strike, 1989), and though many liberals do not favor socialism, some forms of socialism are not contradictory to liberalism. In addition, at least one of the conceptual strands of thought in question, associated with the term "rights," inherits from diametrically opposed conceptions of human nature, as being either fundamentally social, or fundamentally individualist. Perhaps for these reasons, someone with a strong attachment to just one of these concepts (such as justice, or equality, or liberty) might find that the liberal state is unlikely to satisfy, so much does it have to compromise, to deliver fully on any of them. Those favoring the liberal position on equality (or for that matter, justice understood socially) may see it as part of an "emancipatory project" that has not yet been completed, and one that may indeed perhaps need to be continued by conceptual means not fully delivered in liberalism.[7] Let us begin, however, with central liberal concepts.

Freedom, liberty, and autonomy

Liberty in the sense of freedom from impediment is sometimes referred to as "negative liberty"; we can also talk about personal autonomy, referring to the extent to which one is the author of one's own life, as "positive freedom" (Callan & White, 2003). In this line of thinking, liberty, and its counterpart, autonomy, are logical byproducts of the human ability to reason. If individuals are capable of reason and independent decision, their lives and their circumstances within institutions and states should reflect that. Locke gave particular attention to the undesirability of the state intervening in citizen's private lives (following a long and bloody history of the state doing so in regard to religious beliefs); Kant's work addresses (among many other things) autonomy and justice. Among these concepts, autonomy (for learners, notably) has been the subject of much work in applied linguistics in the last decade (cf. Benson & Voller, 1997). So perhaps at this point we can already begin asking a couple of questions, such as, "Do we think our language students are capable of reason and independent decision?" and, "What are the implications for the classroom or curriculum of that?" and turning the matter around, "If autonomy is something that our students should manifest in their lives in liberal democracies, how should the language curriculum (etc.) be structured to support that?"

In a useful discussion of autonomy, Reath explains that initially there were two main understandings of autonomy:

> One is the capacity to guide one's conduct by one's grasp of moral norms. The other is "sovereignty over oneself" – a basic right to self-governance, which is the basis of further rights and standards of justification.[8]
>
> (1998: 587–88)

Reath then makes the connection to liberty:

> [A]utonomy is a central value in modern liberalism and democratic theory. A conception of persons as having autonomy figures in liberal conceptions of justice.... It is the basis of those rights and liberties that are the institutional means necessary for individuals to exercise autonomy – including liberty of conscience, rights of free expression, liberty to develop one's own plan of life ... and rights of political participation.
>
> (ibid.: 590)

Autonomy can also be conceptualized as both inner and outer freedom:

> Freedom ... is a central element in the dominant political ideology of our age, liberalism.... Freedom has an external and an internal aspect: it depends on whether the world is arranged in such a way that someone has many doors open to him, but it also depends on whether he is able to choose, genuinely, which door to pass through ...
>
> How can we promote this inner freedom, the capacity to make genuine choices? One way is to expose people to a wide range of alternatives, so that they are less likely to take it for granted that any one set of beliefs, or any one way of life, must be the right one ... So a government that wanted to promote freedom to choose could do so by encouraging social diversity – by exposing people to new ways of living, new forms of culture, and so on.
>
> (Miller, 2003: 55–7)

Clearly that is what foreign language teachers do:

> One practical manifestation of such a policy would be an education system that encouraged children to think critically about the beliefs and values they have inherited from their parents or imbibed from their social network, and at the same time expose them to other faiths and other cultural values.
>
> (ibid.: 62–3)[9]

A variety of tasks and means have been advanced over many years for the implementation of such concepts in education, including latterly in language education. Miller's words echo those of many language-teaching specialists in their call for wide and diverse curriculum content, and the fostering of critical thinking. Autonomy is clearly capable of being developed through the provision of opportunities for students to engage in self-direction, within an overall school ethos that is not authoritarian and within daily timetables that are not scheduled so as to eliminate choice. The child-centered tradition of Dewey and others lies in this domain:

> The mainstream view sees autonomy as an ideal for mature persons, and children as being gradually prepared for an autonomy that lies substantially in their future rather than their present. But this presupposes a distinction between children and adults that some would reject or at least blur substantially. On this latter view, the compulsory curriculum to which children are normally subjected may be as unjustified as any other of the constraints on free choice that liberals have traditionally deplored. . . .
>
> Egalitarian liberalism is in principle suspicious of the idea that the moral standing of one group of persons (for example, men rather than women, members of one ethnic group rather than another, etc.) differs from those of another in ways that justify greater coercion toward one rather than the other. That being so, the child/adult distinction is an appropriate object of philosophical scrutiny for liberals, and even when it is conceded that the distinction is often morally relevant, its relevance is not so clear to the extent that a compulsory curriculum on the mainstream view has been conclusively justified.
>
> (Callan & White, 1998: 98)

It would seem, then, that if educational institutions are to reflect the sociopolitical ethos of the societies they are within, they should aim for as much liberty, freedom, and autonomy for their members as possible, consistent with their educational aims (and this should apply to child as well as adult students). Language teachers are most likely already to be responding to high expectations for learner autonomy if they work in systems and schools, which, for example, often provide learner choice concerning courses to be taken, some degree of learner input into the selection of topics to be considered in language classes, and a range of options for assessment. Such curricular initiatives and practices are obviously available to a greater or lesser degree across schools systems and among social democracies, however.

Justice

Justice is a central topic in sociopolitical philosophy. We need a theory of justice if we are to do a proper job of deciding whether the societies we work in are just (a decision that I assume in turn has implications for our work, or at least our thinking, as language teachers). That means, among other things, that we should consult the philosophical literature on what justice is, and what a just society is, and then consider our own positions as S/FL teachers.

The fair, or just, treatment of individuals by each other and by those in power would appear to be of great importance for society, and something to be aimed for by political powers and systems. Within the language classroom, teachers are accustomed to examining their interactional practices for such matters as fair distribution of turns at speaking; and grading practices or the development of in-house exams and tests naturally come in for review on grounds of justice or fairness. Where English language teachers and the field as a whole, in its local manifestations particularly, come in for scrutiny, of course, is in regard to the role that language proficiency plays in the passing of important university entrance examinations in many EFL countries, or indeed in regard to the role of internationally recognized tests of English proficiency to entrance into international universities.

A prominent theorist of liberal ideas in education is Strike, from whom I take the following preliminary remarks focused on justice:

> First, certain characteristics of individuals are morally central to a liberal theory of justice... the assumption that persons are autonomous and rational moral agents. But human beings are not borne [such;]... a liberal theory of education must concern itself with how rational moral agents happen.
>
> Second... liberals suppose that justice itself is the chief condition of social stability.... If a just society is to be stable, it will need to promote an understanding of its conception of justice, a willingness to abide by the requirements of justice...
>
> Third, a liberal theory of education will need to concern itself with the fair distribution of relevant social goods.... In our society education and schooling have profound consequences for the distribution of social goods. Schooling itself is an important social resource...
>
> It is to be noted that liberals will not be inclined to think about education by asking first about the nature of the good life for human beings. The reason for this is that liberal neutrality requires that people be free to choose their own conception of their own good. The liberal state has no right to specify what goals its citizens will pursue. Thus, liberal concepts of education are not motivated by a view of the good. Liberal educators are more properly concerned to help students develop and realize their own sense of their own good.
>
> (Strike, 1989: 31–2)

Specialists disagree about the extent to which justice is, or can be seen as, both social as well as individual in nature. Miller gives useful detail on the tension between individual and social positions here:

> Social justice [as opposed to individual justice, is] the idea that we can put in place a set of social and political institutions that will ensure the just distribution of benefits and costs throughout society. This idea first emerged in the late 19th century, and stood at the heart of political debate throughout the 20th . . .
>
> Critics such as . . . Hayek argued that there was a fundamental error involved even in talking about social justice in the first place. According to Hayek, justice is fundamentally a property of individual actions. . . . But if we look at how resources – money, property, employment opportunities and so forth – are distributed across a society we cannot describe this distribution as either just or unjust, since it results not from the actions or decisions of a single agent, but from the actions and decisions of millions of separate people, none of whom intended to create this or any other distributive outcome in particular.
>
> Hayek is certainly right to point out that "social distribution" cannot be attributed to any single distributing agency, given the complexity of any society in the contemporary world. But what he overlooks is that the distributive pattern that we observe around us does, in its general outline, depend upon the institutions we have created, consciously or unconsciously – for instance the prevailing rules governing property . . . the level of public expenditure on education . . . and so on.
>
> (Miller, 2003: 84–5)

In other words, it can be argued that along with individuals being just or unjust, and government dispensing justice, societies can manifest (or not) social justice, and that this is promoted, or inhibited, by the institutions of society, including educational institutions. As teachers, and thus members of such institutions, then, we have a role in the promotion of social justice, in our work in and our influence over the schools we teach in. If Strike is correct, we must also, as language teachers, address ourselves to the matter of how our students "develop and realize their own sense of their own good," (Strike, 1989: 31) presumably both through a language such as English and through the way they learn English in our classrooms.

The most important social-political philosopher of justice in the past century was Rawls (1971, 2001; Rogers, 1999).[10] Rawls tried to develop a conception of justice that accepted the liberal valuing of plural conceptions of morality:

The problem here is how to ground a normative theory of politics in circumstances where people disagree about their conceptions of the good. [One way]... is to put, as John Rawls argues, 'the Right before the Good' (Rawls 1971). That is to say, we can recognize that citizens differ about what they take to be good in human life, but nevertheless they have an interest in the justice of the political framework within which they pursue their own diverse goals. One can argue that it is possible to produce a compelling account of the rules of justice within a diverse society by making some rather minimal assumptions about certain basic human goods... and then to invoke some general principles of rationality to decide upon rules governing the distribution of such "primary goods." Theories of this kind aim to justify a political order by reasoning on the basis of slight assumptions about human goods, while recognizing the pervasive nature of moral diversity in relation to more specific human goals and purposes.

(Plant, 1998: 527–8)

And that is what Rawls does. As Noddings explains,

Rawls builds his theory of justice on a strategy he calls "the original position." In the original position, all participants are fully rational persons, but they have no idea what their actual positions in society will be. They must create the rules by which they will live.... Rawls gives a first formulation of the two principles that he says would result from deliberation in the original position and later adds "priority rules" to fill out his conception.

(1995: 162)

Rawls's principles are:

First: each person is to have an equal right to the most extensive basic liberty compatible with a similar liberty for others.

Second: social and economic inequalities are to be arranged so that they are both (a) reasonably expected to be to everyone's advantage, and (b) attached to positions and offices open to all.

(1971: 60)

Rawls's conception of justice is Kantian as opposed to utilitarian because it assumes that individual rights are not negotiable and cannot be traded off against the maximization of some greater overall utility. His approach is also a bit like Kant's approach to ethics: seeking a rule or procedure that we would all agree is in itself fair, and by us all conforming to it, we would all benefit, that is, we would have an ethical society. His position is that a society that operated according to those two principles would be a just society, and that conversely, social justice is to be achieved by an emphasis on individual liberties, and a meritocratic approach to inequality – that is, it is tolerated to some extent on the grounds that it is needed if society as a whole is to benefit.

This account suggests, in brief, that a just society is a meritocratic society. If the inequalities (mostly concerning wealth, in Rawls's conception) can be justified (i.e., that those who are better paid deserve it because of the contributions they make to society and the consequent overall benefit), then it is a good society, according to liberal theory. Language teachers may recognize this conception of justice if they work in schools that would accept that it is important to give prizes or scholarships to the best students on the ground that this unequal treatment is fair because it serves to encourage everybody to study hard and therefore raises the overall level of achievement. As will be seen later, it reads more troublingly when considered at the level of societal provision of resources to education.

Equality

A substantial concern with equality is a foundational theme at the beginning of the liberal tradition, in the work of Locke. Wringe comments:

> For many, the issue of whether a more equal society is itself desirable has long been settled beyond all further discussion. Such a view may be justified by the observation (cf. Locke, 1689–90, II.2.4: 309) that no one has any reason to regard himself as being of less consideration than anyone else, or accept a set of social arrangements that bear this implication.
>
> (1988: 82)

The demands that liberals oriented to equality make on their fellow-citizens are greater than those made by other liberals. There is a general sense in this line that a lack of equality is detrimental to the ability of individuals in a state to take care of themselves efficiently or participate actively in society:

> More generous expressions of the liberal ethic support various policies of public provision and redistribution. Egalitarian liberals defend social and economic rights as well as civil and political rights, and so demand of their fellow citizens a high measure of mutual engagement.
>
> (Sandel, 1996: 16)

And "if this all seems somewhat distant from the classroom" (an astute observation by Wringe),

> it must be borne in mind that schooling is an important part of
> the process by which the differentiation between those who are
> destined to be affluent and influential and those who are not takes
> place. ... Schools, by virtue of the organizational, curricular and
> other policies may compound and amplify these differences or –
> if such is their aim – take deliberate steps to avoid doing so.
>
> (1988: 87)

In those countries where competence in a foreign language (most
obviously English) is a prerequisite for university entry, it should be
abundantly clear that language teachers are directly implicated in the
maintenance or change in levels of equality among citizens.

Rights

The topic of rights, in general, and as broken down in various forms such
as human rights, group rights, individual rights, or children's rights, is
an important concept in political philosophy;[11] the idea of rights as
something one has is probably part of common sense for most readers of this work. Teachers of adults have usually had little to worry
about in this area, since few educational practices within the adult classroom itself might be seen as infringing on a person's rights; and teachers
of children would not have concerned themselves with this area until
fairly recently, because children's rights are a relatively recent development. On the other hand, language teachers, particularly those associated with the power language of the present world, may have asked
themselves from time to time, "Do I have the right to do that?" where
"that" is a pedagogical practice or concept of some kind, which they
might have felt they were introducing in a way that was somehow dis-
respectful of a culturally established way of doing things in their host
community.

In doing so, in articulating some concern, they would have been in
line with other cultural boundary crossers and inquirers. During the last
part of the 20th century,

> anthropologists tended to side with relativists and view with crit-
> ical disdain many basic conceptions of the international human
> rights framework, such as notions of human nature, universal
> human dignity and conceptions such as "crimes against nature."
> These highly abstracted formulations of humanity and morality
> were seen as the products of an international order dominated by
> western institutions and as far removed from the basic cultural
> conceptions of justice and morality found in non-western locales.

160

In retrospect, we could say that the early 1990s were the high point of cultural relativism.[12] In 1993, a collection of Asian states... issued [a] Declaration [which] stated that westerners should not try to interfere in their internal political affairs since 'Asian values' provide a superior basis for social and political regulation. The communitarian proclamation provoked a hostile reaction from grass-roots human rights activists in Asian countries and elsewhere, and prompted a growing awareness of the extent to which political elites used the ideology of relativism to legitimate their own mendacity....

(Wilson & Mitchell, 2003: 1–2)

The concept of rights, part of the central set of liberal concepts, is important for international aspects of our work. Rights in their initial development as part of political philosophy in the 17th century were based in the idea of a "natural" law that derived from a Christian understanding of the relationship of the individual to God (Fagan, 2005). In the 20th century this original line of thinking was considerably transformed, using the work of Kant, into the doctrine of human rights. The concept of human rights "seeks to define the inviolability of persons against considerations of utility" and to support "the moral entitlement that each individual is owed by virtue of their natural capacity as human beings" (Ramsay, 1997: 146).

> The Kantian conception of human beings as ends-in-themselves and therefore as bearers of rights provides the background for the argument for various justifications of different sets of rights as human rights. These rights are grounded in respect for human agency or autonomy and rest on conceptions of human beings as capable of choosing and pursuing their own projects, ends and values. Hart's classic statement of the equal right of all... to be free is defended as a natural right because it is one we all have if we are human beings capable of choice (Hart, 1955: 189–91). Claims to particular rights are derived from this universal right to liberty held equally by all, to be constrained only if circumstances are consistent with the general principle of the equal right of all to be free.

(ibid.: 147)

The 1948 UN Declaration of Human Rights has established this area, regardless (perhaps actively disregarding) the disagreement among political philosophers of both right and left concerning the legitimacy of the concept (e.g., Burke, Bentham, Marx).[13] The main current entities who resist the concept appear to be oppressive or strongly nationalistic governments.[14]

Some teachers of second or foreign languages will need to make specific connections to this domain of rights talk. At the language policy end of things (as opposed to classroom practice), the rights in question are likely to include positive rights. As English spreads, other languages die; minority communities have tried to make space for the maintenance of their languages by drawing on UN rights discourses and developing the concept of linguistic human rights. Teachers of English in certain circumstances will need to be aware of the rights associated with the national or minority languages whose speakers they should be aiding (through providing an additional language) rather than displacing. (See Rojas & Reagan, 2003; Spring, 2000, for discussion.)

Children's rights

For language teachers whose students are children, it seems obvious that an understanding of children's rights would play into the development of their philosophies of teaching. Past discussions of rights excluded children from the domain entirely, on the grounds of the child's limited rationality. (Of course, this was the same ground upon which women's rights had originally been limited.) On the other hand, one distinct strand of thought associated with ideas of liberty disagreed with the conventional position on children. Godwin (1797/1964: 88) emphasized the child's own entitlements to freedom and dignity. The child, he said, is "an individual being, with powers of reasoning, with sensations of pleasure and pain, and with principles of morality; and that in this description is contained abundant cause of the exercise of reverence and forbearance." It has taken quite a long time for rights discourses to catch up with this view of the child. Rights theorists working in this area (e.g., Lindley, 1986) developed arguments to the effect that the standard criteria used for denying rights to children (lack of rationality, inability for wise judgment) did not do a particularly good job and would exclude plenty of adults! Lindley reviews the capacities of 10-year-olds and argues that, "by the age of 10 years old, non-mentally handicapped children are people and as such they are fit subjects for the Kantian principle of respect for the autonomy of persons as ends-in-themselves" (Lindley, 1986: 122–3, cited in Ramsay, 1997: 183; a formulation which allows us to reconnect to the pedagogical understanding of learner autonomy, of course). In 1990, building on the UN-sponsored efforts in the area of human rights, 192 UN nations agreed to the Convention on the Rights of the Child. (Only two nations have not signed this: Somalia and the United States.[15]) UNICEF's official documents[16] describe the rights in question as follows:

> Built on varied legal systems and cultural traditions, the Convention on the Rights of the Child is a universally agreed set

of non-negotiable standards and obligations. It spells out the basic human rights that children everywhere – without discrimination – have: the right to survival; to develop to the fullest; to protection from harmful influences, abuse and exploitation; and to participate fully in family, cultural and social life. Every right spelled out in the Convention is inherent to the human dignity and harmonious development of every child. The Convention protects children's rights by setting standards in health care, education and legal, civil and social services. These standards are benchmarks against which progress can be assessed. States that are party to the Convention are obliged to develop and undertake all actions and policies in the light of the best interests of the child.

The Convention on the Rights of the Child is the first legally binding international instrument to incorporate the full range of human rights – civil and political rights as well as economic, social and cultural rights.

However, in practice this is not sufficient. Without supporting students in their development of autonomy, and without institutional conditions that support it as well, such rights are likely to rarely manifest in reality. Discussing education in the UK, Ramsay comments:

There is no tradition ... of acknowledging the rights of children and young people to participate in the process of education. Children have no rights to be consulted with regard to educational provision, school choice, school suspensions or exclusions or on any issue relating to their education or problems in school. Children have no formal rights to participation in matters of school policy or administration or to be involved in decisions. ... The basic civil liberties of freedom of expression, association, thought, conscience and religion are severely curtailed for children and young people ...

The content of education, too, fails to promote autonomy in that it does not provide children with the necessary knowledge, understanding and skills to participate fully in a democratic and multi-cultural society or to question and challenge received ideas.

(1997: 186)

Nevertheless, in some schools in some countries, including within some state schools, it is very definitely the case that children do participate in matters of school policy making, through schools councils and as a by-product of the recent international movement for school-community-based management, which has democratized school administration in many countries (even while sometimes increasing certain aspects of state quality-control measures). Similarly, it might be said that citizenship education, a fairly recent development, is intended precisely to provide children with the knowledge for participating in a democratic, multi-cultural society. Such practices, and such developments, do not occur without the considered action of teachers and other educationists. Language teachers, particularly those involved with multicultural education, may find themselves needing to consider whether the curricula they are designing, or implementing, do carry the necessary content to deliver on the rights of children in multicultural societies, in the way that Ramsay suggests. In language classrooms, where content is always an issue (since there must always be a topic for talk), we presumably should consider whether we fully allow for our students' freedom of expression if we have an adherence to the liberal values which some analysts say inform most democratic states.

Criticisms of liberal concepts

Assumptions in the "liberal individual"

Criticisms of liberal concepts, and of their manifestation in education, have been in existence as long as liberalism, of course. Both initially and at present, many of those focus on the implausibility of the basic conception of the individual that grounds liberalism. This is the "unencumbered self" – the isolated individual who is moral and rational, prior to being involved in any society. Ramsay (1997) summarizes the implications of this position drawing on three sources of critique: Marxist, communitarian, and feminist. At the same time she notes that one does not have to accept the whole of these lines of thought "to see that separately and together they present a powerful challenge to liberal political theory.... All point to the inadequacy of the concept of the abstract individual as the starting-point for political explanation and analysis" (p. 12).

The Marxist approach is a re-echoing of Aristotle's fundamental conception of the human being as essentially a "political animal." Aristotle, like Socrates, felt sorry for a person who did not live in a city or a state, for such people were deprived of the socialization and social interaction that would make an individual civilized and thus truly human:

> Real living individuals always exist in some specific social context and it is to this that we must refer in order to understand the nature of human beings already formed in society.... Unlike animals, [humans] have to produce to meet their needs.... This conscious production to meet needs is the distinctive feature of human beings. Production is not an isolated activity, but a social

activity which requires cooperation. Producers are not independent, self-sufficient atoms, but interdependent.

(Ramsay, 1997: 21)

However, this conception also embodies a theory of society (sometimes called "conflict theory"), which, as is well-known, sees society as stratified into classes, and classes that do not have converging or shared interests (again, as opposed to being made up of isolates). This is contradictory to liberalism's conception of society as an "aggregate of individual interests" which can be harmonized (as utilitarians do) to result in a common good.[17]

The communitarian position likewise takes aim at the liberal individual.[18] Callan and White remark:

> As a political philosophy, liberalism grounds the political organization of society on the exclusive values of individual choice and well-being. That is the substance of "liberal individualism."
>
> Communitarian arguments [react against this]. The reaction is motivated by questions that are both ethical and metaphysical. Might not liberalism exaggerate the place of individual choice and well-being in its interpretation of the good and just society? Much of what enriches our lives is found in associations of family, culture, and creed that we do not initially or perhaps ever choose. And if the good society is a place where our lives are woven together by shared adherence to a common good, does not liberalism sponsor attitudes that alienate us from one powerful source of human fulfillment and social cohesion [religion]? Similarly, it may be doubted that liberalism rests on a metaphysically coherent conception of the individual, given the constitutive role of social practices in forming any self....
>
> (1998: 102)

Callan and White note that communitarian arguments can support, for example, "religious exercises in state-sponsored schools." They suppose that if "liberal values are part of a public culture," they would have to be taken into account by communitarians, but "liberties of conscience, speech, and the like would have to be interpreted and limited by an overarching commitment to the good of society as a whole, and the proper place of communal identification in the lives of individuals" (ibid.: 104). Callan and White propose Dewey's work as "the most substantial attempt to construct a communitarian theory of democracy and democratic education that absorbs important liberal elements" (ibid.):

> Dewey believed his democratic ideal was latent in American culture and inseparably tied to the progressive tendencies of

> modern science. But he also knew that the struggle for demo-
> cratic community contended with powerful opposing pressures
> which included the atomizing effects of industrial capitalism, the
> persistence of premodern forms of religiosity, and the shallow
> individualism that liberal thought had . . . encouraged.
>
> (ibid.: 104)[19]

Language specialists have tended to emphasize the importance of teaching and maintaining minority community languages. The emphasis in
liberal political theory on the individuals and their autonomy is, for
communitarians, given too much importance compared with the need to
respect and support communities:

> The liberal theory that emerges in response to the communi-
> tarian revival treats questions about the formation of identity as
> central rather than peripheral, and it registers the decisive role of
> associative ties in the formative process (Macedo, 1990, 1999).
>
> (ibid.: 108)

Basically, the argument being directed against the liberal position is as
follows: "You say you want autonomous individuals; then you must
ensure the conditions, the safe, culturally intact conditions, for them to
develop – but notice that your society is composed of many cultures.
Also consider the importance of the intact family for the development of rational autonomous citizens; and then consider what is necessary to foster that" (cf. Kymlicka, 1989; Okin, 1989). Even group,
rather than individual, rights may have to be supported, such as the
right of a group to the preservation of their language, or education
in it, if some citizens are not to be marginalized in the pluralist state.
Yet these requirements go against the thrust of the original liberal
political theory.

Finally, a third source of critique is from feminism. One of the assumptions of liberal theory is that it applies only to public life, and what is
in one's private life is not open to state scrutiny or control. The family
is included in this domain. However, feminist critique focuses attention
on the family as a place where women's labor is exploitatively not recognized, as a site for the maintenance and transmission of oppressive
conceptions of gender roles or oppressive use of sexuality. When the
liberal state fails to intervene in family matters,

> the state is not a neutral arbiter between individual interests
> [as in the liberal depiction, but] embodies partial interests and
> is systematically biased against women . . . [C]ontrary to liberal
> assumptions, there is not room for a private area of life free from
> power and political interference. Liberal theory obscures how

questions of the family, sexuality, gender, housework, reproduction, knowledge and language are political questions....

Male control in every arena shapes men's and women's perceptions of reality and of themselves. It forms their sexual and gender identities, moulds their needs and wants and limits their aims, expectations and opportunities. If patriarchal interests dominate...then the liberal idea of the abstract or pre-social individual independent of social determinations is again called into question. So, too, is the notion of the autonomous individual as the best judge of their own interests....The idea that women as a group have shared gender interests, and require collective action to realize them, conflicts with the liberal idea of the isolated individual acting to maximize their own interests or to achieve their own good in their own way.

(Ramsay, 1997: 29–30)

Criticisms of the liberal conception of justice

The liberal conception of justice is also subject to critique. Its most recent version, as I mentioned, is the work of Rawls. One problem is the tension between the two crucial elements in liberal theory: justice and equality.

In the realm of education, many challenging analyses and descriptions have been provided of the "justice" that the real world of liberal societies has to offer in respect of the education of the poorest sectors of society. Generally, the poor get disproportionately poorer state education. Noddings (1995) approaches this point by referring to inequalities in physical resources within state education systems and asks whether utilitarian decision making (another feature of liberal democracies, but a position that Rawls is arguing against) would allow the extreme differences in resource allocations that characterize U.S. public schools.[20] Her answer is in the affirmative; so the position that Rawls opposes is bad, from the viewpoint of one concerned about the inadequate extent of a just provision of education in the real world of "liberal democracy." At first Rawls then seems to be the preferred alternative. A strict application of Rawls's concept of justice as fairness would "prevent" such disparities (or call for their elimination). However, as mentioned previously, unfortunately for those valuing equality, Rawls's second major theoretical principle, the "difference principle," indicates that if it could be shown that an economic difference actually benefits the disadvantaged, it can be tolerated.

At this point, those who have seen the remarkably unequal provision of educational resources[21] within liberal states may begin to lose patience with Rawls (cf. Gewirth, 1994). Philosophers of education have a somewhat difficult task in this area. On the one hand, Rawlsian theory is the default setting for discussions of justice; on the other, Rawls had little to say about education, and it is not clear if he considered it one of his fundamental rights. If it were, then Rawls's first principle is, in the real world, so far from applying as perhaps to call into question the relevance of his work. If it were not, then Rawls's second principle can apply, which justifies inequality in educational resource provision, which is itself unattractive to many teachers.

Indeed, the considerable differences between the real world and the assumptions that Rawls must make to get his theory off the ground have been a general focus of his critics. Like many others, Noddings (1995) complains about its abstractness, associated with the fact that it (unlike Dewey's) is not grounded in any real world of political processes. Apparently the criticisms leveled by his contemporaries at this modern instantiation of revived liberal political philosophy are very similar to those leveled by critics (notably Hegel) against the first wave of liberal theorists (Smith, 1989). "His [Rawls's] works do not speak to any recognizable political world and ignore almost completely the real dilemmas and tragedies of our time" (Anderson, 2003: 40). Rawls's original work seems to have assumed a unitary, individualist, and secular culture; this perhaps reflected his upbringing in upper middle-class East Coast America in the mid-20th century. It largely ignores "historically determined differences in social structures – for example, the identity and relative status of different classes, genders, and other groupings considered socially relevant at a given time" (McBride, 1994:110). It also was conceived primarily in terms of what might go on in an abstract single political entity. McBride comments that

> Rawls's decision to conceptualize the problem of justice only within *single* societies and not "internationally," or globally, means that *A Theory of Justice* and much of the philosophical literature parasitic on it will simply neglect some of the most pressing issues of social and political philosophy in our time.

(ibid.: 107)

Rawls's later major work (1993, 1999) attempted to address this, but for some commentators the stretch necessary to bridge his highly abstract theory and the real world is too great. In his final work (2001), he too seemed to have less confidence in the real world, saying that "only a 'property owning democracy' or a 'liberal socialism,' that used government or judicial power to prevent a small part of society from controlling the economy, and indirectly, political life as well would meet the criteria for justice" (Anderson, 2003: 50).

Human rights in tension with liberalism

Even if human rights are now seen initially to derive from the work of Kant, which is usually liberal in orientation, those valuing a broad conception of human rights may need to distance themselves yet again from the origins of this concept, or from a Kantian version of the concept. Liberal conceptions of human rights run into problems caused by the liberal prioritization of negative rights (e.g., to freedom from interference) over positive rights (e.g., right to employment). Civil and political rights were designed to protect citizens from interference by the state. But the focus on justice over equality eliminates the possibility of equal citizenship, since it causes or fails to ameliorate class and group inequalities.

> The moral foundation for both sets of rights was said to be Kantian respect for individuals as ends-in-themselves. But the individuals who require positive rights to resources if they are to be treated as ends-in-themselves are not the individuals of liberal theory. The individual in liberal theory is asocial, isolated, self-sufficient and self-interested, concerned to protect themselves against the conflicting interests of others. It is not difficult to see, then, why rights in this tradition are viewed as boundaries surrounding the individual to protect them from invasion by predators and why we are thought to have only a general moral duty to avoid harm and no obligation to aid....
>
> (Ramsay, 1997: 162–3)

> The individual that is the subject of positive rights claims is a social interdependent being with needs that can only be inter-subjectively realized; this individual requires for their survival and reproduction the co-operation, help, support and productive efforts of other people. According to this view, rights are not individual claims against isolated, antagonistic, self-interested and competitive individuals. Rights and their corresponding duties to avoid harm, protect and aid are organizational, co-ordinating devices which reflect our inter-relatedness; which express our respect for individuals as ends-in-themselves; which govern institutional arrangements for each individual's positive duty to contribute to and positive right to benefit from the collective and co-operative endeavour to satisfy human needs.
>
> (ibid.: 164)

So a person who really agrees with the idea of positive rights, such as the right to employment, a right to health care, and so on, is supporting a conception of rights that goes beyond what the liberal state, or the conception of the liberal individual, can really accommodate.

Interim summary

A fairly long tradition of seeing language as structure, and language learning as psychological and individual in character, has made it unlikely until recently that language teachers would see their work as capable of benefiting from a sociopolitical look. Even to suggest a political dimension to language – to suggest that language was itself other than neutral, or could not actually be separated from its social contexts – would have been unusual, and in some EFL contexts at least, dangerous. But at the same time, given the kind of ethics we expect to manifest in our classrooms, and given the power of the main language we work with internationally, it was presumably only a matter of time before an apolitical position became impossible to sustain, at an intellectual level at least.

Yet many language teachers in many countries still cannot express such positions safely. In addition, so long as the dominant conception of the subject matter we teach is structural, there is less room for an appreciation of how a sociopolitical viewpoint of any kind might play out in the classroom or in other aspects of one's practice as a language teacher. I can appreciate a hesitancy to engage with this perspective. It may be more or less appropriate, depending on what stage in a career a teacher is at, or what responsibilities an English language specialist has. While I insist that the language classroom is itself a political place, the teacher who is doing additional duties as materials developer or test administrator may perhaps see the political dimension more immediately.

As we have observed, the theoretical material that is the core area of dominant sociopolitical philosophy is torn in two directions. Liberal political theory is a wide conceptual domain with an extensive history, and many of its positions overlap, in addition. If a language teacher is operating with liberal humanist goals in mind, working toward the delivery of a liberal education, s/he may well be operating in a way that is consistent with the major concepts I have outlined in this chapter. If the education system s/he is working in allows for student choice, a substantial measure of student freedom, and treats students justly and fairly, it may be broadly liberal in nature. If its language component, let us say, involves English to add an international dimension to the school curriculum, which also aids student perception of an international environment seen democratically as a site for egalitarian participation, then perhaps that could be said to be providing liberal language pedagogy. If such a term were not in use, but the school manifested these characteristics in any case, it would be a good indicator of the way liberal concepts of education have indeed been taken up, or are being moved toward, in many cultures and societies, so that they are becoming unremarkable. If a language teacher is satisfied with the interpretation of those concepts within his or her school and society, and acts out of those concepts, s/he probably has developed that part of his or her philosophy of teaching sufficiently and need explore no further.

Concluding remark

In this chapter I have been concerned with discussions of sociopolitical philosophy, as applied to education, that are fairly mainstream and come under the heading "liberal." And I have taken up some criticisms of them, as well. But the range of alternative positions from which to improve this position is considerable (see e.g., Simon, 2002). In this connection, it is probably important to have a sense of how philosophical traditions change over time. In many cases it seems that a particular position is a complex concatenation of stances and views. Both argument and the real world may make a position less plausible, but the chances are that the argument, or the aspect of the real world that presents the challenge, does so (upon inspection) not to the whole position, but to part of it. The attackers may wish to dispose of the entire position; but even they may be somewhat supportive critics, and in the end may proceed by retaining what they feel is most valuable, while discarding the rest.[22] An individual might be sympathetic to some rather than other parts of the liberal understanding and turn to critiques of liberalism to develop understanding of it without necessarily accepting all of the bases for those critiques.

Critics of liberalism have been in place almost since its beginnings, as I mentioned earlier. The perceived failures of the early (19th-century) liberal states, notably in the area of equality, were a spur to radical social theorists (and educators) of the Victorian era. Those devoted to democracy, as the political manifestation of liberal ideals of equality and freedom, too, found in their desire to retain or advance as much of that as possible, that they were willing to dispense with other aspects of the liberal paradigm. Turning to the other end of the timeline, most recently, the highly stripped-down conception of the individual (as separate, given, not created, and largely culture-free) has seemed to fly in the face of the plausibility of hybrid 21st-century identities. Lindley (1986: 139), reflecting pessimistically on the specific matter of democratic states delivering on a commitment to children's rights, commented: "The problem for liberals is that some values which lie at the heart of liberalism are, in their implications, radical."[23]

In recent years the manifestations of this and similar positions, both the older critiques and more recent ones relating to the nature of individuals in the 21st century, have become quite influential in certain parts of the TESOL field, in applied linguistics generally, and increasingly in the foreign language/Languages Other Than English (LOTE) domain as well.[24] Thus the next chapter takes up and reviews two radical critiques as they play out conceptually in S/FL curriculum theory and from which one might further extract material for the construction of a philosophy of S/FL teaching.

Discussion questions

1. To aid further understanding of the term "liberal" – what would be the features of a nonliberal democracy?
2. Are your students autonomous? Should they be? How about "rational"? Do you have a role in this?
3. How can a language teacher who is a liberal educator "help students develop or realize their own sense of their own good"? (Assume this individual has complete control over her own curriculum and pedagogy, etc.)
4. Equality or equity? Is unequal treatment of students sometimes "fair"? Is what you are doing as a language teacher compounding or amplifying differences among individuals, or diminishing them? Is amplifying differences defensible in a meritocracy? (Are there such things?)
5. As a language teacher, what is your position on positive rights?
6. (For teachers of nonadults) What rights do the children in your school have? Is this reflected in your classroom or in the way your school runs?

Notes to Chapter 8

1 And remember, some philosophers have even developed and run schools!

2 Although, as Fink (1981: 3) remarks, "The programmes of political parties and social movements...when...pushed beyond surface polemics...they become discussions of social philosophies."

3 Hawkesworth (1992: 27): "The central question for political research then is 'who gets what, when, how' (Lasswell [1936])"; and politics "concerns the procedures by which scarce resources are allocated and distributed...between groups who uphold and those who challenge the status quo" (Dove, 1986: 32).

4 "In ancient philosophy, politics also embraced what we call ethics" (Runes, 1983: 257). "Political philosophy evaluates social organization . . . from an ethical viewpoint" (Sankowski, 1995: 693).

5 "As of 2004 in much of the developed world, enough of the goals and values of liberalism are entrenched in governmental and societal institutions that liberalism has necessarily taken on a moderate and reformist character" (Encyclopedia of Political Information; retrieved June 2005, www.politicalinformation.net/encyclopedia/ Political_liberalism.htm). The technical use of the term is not consistent with the recent development of a pejorative interpretation of the terms "liberal" and "neoliberal" in modern political discourse.

6 As early as 1812, when the term was used in the Spanish constitution.

7 If that is so, and we subsequently discover that the educational institutions, or the political systems, are not living up to our ideals, we then must decide what to do, or at least, how to view the situation. Conceptually, we might be able to identify the weaknesses in the systems; or for that matter, decide that the entire conceptual system is at fault and should be replaced. Practically, we may or may not have any possibility of acting to improve matters. If we do, we then need to decide whether we wish our efforts to have an ameliorative function, or whether to work for larger-scale change.

8 Kant is the philosopher most famously associated with this concept.

9 See also Callan & White, 1998: 97.

10 His work is said to represent the beginning of the revival of political philosophy, after a period during which, under the influence of logical positivism, it was argued that almost all political philosophy was subjective and thus useless. Not all commentators agree on this point, however (see Anderson, 2003).

11 And indeed in liberal theory. For Sandel (1996) it is definitional: "In [the] historical sense, liberalism describes a tradition of thought that emphasizes toleration and respect for individual rights" (p. 4).

12 Pollis & Schwab (1980), Pollis (1992); for a swift dismissal of which, see Donnelly (1998, Chapter 2).

13 In the present work, I obviously favor a concern with the origins of ideas, or their genealogy. I note therefore that human rights scholar Griffin (2002: 20) remarks, "The United Nations says little in its declarations, covenants, conventions, and protocols about the grounds of human rights; it says simply that human rights derive from 'the inherent dignity of the human person' [Preamble to the *International Convention on Economic, Social and Cultural Rights*, 1966]."

14 Including those governments who question whether something like an association of nations intended to settle world affairs through negotiation is actually worthwhile. This strengthens the concept in many other individuals' minds, of course.

15 Somalia is widely recognized to be a "failed state"; at time of writing it has no functioning government (www.abacci.com/atlas/politics.asp?countryID=322).

16 www.unicef.org/crc/crc.htm, retrieved July, 2005.

17 Thus human nature is not inherently egoistic or competitive; this, and indeed all conceptions of human nature, are the products of societal systems at a particular point in history; or are ideologies that reflect the interests of those who get to say what human nature is, at a particular point in history. Thus "rationality, autonomy and [the] sovereignty of the individual's expressed desires" (Ramsay, 1997: 24) are also called into question by this form of social theory.

18 "The paradigm communitarian argument remains Hegel's critique of Kant's moral (and his derivative political) theory. Kantian ethics celebrate the sovereign rational agent...Hegel argued that Kant's moral conception empties the ethical life of substance because the abstraction it enjoins would blind us to the particular obligations we incur as members of ongoing communities, with distinctive histories and conventions that inform our very identities" (Taylor, 1975: 365–88).

19 Critics (e.g., Callan & White, 1998: 105; Kymlicka, 2004: 127) say that communitarians fail to do justice to postmodern, highly plural, multiethnic or indeed multination states.

20 The matter of the degree of this, changes in it, and similar patterns in other countries is the subject of continuing investigation. See e.g., Murray, Evans, & Schwab (1998) and articles in the *Journal of Educational Finance*.

21 The provision of *different* resources is another matter. Independent of resources, though reflecting the ideologies of liberal societies in the 20th century, inequalities in the area of curriculum have often been seen. Even Dewey advocated different educations for children according to their different interests; but this can be turned to the advantage of those who wish to perpetuate social inequality. Addressing this point, Noddings (1995: 176) advocates an "education organized around a finite number of broad talents and interests, augmented by serious inquiry into common human problems" to foster meaningful equality.

22 This is how Strike (1989), for example, characterizes the liberal position: as a "research program," drawing from e.g., Lakatos and the philosophy of science concerning the nonrefutation of theories.

23 Cf. Ramsay (1997: 254): "Liberal concepts cannot just be expanded within a liberal theoretical framework and within a liberal social context. There is a point at which they collapse back upon themselves because they are necessarily limited by the concept of the individual and a commitment to individualism that is at the heart of their theorizing. To bring forward the emancipatory project liberalism once embarked upon, we can retain the idea of respect for the equal worth of each individual, but we must jettison the liberal conception of the individual and all that follows from it."

24 Considerably more prominent, for example, than those influenced by communitarian positions, although presumably bilingual and multicultural education implicitly draw on a communitarian philosophy.

9 Radical alternatives

Background

This chapter follows on from the preceding one in developing discussion of matters of justice and equity in and through education. If you are not satisfied, as a teacher, with the philosophical concepts outlined in the previous chapter, either in theory or as they manifest in practice – particularly if you are dissatisfied with the inequities that manifest themselves in your society and education system, or the lack of democracy you find in it, then, as a teacher in search of a philosophy of teaching, it would be natural to explore the philosophies of pedagogies that attempt to respond to such inadequacies.[1]

The history of education, and the history of S/FL teaching, are full of reactions intended to correct inadequacies. There have been more than a few reform movements intended to correct misperceptions concerning how we are capable of learning, how we are best able to learn an additional language, the role of learning in society, the role of language instruction in the world, and so on. Thus we should not be surprised that critique continues and infuses certain perspectives on language learning and teaching, either in themselves or as they relate to conceptions of human nature, school, the role of the teacher, the nature of society, and so on. That being the case, it is essential that a work (such as the present one), which proposes to contribute to teachers' developing philosophies of teaching, consider such critical traditions.

In the East, in China, the earliest educational tradition is clearly founded on a fairly extensive critique of the order of the day, in man[2] and under heaven. As alluded to in Chapter 2, Confucius's teaching was a response to the condition of persistent warfare among the various states that made up what later became China. Because men of influence had not cultivated themselves, and ignored rules of propriety, states were ill-governed and the people suffered. Confucius persistently offered his advice to the powerful in several of those states, but finally, rebuffed by all, he set up an independent educational institution to teach the *right* way to do things, in the face of general unrighteousness. After periods of being ignored or decried, his position was returned to on several occasions as one way to restore good government, notably in the neo-Confucian era of the 1300s.

Similarly, in the West, after the Middle Ages, the modern period opens with humanism, an educational movement intended to redress incorrect conceptions of the nature of man; Comenius's ideas (to take a language specialist we have mentioned) were intended to correct misconceptions in this area; and Rousseau's ideas were an educational response that radically altered practice on the basis of a far-reachingly different conception of (the) human being. As the West caught up with the East, both in terms of economic development and in terms of understanding the importance of education for the state, radical and/or critical reform movements repeatedly attempted to use the power of education to correct or improve social conditions, or our ability to learn in general.

Within the last century, one of the more successful educational traditions of critique in the English-speaking world, the Progressive Movement, has seen a number of its ideas become mainstream, or to some extent become submerged in the mainstream. Though there are still tensions between back-to-basics and child-centered approaches, many of the ideas of Dewey, notably an activity-centered curriculum, have become taken for granted by specialists in TESOL.

However, there are traditions of critique further out than this, which have *not* become part of the mainstream. I referred in Chapter 4 to reconstructionism, a movement in U.S. education of the 1930s that was critical of Dewey and the progressivists for not going far enough. This position was not taken up broadly, even though some of the impetus for social reform (and some associated understandings of curriculum) did get absorbed into some parts of state education systems around the world. These and other more extreme positions of social critique were restated in the 1960s, drawing on, but greatly developing, radical positions that had coexisted with such positions or even preceded them. These involved discussions of class (initially), with gender as a major theme developed in parallel, but with its educational manifestations coming a little later. In this chapter, I will review the older lines of critique embodied in radical approaches to education and then discuss their manifestation in approaches to and concepts of S/FL learning and curriculum that reflect class and gender.

Free libertarian schools

We have seen (in Chapter 3) language teaching embodying humanist ideas, and trying to support liberal forms of learning through helping students become familiar with uplifting literature. With Clark (1987) we have identified the inheritances of reconstructionism and progressivism within the widespread communicative approaches in ES/FL (in Chapter 4). The upheavals of the late 1960s introduced radical ideas more explicitly into S/FL teaching, and one tradition, critical pedagogy, has become quite well known. As with a number of other topics discussed in these pages, this matter involves a philosophical position or school, a pedagogical movement associated with it, and manifestations in language teaching. Since the present work is not a Methods text, but emphasizes the philosophies of educators so as to foster the teacher's own development of one such, I will start from the philosophical end of this matter, again using a somewhat historical perspective.

In the global world of the 21st century, if we are dissatisfied with the state of the world – perhaps with aspects of what has been called "modernity" – and want to pursue and explore that sense or feeling, we have a range of dissident analyses to turn to. In a sense, all nonmainstream cultures are a critique, through a standing aside and dismissing of the dominant way of the world. Particularly noticeable when appearing within developed countries, traditional indigenous cultures reject as inadequate much of what the mainstream modern world has to offer. In the world as a whole, religious traditions often offer a comprehensive alternative, including often scathing criticism of the dominant patterns of the modern world, and they have associated with them their own educational traditions and school systems. But besides those traditions, which consciously stand aside from the mundane world of money-making, materialism, and individualism, there is a broad trend of thought that engages with it, and critiques it, at the sociopolitical level (rather than being culturally or religiously apart).

Let me turn now to the educational movement associated with this position and begin to identify a sector of education within which it emerged and the stance it took. Most of the time in this text, I have not distinguished much between state education systems and nonstate systems. Of course, organizations other than the state have always produced or supported schools, as appropriate to their own objectives. In addition, educational institutions have often had the capacity to oppose themselves to dominant forces in society. Humanist schools in the early Renaissance in Europe, for example, could be seen as inherently opposed to conservative trends associated with the Catholic Christian church. In Korea or China, various independent academies promoted ideas at odds with those of the ruling elites at various times. Thus, in times and contexts of strong states, the nonstate sector can more easily accommodate educational critique, if any is possible at all.

Now as I reviewed earlier, by the 19th century, education of and for "the masses" had become a possibility for the first time, though mass education was initially only within the lower education sector. Schools were for children; universities however were still for elite adults; what about those adults who had missed school or for whom school had never been an option? For the first time, "adult education" came into existence as different from university education. And while developing regular school systems were increasingly coming under the control of the state, new forms of adult education, less structured and more elusive, were not. Adult education for the poor in various countries came under the influence of trade unions, while religious organizations whose intent might not have been congruent with those of the state (such as missionary schools in many places) were also active in this area. Thus, there are two sectors within which this story plays out: historically, first most prominently in the independent elementary sector; subsequently, more obviously in the adult education sector.

Let us pick up the historical story in Europe. The decline of the French Revolution into dictatorship initially discouraged many progressives in Europe. However, rapid social change through discontinuity rather than reform continued to be seen as a possibility, so that the first part of the 19th century saw a flurry of revolutions (Germany, 1848; France, 1849; the Paris Commune, 1871; Italian uprisings in 1860) accompanied by a range of strands of critical thought about society, including about education. In due course, specialists who studied the structures and elements of society at that time, and who did so with a view to improving on them, naturally focused with interest on the burgeoning new features of society, which had either not hitherto existed at all, or had not previously been the strong forces of change that they had now become.[3] I refer to businesses, companies, firms, entrepreneurial activity, and, in short, capitalism. Some alternative theories of society focused on the economic organization of society and ways that it could be made better; a broad model of an alternative society that critiqued the existing arrangements developed within early social theory, known as socialism, and a movement for social change became associated with it. Optimistic analyses of how such a form of society might come into being were developed. There were a variety of such "socialisms";[4] perhaps one unifying characteristic to note was their opposition to the individualist analysis of liberalism, discussed in the previous chapter.

A crucial divide was to manifest itself between those who favored using the power of the state for social change and those who did not. Both made use of critiques of society founded in egalitarian concepts, but initially had little to say about the style of education, though plenty about the institutions of education. Those who wanted to use the levers of power of the state to complete radical social change became known as communists. Under Lenin, following the revolution in Russia, the same attitude to state education that was found in, say, Prussia could also be found there – that is, an indoctrinary attitude and authoritarian practices.

Those who were against the state in any form were inheritors of the emphasis on freedom of the liberal tradition; they constituted the "left wing" of socialism (Kropotkin, 1910). This line of libertarian socialists eventually became known as anarchists, and their educational interests manifested in continuing a tradition of small independent schools run by dissident educators of various affiliations. They extended to such institutions a concern for nonhierarchical methods of school organization, and a great desire that teaching itself be noncoercive. The term "free schools" is typical of this tradition.

Earlier in these notes (Chapter 3), I alluded to a variety of independent experimental schools that took inspiration from the ideas associated with Rousseau. Such initiatives continued to occur though the sources of ideas shifted. By the middle of the 19th century, some schools, notably in France,[5] made use of or allied themselves with the antiauthoritarian tendencies I have just alluded to, which at this time were going under the heading "libertarian" (even though previously they might have used a term such as "anarchist," associated with the theorist and activist Proudhon).[6] They drew on the ideas of "integral education" – a form of education that would be for both mind and body, have a vocational character, and aid in advancing the position of working people. It would, to that end, be anti-individualist, decentralized, and cooperative; and quite likely, involve adult education as well. These ideas about the content and structure of schools were taken to Spain by Francisco Ferrer, who was successful in popularizing them during the first decade of the 20th century. "By the end of 1905 there were fourteen schools in Barcelona alone which were modeling themselves on Ferrer's school, together with another thirty-four in Catalonia, Valencia and Andalucia" (Avrich, 1980: 26, cited in Smith, 1983). Ferrer also established an associated international organization, and journals and periodicals spread the ideas. In 1909, Ferrer was tried on false charges by the Spanish authorities for political reasons and executed, which served to spread his ideas further. Ferrer schools were started all over Europe and in South America, China, and Japan. "The most vigorous response of all came from the United States" (Smith, 1983: 6). According to Smith, during this period, the growth of radical ideas and "syndicalism" (i.e., trade union activity) among teachers in state schools led to "the argument that state schools could be reformed along libertarian lines from within" (p. 13).

In theorizing the modern school, Ferrer (e.g., 1913) pulled together many ideas that were radical at their time but are commonplace nowadays: coeducation, active learning, a scientific approach (inquiry and data analysis) applied throughout the curriculum, the same emphasis on the practical as well as the theoretical, and the use of the actual environment as a learning medium (resource centers, school trips, and the like).

In this line of discussion, Smith (1983) sees a gradual move away from the vocational emphasis of early integral education toward the theoretical development of a general core curriculum that would be consistent with anarchist or libertarian principles. This he finds in the educational writings of Kropotkin (e.g., 1899/1974) and also Tolstoy (1967) who was actively involved in running an experimental school for several years. These authors placed much emphasis on motivation, and motivating conditions leading naturally to learning without much in the way of direct instruction or external (punishment or reward) motivation. The conditions concern (a) "love, support and emotional encouragement" of students, and (b) freedom – an absence of coercion, an "approach to the freer conditions on which cultural learning took place" and a redefinition of the teacher–student relationship to one more egalitarian, in light of that (Smith, 1983: 72). Perhaps particularly important for language-teaching specialists, theorists in this line, whether of the 19th century or the 20th (e.g., Holt, 1976; Neill, 1960/1993[7]), recognize a natural inclination on the part of children (at least) to learn, and believe that students can "naturally" organize their learning experiences, and will indeed learn in a somewhat unconscious and natural way if placed in the right educational environment. Paul Goodman (1968) was one of a number of such theorists to hold up L1 acquisition as characteristic of the kind of natural learning that he and other radical educators of this kind wanted to see generalized to all kinds of learning. Holt in particular, though others wrote similarly, looked to the "natural" characteristics of child development, and children's natural and persistent behavior to explore and thereby learn the world around them (including the language around them) as a basic model for the kind of learning they would like to see in schools. And by comparison, they rarely saw this sort of thing in regular schools. For them, says Smith,

> there was something in the school environment itself which enhanced self-consciousness with respect to failure. That something was, of course, the whole business of assessment, marks, grades, the stress on achievement, the constant implicit reference to competition, and the nearness of potential penalty.
>
> (1983: 75)

The emphasis on egalitarian and supportive relations between teacher and student, on a group orientation, and on nondirective pedagogical techniques were certainly radical when they first manifested themselves in free schools and the modern school movement of the late 19th century. But with the considerable social changes that took place during the 20th century and accelerated during the 1960s, by 1976, Holt was able to find what he regarded as an excellent example of a pedagogy which respected the natural processes of learning (exemplified in L1 acquisition) in some state elementary schools (for example, in Denmark).[8] Smith's further theorizing of this places the emphasis on shifting the function of teaching from direct instruction to the provision of feedback. Using the terms of psycholinguist Ken Goodman (1967; later incorporated into such developments as the Whole Language Approach), he notes that for the teacher, "the problem...is how to fit in with the psycholinguistic guessing game" involved in learning to read. "Teaching functions take the character of feedback...designed to help a learner improve on an already existing performance. The learner makes his move first and only then can the teacher offer advice....The teacher should not talk too much, and must respond to the developmental needs of the learner (Smith, 1983: 83). Learner initiative and choice are to be emphasized, as means of developing and nurturing the free will that is crucial for individual freedom.

This tradition continued and even penetrated U.S. state schools in the late 1960s, with a small number of state schools finding conditions allowing them to adopt more radical practices (Miller, 2002; Neumann, 2003). Although greatly diminished in number, a handful persisted (e.g., Basile, 2004) and this work has probably fed into the uptake of the "charter school" concept by those seeking radical school alternatives that can benefit from state support (Rofes & Stulberg, 2005).

The traditions of sociopolitical critique and antiauthoritarianism were unified for one part of the old left (anarchism) but not for the other (communism). Studies of education in the Soviet Union comment that despite early attempts in the 1920s, which reformed education in progressive and Montessori-like directions (along with the abolition of uniforms, examinations, grades, etc.), subsequently under Stalinist influence and with the desire to build a strong state through state education, political critique ceased to manifest interest in freedom at the classroom level or within the organization of schools.[9] Even outside of such countries, the availability of Marxist lines of sociopolitical critique was much greater than of those inspired by Proudhon or Bakunin. So educational philosophy of the 20th century that drew on alternative social theories, and on critiques of existing political systems, tended to draw on developments of Marxian theories.

Critical pedagogy

During this period, elements of socialist forms of political organization flickered in and out of existence but (contrary to the expectations of Marxist-inspired actors and analysts) were not long-lasting. By the middle of the 20th century, theorists addressed themselves to the matter of why earlier analyses had been overoptimistic. These forms of alternative social theory acquired the label "critical theory." Somewhat in parallel with them,[10] a theory and practice of curriculum and instruction that set itself in accord with radical efforts for social change was

developed in Brazil in the 1960s by Paulo Freire. This was "critical pedagogy." For some specialists (e.g., Shotton, 1992; Smith, 1983; Spring,
1975, 1994) this, in its opposition to oppression of all kinds, is sufficiently akin to the libertarian traditions just mentioned for it to be
discussed alongside them.[11] For SL specialists, it is this educational tradition that has become most popular among those drawing on radical
social philosophy. It is perhaps not surprising that this has had considerable influence within S/FL studies, because unlike most educational
"innovations," it begins with and is directly concerned with language,
specifically literacy; not only that, but it takes culture as its central focus;
and was initially located in the second of the two possible educational
sectors hospitable to alternatives: adult education.

Low literacy rates and poverty have tended to go hand in hand, and
throughout the latter half of the 20th century, many agencies in poorer
countries have worked within adult education systems to try to foster
greater literacy. In understanding the development of the critical pedagogy movement, it is important to be aware of the role played by the
Catholic Church in promoting adult literacy classes. In South America,
after World War II, the church became radicalized, and began to more
strongly articulate the critique of material society that is implicit in some
Christian teachings. Various strands of influence, both the Christian and
the socialist, were taken up and developed both in practices and in theories, by Freire. In Brazil, citizens had to pass a literacy test in order
to have a vote; typically the poor were thus disenfranchised, so literacy education became an important means of fostering peaceful social
and political change there. Unfortunately, as some say, if voting led to
radical social change it would be made illegal, and so it more or less
proved. Following a right-wing coup, Freire was first imprisoned and
then exiled.[12] As a result, circulating in the English-speaking world from
the late 1960s on (to an extent that they did not, at first, in the Brazilian
Portuguese or Spanish-using areas), Freire's ideas entered foreign language education and ESL education in the mid- to late 1970s. Where
they came from is made apparent in the analysis of Taylor (1993), from
whom the following long quote is taken:

> The genius of Freire was to bring together a range of pedagogies
> and learning/teaching techniques to create a method of teach-
> ing which is now known throughout the world as the "Método
> Paulo Freire," a method which is both a process of literacy acqui-
> sition and a process of conscientization. It is based on the simple
> but fundamental technique of *problematizing* or "problem pos-
> ing," and is therefore the antithesis of Banking Education which
> seeks solutions or gives answers. It consists of daring to interro-
> gate what is given, bringing into question known structures, and

examining conventional or taken-for-granted "explanations" of reality. It discovers and then reacts to [the] possibility of "contradiction," identifying ways in which things can be said, done, or exist differently.

In *Education: The Practice of Freedom* [1967/1974], Freire explains the details of his method which has changed very little over the years. It is a three-stage investigation, which poses three fundamentally different questions. First, there is a NAMING stage where one asks the question: what is the problem, what is the question under discussion? Second, there is a REFLECTION stage: why is this the case? How do we explain this situation? Finally, there is the ACTION stage: what can be done to change this situation? What options do we have?

It is a pedagogy which describes certain processes of learning rather than prescribing certain required outcomes, acceptable results or attainments. In the jargon of educationalists, it is process-centred, not product-centred.

"It is a permanent, critical approach to reality in order to discover it and discover the myths that deceive us and help us to maintain the oppressive, dehumanizing structures. It leaves nobody inactive. It implies that people take the role of agents, makers and remakers of the world" (Freire, 1971: 24).

The three-stage structure of the method, however, was not Freire's creation. It parallels a process popular in the 1960s within the Basic Ecclesiastic Communities (*Comunidades Eclesiales de Base: CEB*) in Brazil. As the basis of the social education programme, especially in the literacy campaign broadcast nationwide by the Church's Basic Education Movement (MEB), they used a method known widely as *See-Judge-Act*: what is the case, why is it so, and what can be done about it? The method found favour, particularly within the Catholic Church, partly because it was simple and practical, and partly because it represented the secular application of the three stages of prayerful meditation as taught within the Jesuit tradition. . . .

Freire was thus using a tried and tested method, as Cartesian as it was Catholic, within a learning context which was equally well known to many people both through the CEB and through the trade unions, that is in the *Culture Circles*. These groups became very much associated with his method, although the idea behind the Culture Circle is again, as we have seen, neither new nor particularly South American. What Freire saw was the potential of such a group for the Portuguese lessons which he gave to workers and peasants. Later, it seemed a natural context for his literacy programmes. Only very much later did he see the political possibilities which the CEB had been deliberately exploiting for some time [cf. Fernandes, 1985].

(Taylor, 1993: 73–9)

Although Freire was later unhappy about the development of his ideas into some fixed "Freire Method," an initial understanding of what his ideas imply for practice can clearly be obtained from a sketch of the typical procedures he instituted in literacy classes. For him, it was very important that the curriculum begin with the concerns and issues of the students. For beginning literacy, the core words should relate to the issues of the students' lives and the things in their lives that were problematic and that they might be able to change and improve through the tool of literacy and the changed consciousness that would come from that. When literacy courses were delivered within the students' home communities, the instructional team spent time living in the community to develop an ethnographically grounded base for the curriculum. A characteristic feature is the use of images (pictures, or later, photos) of certain aspects of the students' lives. But in addition, since one underlying goal of the approach is to foster the freedom of the students, the students themselves play a substantial role in the development of curriculum content and even materials. The pictures, for example, are used as projective devices; through commenting on them and discussing them, students develop or articulate some aspects of the topics or language content they wish to learn and wish to be able to command.

One of the first S/FL specialists to research and develop the application of these ideas to FL language teaching was Crawford, in her 1978 dissertation.[13] There she discusses 20 principles, from which I extract the following particularly important and indicative items, as follows:

A. The purpose of education is to develop critical thinking by presenting [students'] situation to them as a problem so that they can perceive, reflect and act on it (p. 73);
B. The content of curriculum derives from the life situation of the learners as expressed in the themes of their reality (p. 78);
C. The learners produce their own learning materials (p. 99);
D. The task of planning is first to organize generative themes and second to organize subject matter as it relates to those themes (pp. 101–2);
E. The teacher participates…as a learner among learners (p. 104);
F. The teacher…contributes his/her ideas, experiences, opinions, and perceptions to the dialogical process (p. 104);
G. The teacher's function is one of posing problems (p. 105);
H. The students possess the right to and power of decision making. (p. 107).

At the same time, the first manifestations of this line of curriculum theory began to appear in the ESL literature (Moriarty & Wallerstein, 1979, 1980; Wallerstein, 1983a, 1983b, 1983c).

The mainstream critical pedagogy literature has two somewhat distinguishable strands: One is fairly closely oriented to the classroom, to student–teacher relations, curriculum and materials, and teacher values; the other is more concerned with the social and political structures surrounding schools and curricula. The former descends fairly directly from Freire's own work and notably also the work of his sometime coauthor Shor (e.g., Shor, 1992; Shor & Freire, 1987); the latter, while clearly influenced by it, also has strong connections to what in the 1970s was called the "new" sociology of schooling, and also to critical social theory directly; it is often associated with the names of Giroux (e.g., 1983) and McLaren (e.g., 1994).

In S/FL teaching, critical pedagogy initially manifested itself mainly in terms of curricular and classroom practices. Subsequently it has also developed a small literature paralleling the more abstract sociopolitical critiques of Giroux and McLaren, in some of the writings of Pennycook, for example (e.g., 2001). And as Freire was from the Third World and worked with avowedly anticolonial governments in Africa, it is noteworthy that critical S/FL pedagogy has its own anti- or postcolonial wing, exemplified particularly by Canagarajah (e.g., 2002). The ideas are also not confined to just English language teaching: See Osborn (e.g., 2006) who uses the term "world languages" (replacing what used to be called "foreign languages" in L1 English countries) in discussing the implementation of this approach in language curricula generally.

Although I have tried to present this set of ideas in a linear sequence, that is (as ever) only for purposes of expository convenience. The real world is too messy for linearity to do justice to it, and a variety of disconnects and dropped stitches should be pointed out in the story. First of all, the libertarian tradition has tended to have comparatively little to say about the specifics of classroom practice. It has more to say about broad curricular perspectives (e.g., integral education) and puts much faith in its ability to discern "natural" and inherently essential characteristics of human beings regardless of sociohistorical or cultural circumstances.[14] Accepting what we might call an anarchist theory of (educational) administration, it also assumes that providing schools are radically self-governing, the teaching will take care of itself.

The critical pedagogy tradition manifests its bifurcated nature in an ambivalence about state education (as opposed to the fear of it shown by the libertarian tradition). First of all, Freire himself is often quoted as saying that schools (alone) cannot change society, and as favoring adult education as a site of radical teacher action over the primary or secondary sectors. On the other hand, critical pedagogists of the McLaren clan accept the state and state education. Indeed, they regard themselves as rebutting an immediately preceding position (of the "reproduction" theorists, e.g., Bowles & Gintis, 1976) who argued that state schools simply reproduced the existing inequitable structures of society and were not viable sites for political action.

Perhaps because of the diversity of S/FL teaching sites, critical S/FL pedagogists do not seem to have committed themselves explicitly about these issues. Crawford-Lange wrote with U.S. "foreign" language high school teachers in mind, and seemed to think they had the necessary freedom of action, which perhaps they did in the late 1970s. Wallerstein's initial work was in EFL refugee camp settings, where language teachers often had curricular control (but see Tollefson, 1989); most of Auerbach's work relates to adult ESL for immigrants (where again, teachers and curriculum developers are indeed more or less independent of hierarchical administrative structures, even if their funding is evanescent and depends on governmental concerns for social justice, an inconstant source). Wink (1997) seems particularly to have elementary teachers in mind. Certainly, the bulk of the literature is directed to the ESL market rather than to the EFL scene. The latter area is considered culturally a hard nut to crack, and anecdotally one expects EFL teachers to be under greater administrative control than ESL teachers.[15]

And finally, just as mainstream critical pedagogues do not engage much with psychological theories of learning (although they do derive some strength from social theories of learning) so, too, is there something of a disconnect between critical S/FL pedagogy and psychological theories of learning or SLA,[16] even though task-based curriculum and methodologies appear to be held in common by both lines.

Feminism and feminist philosophy in education

Teaching, it has been said, is a feminized profession. Certainly teaching was one of the first professional areas to be extensively penetrated by women during what has been called the first wave of feminism. At the same time, women are very disproportionately to be found in the lower ranks of teaching. Higher administration is more obviously male; the professoriat in general is more male than female. However, such gender-related differences may become more vivid for some language teachers – the international, cultural, and boundary-crossing aspects of ES/FL teaching may force us to recognize that some of our taken-for-granted values are absent in other EF/SL countries. While political divides are not always salient for the boundary-crossing ES/FL teacher, differences in attitudes to gender and differences in what is considered appropriate behavior for male and female teachers and students can be very vivid. Teachers from "first circle" English-using countries, who may not have thought of themselves as feminists, may find, upon moving outside the West, that they are.[17] This is an area for which there is a developing ES/FL pedagogic and curriculum theoretical literature, although feminist philosophy of education is rather scanty. Given the gender-related characteristics of language teaching as a field of work, I believe the topic of the present chapter is, in and of itself, important for teachers who are developing a philosophy of teaching; it also follows on, to a large extent, from the discussion of liberal sociopolitical philosophy of education, and responds to the sense that many aspects of that liberal project are yet to be attained.

There are a number of different definitions of feminism. Lather, a prominent feminist educator, remarks that "the central premise of feminism is that gender is a basic organizing principle of all known societies and that, along with race, class, and the sheer specificity of historical circumstance, it profoundly shapes/mediates the concrete conditions of our lives" (1987, reprinted in Stone, 1994: 242). It goes along with the position that most cultures in history, including to a substantial extent present Western culture, are or have been patriarchal.[18] From a feminist point of view, philosophy itself appears not to be just philosophy, but largely, philosophy espoused by men, from a male point of view, and possibly at the expense of women (Leach, 1991; Martin, 1982). So, although up until this point I have hardly mentioned the gender of philosophers and philosophers of education,[19] I should at least now note that almost all of them have been men.

Within the source areas I am drawing on in this work (mostly philosophy), it may be seen that the feminist position is almost inevitably a broadly critical one, that is, it is embodied in critiques of matters that have otherwise been taken for granted, or taken to be "un-gendered." Gender, male and female, has certainly been the subject of inquiry and theorization by philosophers. The philosophical theory of gender has, for most cultures and most of human history, turned out to be not much more than a high-flown version of what has passed for common sense in patriarchal cultures: namely, that women (and men) have certain inherent characteristics that suit them best each for their common roles in patriarchal societies (women are inherently nurturant, men more likely to be violent, etc.).

This position is referred to as an essentialist position and feminists would say that it tends to be used against women. Feminism naturally favors an antiessentialist position, against the view that women always and essentially have one specific set of properties (and likewise against the view that men always can be seen to have a specific group of characteristics).[20] This does not mean that current feminism finds no difference between men and women. Feminist philosopher of education Noddings (1995) is helpful here. Her position is subtle and cultural–historical: Where differences appear they are understandable; the existence of differences does not mean that one category is superior to another, nor that there is no overlap; and finally, it does not mean that differences, when they exist, are not subject to alteration through education.

While the philosophical history in this area is not so encouraging, perhaps we can be a little more optimistic when looking at the history of education. The beginnings of improved (or any) education for women[21] coincide with the European Enlightenment and the initial writings and action of early feminists such as Mary Wollstonecraft (1792/2004). The picture painted by some authorities (e.g., Nash, 2005; and taking the United States as a case) is one of an initial improvement from a very low start, with a backlash setting in around the time of the suffragette movement at the very end of the 19th century. That the story is one of ups and downs suggests the need for continual struggle, rather than one in which the goal is won or lost on one occasion only.

Points of feminist critique in philosophy and education

I will summarize swiftly key points from three recent overview remarks, the first concerning feminist philosophy, the second concerning feminist philosophy of education (these two being somewhat retrospective), and the third concerning very recent feminist educational thinking in general (and thus prospective, or sensitive to the latest developments).

A recent overview of feminist philosophy focuses on four areas, in which "the most influential conceptions and controversies have evolved... in recent years" (Nagl-Docekal, 2004). They are: philosophical anthropology, aesthetics, theory of science and the critique of reason, and the philosophy of law. The first of these areas provides a basis for the feminist position that there is no natural order of the sexes: Women (and men) do not have any particular essential characteristics "by nature." The second is not relevant to us (it deals with the question of whether theories of beauty that have been developed so far reflect a male sensibility or perspective).

The third area addresses the way reason and rationality have been developed from male perspectives, such that women have often been described as less rational than men. This line of analysis leads to the possibility that much scientific knowledge is itself infused with perspectives, or indeed bias, that arise from associations with the partial perspectives of just one gender. This area is closely related to epistemology (see also Pendlebury, 1998). Some feminists would accept a "naturalized" epistemology (one that rejects foundationalism, self-evident premises, or basic observation statements) – others dispute mainstream epistemology's emphasis on rational autonomy and associated methods for arriving at legitimate claims to knowledge, and criticize the Cartesian epistemological subject for being a mental mechanism rather than a full-bodied subject. The alternative (one, at least) is the view that a conception of the epistemological subject as a real person, an insider with all associated biases, is just as valuable. This is a view often referred to as "standpoint epistemology."

Finally, the fourth area, the philosophy of law, could be seen as developing from the questions, "Why is it that law does not prevent the many injustices that women suffer from, all over the world?" and then, "What is needed to arrive at a more equitable society for women?" – here the implications concern social and political action. This seems to have close links to the analyses of the conditions of women and girls in schools. Feminist researchers of classrooms and schools have pointed out that girls do not get equal time in classrooms, get harassed, and yet are not taught about gender issues or how to deal with sexism, and in some cases have concluded that girls have better opportunities in same-sex schools (AAUW, 1995; Vandrick, 1994; cf. Stabiner, 2003). This perspective leads to the same question: "How can things be changed to improve matters in this area, whether in schools or in society in general?"

I now draw on a review of feminist philosophy of education (Martin, 1998). In summarizing this, I again am hoping to quickly provide a sense of the general domain of inquiry (before narrowing down to language). Martin is a preeminent figure in feminist philosophy of education, and her central concept is what she calls the education-gender system, which, like most feminists with an interest in education, she sees as implicated in reproducing patriarchal culture. While changing education may not itself change society, trying to change society while ignoring its education system seems ill-advised. However, while feminists and feminist philosophers have written, thought, and acted in respect to many aspects of this, the subfield of feminist philosophy of education is a little underdeveloped at present, she says:

> Today, however, there is an education gap in the feminist philosophy text. Books in the field pay little attention to the subject of education and rarely cite feminist research in this area.
>
> (Martin, 1998: 441)

This subfield has been active since the 1980s, but as yet is not as prominent within philosophy of education as feminist philosophy is within philosophy as a whole. Nevertheless, as a philosopher of education, Martin naturally believes that what we might call "active" philosophy in this area is certainly needed, as the basis for the transformation of education toward feminist goals.

In Martin's view, society "takes for granted the idea that the function of education is to transform children who have heretofore lived their lives in [the home] into members of the [wider world]." But "the public world and the world of the private home are gender-coded." This in turn makes the education system "gendered." Since the day-to-day world was "historically speaking, a male preserve and to this day reflects this fact" (ibid.: 442), education tends to prepare students for a male-dominated world. At the same time, it is either silent on or projects negative attitudes toward home and its distinct culture.

Martin identifies three main strands of feminist philosophy of education (while acknowledging both historical work and a variety of relevant material from just across the boundaries of the subfield, much of which is in Stone, 1994). The first of these "has been devoted to reclaiming, reconstructing, and reinterpreting historical theories of the education of girls and women" (p. 445). That is, it (a) looks at classical authors in philosophy of education, including Plato and Rousseau, for example, from a feminist point of view; or (b) looks at the work of earlier feminist educators, such as Montessori or Louisa May Alcott, from a philosophy of education perspective. The second strand is the extensive literature developed following Noddings's articulation of an "ethic of care" as central to the work of teachers. As the title of Noddings's 1984 book indicates, this is a position represented as a "feminine approach."

The third strand is what Martin refers to as the development of a "normative philosophy of education for both sexes" (p. 446), that arises out of some of the critique applied by feminist philosophers to education. Within this are five components:

1. Feminist critiques of dominant educational paradigms, such as the concept of the "educated person" and liberal education (Martin, 1992); [and of] standard philosophical analyses of teaching (Laird, e.g., 1995); and critiques of individualism in education (Rohrer, 1994);
2. Analyses of education that relate to gender directly. This includes treatments of educational equity and sexism, the women's movement, affirmative action, and coeducation;
3. Feminist discussions of specific curriculum areas, such as physical education, sex education, the teaching of literature, and science education;
4. Curriculum theory and practice specifically intended for the education of girls;
5. Broad proposals for the complete reengineering of educational systems on feminist principles (Martin, 1992; Noddings, 1992).

For the final item in this set of overviews, here are some of the topics that feminist educators think are important in recent work in the area, as identified by several prominent specialists:

> Feminist educational thinking views the intersection of education and gender through a variety of lenses: it examines schools and universities as sites for the enacting of gender; it explores the ways in which conceptions of gender shape the prohibition of state-supported education; it highlights the resistances subordinated groups have developed around ideas of knowledge, power and learning; and it seeks to understand the relationship of education to gendered conceptions of citizenship, the family and the economy. Thus feminist educational thinking is fundamentally political; it fuses theory and practice in seeking to understand contemporary education with the aim of building a more just world for women and men. In so doing, it acknowledges the reality of multiple feminisms and the intertwining of ethnicity, race and gender.
>
> (Weiler, Weiner, & Yates, 1999: ix–x)

And this area, naturally, has been impacted by some of the developments in the world of ideas alluded to in Chapter 6. The same authors continue:

> Feminist educational thinking is influenced by developments in feminist theory more broadly and by the changing global educational landscape. In terms of theory, both post-structuralist and post-colonial theories have profoundly influenced what is conceived of as "feminist." As is true elsewhere, current feminist educational thinking takes as central the intersecting forces that shape the educational experiences of women and men. This emphasis on the construction and performances of gender through both discourses and material practices leads to an attitude of openness and questioning of accepted assumptions – including the underlying assumptions of the various strands of feminism.
>
> (ibid.: p. x)

Feminist pedagogy

Feminist philosophy is, among other things, a theorizing of practice – in this case, the practice of a movement. It also consists of analyses of concepts central to feminism; and feminist philosophy *of education* similarly tackles concepts crucial to feminist *teachers'* practices. This philosophical work thus contains much of potential importance to the well-grounded development of a teacher's practice; but feminist teachers naturally did not wait for the full development of this kind of work before entering a classroom. Much that is theoretical or philosophical already was coming into being as feminist pedagogy developed in parallel with feminist philosophy of education, so there is considerable overlap. It is now time to consider what can be said about this area of general educational practice, and whether there have been manifestations of this kind of thinking in the ES/FL area.

Mainstream education specialists in feminist pedagogy have drawn substantially from the initiatives fronted under the heading critical pedagogy that were reviewed in the previous chapter. Stone, for example, introducing a collection in the area of feminism in education, refers approvingly to "critical feminist pedagogy" (1994: 2); similarly Weiler, in an often-cited critique of critical pedagogy[22] from a feminist point of view, begins by noting that, "Feminist pedagogy as it has developed in the United States provides a historically situated example of a critical pedagogy in practice" (1991/1995: 24). There are some notable points of disagreement, however, between feminist pedagogues and the older critical pedagogy literature (besides Weiler, Ellsworth [1989/1994] is probably the most cited complainant). The principal charge is the dependence of critical pedagogy on rationalist universalist decontextualized assumptions – which is to say, its original ideas were of their time.[23] Weiler makes an important point:

> The pedagogy of feminist teachers is based on certain assumptions about knowledge, power, and political action that can be traced . . . to the political activism of the women's movement in the 1960s. This same commitment to social change through the transformative potential of education underlay Freire's pedagogy in Brazil during the same period.
>
> (1991/1995: 29)

These two approaches had in common that they were developed on and with *homogenous* groups who already had a measure of commitment or oppositional consciousness. Freire's literacy culture circles were part of informal adult education, not part of regular schools. The consciousness-raising groups of the women's movement were similarly far from regular institutions, as Weiler says. But an important development of feminism since the 1960s has been its move into postsecondary educational institutions, in women's studies programs and other "hierarchical and bureaucratic structure[s] of academia" (Weiler, 1995: 32). The feminist teacher is faced with "heterogeneous groups of students within a competitive and individualistic culture" (ibid.). Weiler cites bell hooks: "The academic setting, the academic discourse (we) work in, is not a known site for truthtelling" (Weiler, 1991/1995: 32, citing hooks, 1989: 29).

Within this overall framework, curriculum occupies (as ever) a central place. Noted feminist scholar Tetrault (2004; see also Maher & Tetrault, 2001) identifies five phases of curriculum development that might be passed through on the way to a feminist pedagogy. In the first, male-defined curriculum, it is assumed that male experience is universal. In the second, a "contribution curriculum," women are token figures, tossed in as indicative of women's "contribution."[24] Tetrault's third variant is the "bifocal" curriculum. This is "open to the possibility of seeing the world through women's eyes," but "thinking about women and men is dualistic and dichotomized" (p. 167). Fourth, in "women's curriculum" it is "women's activities, not men's, [that] are the measure of significance." Within this most recent area of development (as Weiler, et al.'s earlier quote suggests), a "pluralistic conceptualization of women" is called for . . . "Historians ask how the particulars of race, ethnicity, social class, marital status, and sexual orientation challenge the homogeneity of women's experiences. Third World feminists critique hegemonic 'Western' feminisms and formulate [alternatives] . . . " (p. 170). The fifth and final phase is "gender-balanced curriculum." This is "conscious of the limitations of seeing women in isolation and aware of the relational character of gender," and in it, the "pluralistic and multifocal conception of women that emerged" in the previous phase "is extended to [all] human beings" (p. 172). In this sense, it reflects an inclusive feminism (hooks, 1989; cf. Zack, 2005), in which what is good for women is most likely good for men, too.

Narrowing now to the realm of ESL, we can consult the work of Vandrick (1994, 1998, 2003). In her 1994 article, she first outlined the background to this area, and then went on to provide a useful summary of ESL feminist pedagogy developments up to that point in time. In Vandrick's view of feminist pedagogy, the classroom ideally functions as a "liberatory environment, in which students also teach, and are subjects not objects; and in which consciousness could be changed, and the old weaknesses (racism, classism, homophobia, etc.) expelled" (Vandrick, 1994: 76, citing Shrewsbury, 1993: 8). Vandrick uses the very popular term "empowerment" to refer to how students in such classrooms are enabled to develop "enhanced autonomy but at the same time, mutuality; discovery of own voice . . . authenticity" and also speaks hopefully of establishing "community" in such classrooms. Here perhaps a tinge of essentialism is creeping in, as it is implied that women have a particular need to build connections with each other (as opposed to men).

Within such a classroom, leadership would be liberatory, acting on feminist beliefs. The practical implications of this require teachers to:

- alter the curriculum;
- give faculty feedback on equitable teaching practices; and
- teach feminist process: sharing feelings clearly and personally, helpful feedback, group process skills, conflict resolution, cooperation, networking, being inclusive.

And though there cannot be one "specific set of practices" (Vandrick, 1994: 84), nevertheless the feminist ESL teachers should:

- have a curriculum that is bias-free;
- have materials that avoid stereotyping; raise consciousness concerning the gendered nature of English;
- be aware of gender-related differences in learning styles;
- give female students equal time and treatment in class;
- provide help for male students who are incompetent in this domain;
- explore cultural differences in this area;
- be a role model;
- not tolerate sexist behavior among colleagues;
- "put the feminine at the center of your teaching" (Carson, 1993: 36); or
- "practice affirmative action in the classroom" (ibid.).

Resistance and "the man question"

The heading of this subsection alludes to what I suspect are a couple of obvious questions that may have come up for some readers. First of all, it is certainly the case that the literature in this area regularly comes to grips with the fact that many students will resist the basic premise of this kind of pedagogy. Thus, feminist teachers are accustomed to encountering resistance from their students, whether they are male or female. These teachers are more likely than critical pedagogy specialists to emphasize their own authority in the classroom (Duncan & Stasio, 2005). And indeed, the majority of pedagogy conducted in this general tradition takes place under the relatively favorable circumstances of postsecondary education, often in sympathetic programs such as Womens Studies. Accounts of it in elementary and secondary schools are rare – though not unknown (Digiovanni & Liston, 2005; Sattler, 1997); and the same is true for EFL contexts (McMahill, 1997).

Then there is "the man question": What, if anything, can a male teacher say or do in this area?[25] Well, men can be feminists, of course, and many are. It seems to me that feminist men teachers and administrators should adopt a supportive stance toward feminist women teachers. With care, they can engage in discussion of issues and practice in feminist pedagogy. I note that a female, white, middle-class academic in our field recently addressed the matter of whether she could only address issues of oppression related to gender in her work and teaching (since she was not black, lesbian, or working class). She wrote:

> Given my protected position, is it my responsibility to speak out on racism, classism, and homophobia? Or is it presumptuous of me to do so? All I have to guide me is my belief that it cannot be wrong to speak out against prejudice and discrimination. But it is my responsibility to educate myself, to listen to people of various backgrounds, to be reflective, to work collaboratively when possible, and to accept constructive criticism. It is my responsibility to keep trying to understand how various forms of oppression intersect and interact and to support TESOL colleagues of all identities.
>
> (Lin et al., 2004: 493)

If we follow the analysis of Gore (1998), we may find that critical and feminist pedagogues are quite close in terms of the techniques they use. Gore claims that "naming what is unique about these practices... has not been a strong feature" (p. 273) of the literature in question. She asks, "would a woman with a commitment to critical pedagogy teach a class very differently if she were instead committed to feminist pedagogy?" (ibid.). Her answer seems to be no, particularly as she observes the "explicit broadening of both critical and feminist agendas to encompass all oppressed groups." (ibid.). But this is a difficult area, in which the plausibility of the male feminist instructor is clearly in question at the outset; thus, though sensitive, it is an area in which further discussion and empirical report is greatly needed.[26]

So long as feminism is a nonmainstream option, we should not necessarily expect to find a large literature emanating from it in our field. Nevertheless, there continue to be steady, if small, amounts of publications and presentations appearing (e.g., Moffatt & Norton, 2005).[27] The area will remain important for those whose philosophies of second/ foreign language teaching depart from the mainstream on grounds of equity and justice.

Concluding remark

In a recent course I taught in this area, for at least half the junior teachers involved it was their first substantive exposure to such ideas. Clearly it is a truism that alternative ideas are marginal to the mainstream, but even in the Internet age of the "long tail" (Anderson, 2006; or Pareto distribution), it bears repeating that nevertheless the margins can in fact be totally invisible from the middle of the mainstream. Merely to articulate the full historical record is itself an act of resistance, and one that could (at least from a meliorist perspective) improve the center. (My students point out, however, that equally important are vivid and recent accounts of practice; cf. de los Reyes & Gozemba, 2002.)

Sharing alternative visions of education as incorporated in, or arising out of, an alternative vision of society is, I believe, an important corrective to the Methods-driven search of many devoted but frustrated language teachers. Experiencing difficulty in the classroom, such individuals have become convinced that "there must be a better way," but tend to blame their own lack of technique or familiarity with the "latest" teaching methods. Not only (as I have said before) is the search for a better Method fruitless, it also leads to self-blame. The searching teacher should trust their intuition that something is wrong: Only they should note that what is wrong is school and society, not themselves and their techniques.

Discussion questions

1. Are there any problems you would like to solve about (English) language teaching in your vicinity or in your experience, where the problems you see relate to larger societal problems? Does having this orientation mean you are "critical" (in the sense that it has been used in this chapter)?

2. Would you like your students to be able to use the second or foreign languages they are learning to improve their own lives or the lives of others, in their own country or in others? If so, how should "improve" be understood if you are likely to favor a critical or feminist position in your philosophy of teaching?

3. Must a philosophy of (language) teaching interact with a theory of society? Why (why not?) and in what respects or areas? What is your "theory of society"? (That is, what are the key features of society in general, or your home culture/society – what makes it "tick," in what respects does it "work" or "not work"?) How does this relate to you as a teacher of languages (if at all)?

4. What is the relationship (if any) between knowing the dominant language of (a) society and citizenship?

Notes to Chapter 9

1 Prior to the increasing recognition of hybridity and the poststructural contexts of globalization, it was common to refer discussions of inequity and social justice to three categories: class, gender, and race. The reader will note that I address the first

two and omit the last. This is primarily because of the lack of race-related discussions in our field, the difficulty of placing the concept in an international context, and indeed my own difficulty, as a White, in addressing the topic. The resulting complexity of the topic means I cannot treat it adequately in the present work. For new material in this area, see Curtis & Romney (2006), Kubota & Lin (2006).

2 I use the term deliberately here, given the historical context.

3 Such thinking might not have discriminated among the possible disciplines that provided a framework for it. Social and political philosophy was only just beginning to develop into sociology or social theory – the 19th century being the time of the beginnings of the social sciences.

4 The term was first used in 1827 to refer to the views of Robert Owen, an educational philanthropist.

5 Smith (1983) refers to the "Beehive School" of Sebastien Faure, and Paul Robin's school at Cempuis, from the 1880s on.

6 The shift is attributed by Smith (1983) to Faure and was indicative of a concern with broad social experimentation rather than just political activity.

7 For a more recent review of Neill's school and practices, see Appleton, 2000.

8 Danish schools continued to provide a home for noncoercive pedagogy: see Dam, 1995.

9 "Educational liberalism had some effect on Soviet education in the period immediately following the 1917 revolution. Since the Stalin era, however, most educational decrees have advanced the cause of educational conservatism" (Dupuis, 1966: 203; see also Huxley, 1946). "Some Soviet educators advocated a revolutionary reassessment of schooling itself, [e.g.,] Shulgin, director of the . . . Institute of Pedagogy in Moscow from 1922 onward. In many ways, Shulgin's ideas on education resembled those of the progressive movement. . . . At the end of the 1920s, the climate of education began to change. . . . Soviet education returned to a traditional model, with the reassertion of teacher authority, a traditional curriculum and an elimination of democratic organization" (Small, 2005: 160–61).

10 Though drawing less on well-known critical theorists than the name might suggest (Taylor, 1993).

11 Smith remarks, "Freire does not follow Marx in important respects . . . [but] Freire cannot be said in any general sense to be an anarchist. Nevertheless, when we look at his educational position we shall find that it bears a distinct resemblance . . . " (1983: 107–8).

12 Initially to Chile, which shortly thereafter suffered a similar fate as Brazil; Freire then spent some time at Harvard University before securing a position in Switzerland, where he remained for about 15 years.

13 She went on to develop them in two further publications: Crawford-Lange (1981, 1982).

14 But see May (1994).

15 But see Shin & Crookes (2005a, 2005b)

16 For example, prior to beginning a study of a Freirean literacy program, Purcell-Gates & Waterman (2000: 223) comment, "Many of the critical theorists who advocate such radical educational change have little real knowledge of the complex cognitive and linguistic processes involved in literacy acquisition and how different methods of teaching reading and writing adhere to, violate, or interact with these processes."

[17] At the time of writing, some of the most startling differences face those English teachers who either come from or move to certain Islamic countries.

[18] In that sense defined by the *Oxford English Dictionary* as "Relating to, characteristic of, or designating a society or culture in which men tend to be in positions of authority and cultural values and norms are seen as favouring men. Freq. with pejorative connotation."

[19] Within philosophy of education, correctives include Titone and Maloney (1999); for philosophy in general, besides specific works, there is the *Society for Women in Philosophy* and the journal *Hypatia*.

[20] Weiler (1991/1995: 40) writes, "Fundamental to recent feminist theory is a questioning of the concept of a coherent subject moving through history with a single essential identity. Instead, feminist theorists are developing a concept of the constant creation and negotiation of selves within structures of ideology and material constraints."

[21] Outside of elite individual cases across all cultures, that is.

[22] E.g., Schniedewind (1993).

[23] Similar complaints are made against feminist pedagogy, in some of whose writings it appears that feminist teachers are already enlightened and never oppressive.

[24] Still the dominant model in, for example, U.S. elementary curricula (according to Digiovanni & Liston, 2005).

[25] Osborn (2006: 18), in a work on teaching foreign languages with an emancipatory orientation, notes that much more work pertinent to gender in language teaching is needed, but comments that "as a male scholar" he "cannot offer the perspective that will be needed."

[26] See Schacht (2000) and Jones (2003) for two contributions, though they raise as many questions as they answer.

[27] And in mainstream education, articles in successive issues of *Feminist Teacher* (e.g., Digiovanni & Liston, 2005; Weisner, 2005).

10 Some continuing tensions for S/FL teachers

Being a feminist/critical teacher in the academy is not a career move.

(Lewis, 1998: xiv)

In a regime of LEA [Local Education Authority] patronage and preferment, such as conditioned many teachers' responses to the progressive "revolution" of the 1960s, 1970s, and the early 80s, the impact of external power was on the individual: a teacher conformed, succeeded and got on, or he/she did not, but others in the same school might respond differently and thereby have totally different career paths.

(Alexander, 2000: 145)

Although actions are usually grounded in beliefs, this is not always the case. Some teaching practices are based on tradition or routines for which the rationale has long been forgotten.... At the same time, teachers may sometimes be required, through legislation or policy directives, to adopt practices which they do not believe in or which they oppose ideologically or professionally.

(Marland, 1997: 20)

Introduction

The realities of most schools and even universities around the world, as places in which we try to implement our philosophy of S/FL teaching, are rather discouraging, generally. Inasmuch as a materialist world view that is unappreciative of learning seems dominant, even teachers fully in line with mainstream cultural values may feel that their students or society as a whole do not appreciate their efforts to fully act on their beliefs as teachers. And if one's view of teaching, and of the role of second or foreign languages in one's home country or host cultures is *not* consistent with mainstream voices in more substantive ways, then one may be in a fairly difficult position at times. Even the minimum aspirations of a teacher, to fair pay for a fair day's work, or a nonviolent workplace, are often not to be found in many countries, including the most developed.

I do not think that teacher preparation or induction programs do enough to emphasize the difficulties of living up to any of the higher aspirations of teachers. This is probably indicated by the drop-out rate of new teachers, which in most countries is worryingly high. An enormous amount of public and private money is being wasted on training teachers who stay just a few years in the business.[1] At the same time, higher-level teacher development programs in our field may exacerbate the contradictions faced by more senior teachers because the default expectation held for the language-teaching professional by the academics who dominate the field is of someone with a fairly high degree of professional autonomy. Why otherwise would they lay on classes apparently intended to prepare teachers with graduate degrees, so that they can be capable of language test design, curriculum construction through needs analyses, of program evaluation, of conducting at least small-scale research projects, and so on? Yet do most graduate-degree holders in our field have these kinds of responsibilities and the autonomy that goes with them? I would like to think so, but I am not so sure.

Second or foreign language teachers often seek advanced degrees, including in foreign countries, to improve their skills and knowledge, and in the case of English or other FL teachers, to increase their knowledge of the target culture. They also do so to increase their pay and the quality of their teaching career. Increasingly, I tell them that this is a time to take stock and to face up to the realities of the profession within which they have embarked (one might hope) on a career.[2] Should they really go back to the high school that they left? Should they really stay in "lower" education? (Conditions are often better in higher education.) Should they perhaps consider a move to adult or proprietary education, where there is sometimes greater curricular freedom? If their educational philosophies include some of the points raised in the last chapter, should they not perhaps really seriously consider the small alternative sector?

Such suggestions are made with the intent of helping to minimize the amount of compromise and tension that language teachers will experience in future phases of their career. Once one has fully articulated a philosophy of teaching, instead of just going along with the existing textbooks or ministerial directives, albeit with a faint sense of unease that things ought not to be this way or ought to be better somewhere, there is no absolute going back. There is getting out, of course; there is switching to "I'm only in this for the money," "retiring on the job"[3]; and then there is, centrally, both resistance and compromise in the face of tensions between reality and one's philosophy of teaching. In the most favorable conditions, resistance is constructive and results in change. And educational change, though often long in coming, is an area which has its own large literature. I allude to this at the end of the chapter, but devote more attention to intermediate level responses, because I think the field of ELT is insufficiently sensitive to the constraints that the majority of English teachers are under.

Tension/control

The tension between ideal and actuality results primarily from teachers' lack of control of their work. Now of course, if they are the slightest bit student-centered, their practice cannnot be decided on single-handedly, without student input in some form. But aside from that, the institutional and social context of language teaching intrudes greatly, though perhaps in some cases legitimately, on teachers.

Starting at the top, as it were, we need to acknowledge that if we are in the state sector, we are very much within an area of power that is seen by most governments as a domain within which they can legitimately exert authority almost without restraint:

> Pedagogy [is] the ultimate prize for any government wishing to secure a level of control of the educational process as close to absolute as – given the stubbornness of the human spirit and the wayward chemistry of classrooms – is feasible.
>
> (Alexander, 2000: 142)

This was not always the case. When states (i.e., ruling elites) were less powerful vis-à-vis their citizens, their control over education was similarly smaller. In less developed or periphery countries, it is still common to refer to "rural education" as a separate sector, and for example (writing of China), Thøgersen (2002: 11) remarks "as rural communities were left to organize and fund their own schools they were also able to exert considerable influence over them."[4] In a handful of influential countries (most obviously the United States and the UK), there was for a substantial part of the 20th century a fair measure of local control of education, but this was not the case for most other nations.[5] In any case, this pattern has clearly changed and in addition, the states of developed countries at the beginning of the 21st century are even more powerful, with respect to their citizens, than hitherto. This will, of course, not result in tension for those teachers who agree with the position of the government of the day. However, governments change and their positions are not constant.

Moving on, another tension occurs in those countries where English proficiency – or unfortunately, a proxy, namely "scores on tests of English proficiency" – are used as a major entry criterion to higher education institutions. There, teachers of English are under enormous pressure to teach exclusively to the test. In general, because of the nature of

English as an actual or perceived language of power, teachers of English in secondary education face particularly strong tensions.[6]

Also, because of the nature of English, though this can clearly apply to other subjects depending on context, there is a tension between liberal and instrumental education. This is the same more general tension expressed in the differing emphases articulated by changing governments, concerning whether the primary function of state education is to train children to be useful employees, or to be useful citizens. If school is primarily to fit a person for a job, it might be said that, in fact, private industry has successfully outsourced its training needs to the public sector. But when, as is sometimes the case, true communicative proficiency in English, or some component of English (written business English, for example) is a real need in a particular position of employment, then English teachers are certainly again under pressure to "deliver the language."

This latter tension or pressure is less likely to be felt as legitimate by the high school or university teacher by comparison with the proprietary sector teacher. For the latter individual, it is a likely part of the standard setting; in fact, it is also the primary justification for some companies having in-house language-training units. There, perhaps, one may as well give up any hope of providing education, as opposed to training.

A certain amount of research attention has been given to teacher control; the results (for the United States) are in general unsurprising. Ingersoll (2003: 88) notes that in his surveys of U.S. schools, in "large public schools ... only 41 percent of the teachers reported, on average, a great deal of influence over decisions concerned with academic instruction, and just 14 percent reported having equivalent control over social decisions." Teachers at small private secondary schools reported greater (51%) control over academic decisions, but less over social decisions. However "relative to their principals, the private school teachers were no more empowered than the public school teachers" (ibid.: 93).

Finally, here is another source of tension:

> When the individual makes his[/her] choice and advocates one philosophy, his[/her] problem is only half solved. As soon as [s/]he joins a teaching staff [s/]he encounters other points of view.
>
> (Dupuis, 1966: 290)

Unfortunately, it is usually the case that schools are "contested sites," and rarely the case that a teacher's colleagues agree among themselves about formal versus functional approaches, the role of the teacher, and so on. Where rational argument might be useful, so too might a philosophy of S/FL teaching.

Compromise

There are many ways to relieve tension. Most are practical (exercise, meditation, sleep, etc.) and thus not usually the subject of philosophical exploration. But most of the mental aspects of handling a contradiction between one's aspirations for a rewarding life and the realities of human existence come under the heading of "compromise." We do it, but it often seems to be presented as negative. Focusing down to a teaching situation: In truly difficult circumstances, we are obliged to teach, use materials, behave as a teacher in ways that fully contradict our beliefs, values, and professional principles. And in those cases, we eventually may decide to cease teaching; though alternatively, again in bad situations, we may be obliged (for economic, or even legal reasons) to continue nevertheless. Is there any way to understand this sort of situation (of extreme compromise) that will make it more manageable?

Everybody (or at least, everybody who has principles) compromises some of the time. And the topic of compromise seems to me, on the face of it, to be a topic under the heading of morality that I would have thought was characteristic of human existence in the modern (or postmodern) world, with its great concentrations of power. If so, there should have been an extensive literature on it; but that proves not to be the case, as the handful of scholars who have addressed the issue in detail (e.g., Benjamin, 1990) observe.[7] In what follows I summarize a chapter from Benjamin (1990) and try to extend it to educational and ES/FL cases, in the apparent lack of ES/FL-related literature.[8]

Toward the beginning of his book, Benjamin identifies various meanings of "compromise," thus enabling us to set aside the kind of compromises that occur in bargaining over the price of something, or when two more or less equal parties are trying to solve a problem and each gives up something so as to effect an agreement. These sort of compromises are not problematic. It is compromises that involve giving up on principles that worry us. Why is this so? It is because, says Benjamin (following, e.g., Taylor, 1981), of the countervailing concept of "integrity," and in particular, because of the positive idea of a life and a self that is integrated, coherent, and thus makes sense.

Benjamin identifies several categories of moral compromisers: the moral chameleon, the hypocrite, the weak-willed, the self-deceiver. These are all cases where "a loss of integrity is attributable . . . to weakness or corruption from within." Importantly for us, he also identifies cases where this loss of integrity results from pressures from without, where individuals are coerced into "acting . . . and talking, in ways that are at odds with [their] most deeply held and cherished convictions." Such a person is "coercively alienated from her authentic values and principles" (1990: 50).

The elements of integrity are three-fold: "(1) a reasonably coherent and relatively stable set of highly cherished values and principles; (2) verbal behavior expressing these values and principles; and (3) conduct embodying one's values and principles and consistent with what one says.... Taken together they constitute the formal structure of one's identity as a person" (ibid.: 51). However, integrity is not sufficient for morality. Being a "virtue of form," it is "in a sense secondary" (Rawls, 1971/1999: 519); and so, "that moral compromise may compromise aspects of a person's integrity is, therefore, not a decisive consideration against it" (Benjamin, 1990: 54). At this point, Benjamin starts to shift ground, to a more complex vision of integrity.

Benjamin takes up remarks of Williams (1973) to argue against a position that emphasizes integrity at the expense of "wholeness." The world is complex, and "internal conflict is a feature of human life" (Benjamin, 1990: 56). There are often gaps between duty and desire. "We add or accumulate values and inclinations without fully extinguishing those that preceded them and that, for the sake of integrity, we may now consciously disavow" (ibid.: 56–7). By now Benjamin seems to be saying that integrity (in a narrow sense) is impossible. "A complete and fully integrated set of moral values and principles is, I will argue, unattainable" (p. 57). I suppose this explains why there are so many moral compromises. One would not compromise much at all if one were not pulled in several directions at once. A teacher might say, "I want to teach in accordance with my values, which have become clearer to me over time, but I want to keep my job because I have responsibilities to support my spouse and children."

"Conventional wisdom says that in cases of conflict one's moral values and principles are of overriding importance. This however, may be profoundly alienating and destructive of overall integrity.... The claims of morality, if omnipresent, unremitting, and overriding, may force us to relinquish commitments to develop certain morally unobjectionable skills or talents or to complete certain similarly unobjectionable undertakings and in some instances, our reason for living" (Benjamin, 1990: 58). A researcher might say, "I don't want to receive research funding from the military budget because I suspect that in carrying out the mandated research I may be helping war; but if I don't take the money, I won't be able to complete other research that might actually have some genuine and general benefit." However, Benjamin also says, "in some circumstances moral requirements will indeed be overriding" (ibid.) and does not seem to explain how we are to judge whether they are or are not overriding.

"Overall integrity ... has diachronic as well as synchronic dimensions. It requires that our values and ... conduct ... cohere not only at a particular time but also over time. Thus it is difficult to see how they can remain perfectly consistent without being hidebound and unresponsive to new situations and knowledge" (ibid.: 59). Thus, a language teacher might say, "I want to teach students to communicate [I have a responsibility to help them really learn English], but I also want them to pass the entrance exam [I have a responsibility to help them succeed in life; also this is what the school expects of me and puts me under some pressure to achieve]." Benjamin comments: "If, as I have indicated, integrity has social as well as individual importance and involves wholeness as well as consistency, an optimally integrated life (as opposed to the fantasy of a perfectly integrated life) will in the modern world require a certain amount of both internal and external compromise" (ibid.: 59).

Benjamin goes on to work more closely on the diachronic aspects of integrity. We are now talking about how to make sense of one's life. "Central to the process of shaping a morally integrated life is the notion of an enacted personal narrative" (ibid.: 63–4). Here Benjamin picks up the work of MacIntyre (1981; a prominent modern ethicist) who emphasizes the importance of narrative. (Bear in mind that teachers' knowledge, and indeed, a philosophy of teaching, may be stored, or produced, in narrative form.) He quotes MacIntyre:

> "What the agent is able to do and say intelligibly as an actor is deeply affected by the fact that we are never more (and sometimes less) than the co-authors of our own narratives ... We enter upon a stage which we did not design and find ourselves part of an action that was not of our making."
> (MacIntyre, 1981: 199, cited in Benjamin, 1990: 72)

Benjamin comments, "To acknowledge this feature of the human condition is to make room in one's outlook for a certain amount of mutual accommodation.... Those who categorically reject all such compromise with high-minded appeals to integrity often fail to appreciate the limitations and complexities of integrity.... We must regard our integrity as a matter of degree and not all or none.... Compromise in such circumstances, when incorporated into a true and coherent narrative ... does not threaten integrity but rather preserves it" (Benjamin, 1990: 73–4). I would not wish to discourage language teachers from aiming to implement their philosophies of teaching as fully as possible, but I can also say that totally uncompromising individuals may be perceived as rather unrealistic, either in general, or at a particular point in time. The diachronic emphasis of Benjamin's is the most important, for me. A life extended over time, like a rope over a chasm, is likely to exhibit some internal tensions; and this needs to be understood, not dismissed.

Resistance

The heading "resistance," in discussions of education, tends to refer to students resisting teachers, and quite often, teachers resisting other teachers' new ideas or top-down reform efforts. It also has a use in some of the more theoretical literature of critical pedagogy, particularly because of the prominence of Giroux's (1983) book, which includes the word in its title: *Theory and resistance in education*. Unfortunately, all the author means by using this word is that his analysis suggests teachers *should* resist the antidemocratic trends of education in the United States in the 1980s; as Giroux recognizes in the second edition (2001: xxiii), he did not explain *how* teachers in positions of comparative weakness could resist. Yet, to be fair, Giroux's development of theory is itself a step toward resistance. Janeway (1980) has the following lines:

> Confrontation can't always be avoided by the weak, nor should it be. But before it begins there will be a stage in which the weak look consciously at the world-definitions of the powerful and find them questionable.... Until this happens, the governed will be unable to think away from standard definitions, toward alternative explanations of events which point to alternative actions.
>
> This attitude on the part of the ruled is usually given a rather unpleasant name: naturally enough, since it is being defined by the powerful. It is seen as *mistrust*, which can run on through *alienation*, or *disaffection*, which leads on to *disloyalty* – and fetches up at *treason*. [pp. 160–61]
>
> If, in the face of repression, the governed can still hold to mistrust, they will not, of course be *safe*; but they will preserve the inner citadel of the self and with it the capacity of judging the exterior world in terms of their own interests. It may be that they are reduced to minimal action, to "disguised disobedience" which will be renamed pejoratively by their masters, but testimony from those who have survived under [the worst conditions] tells us that resistance begins here and that survival does too, with this first and last power of the weak. Dissent is the intellectual steel which strengthens the self...
>
> (Janeway, 1980: 206)

So it may be that these perspectives and the emotions associated with them are a necessary first step in resistance. Sometimes the only steps possible, under the most difficult conditions – just continuing to exist, continuing to occupy a position – is also a form of resistance. Refugees interviewed by Peteet (2000: 195) said, "'We are all in the resistance. Just to sit in these camps is a way of resisting,' registering a refusal to go away or, more precisely, to be moved."[9] Less dramatically, the point is also acknowledged by prominent U.S. curriculum specialists Walker and Soltis as follows:

> Teachers...who take the most active roles in shaping their own curriculum in systems with strong central control...[may] feel doubt and uncertainty; they may also feel uneasy about whether they have an obligation to inform colleagues and administrators about their deviations, and, when they do, they may receive what they feel are disapproving looks or even open criticism or official reprimands. For innovative teachers in conflict with the official curriculum, the experience is usually a chronic, nagging inhibition rather than a direct confrontation.
>
> (1992: 5)

Going on from this, in the present case, an area the field needs to know more about is how, in practice, teachers deal with the tension between their beliefs and the pressures or curricular imperatives imposed institutionally. Though there may be a scattered historical literature pertinent to this subject, the sensitivity of the topic is the probable reason there is rather little current discussion of it, let alone empirical study.[10] Nevertheless, Reagan and Osborn (2002) refer (over)confidently to "curricular nullification" in several forms – subtractive and additive forms, dissonantal and harmonious versions, intentional or consequential forms – and also consider whether the results are ethical or not. Overall, their claim is that:

> [language] teachers effectively proclaim and use their own veto power over any mandate, curricular, legal, administrative, or otherwise, which they believe to be in conflict with their professional and ethical responsibilities.
>
> (2002: 87)

Presumably they would admit that this is not by any means always a "veto," but when conditions of administrative or legal scrutiny are not great, and when students can be trusted not to turn in the "vetoing" teacher to the authorities, teachers can presumably modify the existing curriculum in a variety of ways. "Subtractively," they may fail to engage in "behaviors that are curricularly and institutionally mandated, including the omission of required topics from the course or syllabus" (ibid.); and likewise they may of course add material "with the intent of contradicting, opposing, or nullifying objectives." In most cases, these are probably acts of what Reagan and Osborn call "dissonantal curricular nullification," which occurs when there is "a conflict between the curriculum and the teacher's own value and belief system" (ibid.). They refer to the concept of professional ethics (citing Strike & Soltis, 1992) that indexes "professionally recognized, appropriate, and sanctioned behavior." It would be in accord with this standard, presumably, that a teacher would engage in ethical curricular nullification.

Bushnell's (2003) interview study of "veteran New York City schoolteachers" is one of a handful of empirical investigations of teacher resistance and is not particularly encouraging. In this school district, as in most others in the United States, there have been increasingly controlling curricular directives, associated with a change in this country's education system from one which was decentralized to one in which there is much greater central governmental control through "the surveillance of standardized curricula" (p. 262). (In this, the United States, having previously been an outlier from the majority of state education systems, has come into line with systems established following the model of Napoleonic France in almost all developed countries.) However, the district Bushnell studied was large and:

> Superintendents are challenged to ensure that every teacher in every classroom follows every mandate. These conditions may have fostered the attitude some current teachers hold toward curricular, pedagogical, or other reforms with which they do not agree: If they wait long enough, the disputed reform likely will be supplanted by a new "latest idea".... [H]owever, the incomplete monitoring of teachers also limits their opportunities for innovation as poor practices may not be rectified through the introduction of potentially inventive pedagogies.
>
> (2003: 266)

An interesting point is that,

> one teacher found that by working in socially subordinate and neglected classrooms, she operated outside of the viewing interest of administration.
>
> (ibid.: 265)

Bushnell does not mention the extent to which this teacher deliberately chose such a school, or once within such a school, chose a subordinate program. Historically and politically, of course, resistance groups have sometimes deliberately moved to such sites to develop operations; resistance has sometimes arisen naturally from within such sites precisely because of their neglected and impoverished conditions. However, she continues that,

Most of the resistance I heard was water-cooler discourse –
teachers complaining about their lack of autonomy, decision
making, and authority – that did not evolve to action.

(ibid.: 266)

A less visible form of resistance is "appropriation." The term has been
used somewhat in applied linguistics, concerning the use of linguistic
material, or even language varieties, in creative ways that may not be
consistent with the original ownership or orientation of such material.
Even its common-sense meaning allows a sense that pertains to a particular kind of resistance, which subverts or coopts an originally oppressive
or unwelcome act or entity. To some extent it may be that the growth of
the field of language awareness in the UK was partially a response to the
National Curriculum's original emphasis on speaking English properly
(cf. Hawkins, 1984; Wallace, 2003: 65). If I am right, this is a broad and
temporally extended act of resistance, in which a governmental directive
to language teachers to give attention to a particular dialect of English
was extended, through the intervention of other curriculum specialists
and academics, toward giving attention to that dialect as one among
others, and eventually to a broad range of issues that allowed space for
sociopolitical issues, and so on.

It is important to emphasize the breadth of this example of resistance
by informed educators. By comparison, Bushnell (2003) basically finds
that "veteran New York City schoolteachers" had very little practical
opportunity to resist, individually, increasingly controlling curriculum
and administrative initiatives. While it was true that the school area in
question was so large that individual teachers could escape the attention
of supervisors, Bushnell also found that they were "complicit in their
own subordination" (2003: 251) in that they were more inclined to wait
out change than directly challenge the situation.

Edelsky and Johnson (2004, see also Edelsky, 2005) provide a partial
account of the work of a state elementary teacher who was able to
resist the implications of mandated phonics texts and curricula. Key
circumstances permitting this included:

locally specific leeway (an overburdened administration unable
to police the new curriculum mandates, disorganization at the
district level, and so on) that has enabled them to "dance around
the legislation" ... like-minded colleagues in the building and
in a [local organization]. ... Leeway, however, was most likely
attributable to her disinclination to ask permission, her ability to articulate in ... terminology [of the mandated curriculum]
what students were learning from her "deviant" teaching, her

> reputation...and the increasing number of students who were passing the state test.
>
> (2004: 128)

This "dancing around" is consistent with a less confrontational perspective that Osborn (2006: 14) articulates: that of a "companion methodology." "When a supervisor comes to observe," he says, "many teachers will choose activities and formats that are most conducive to the appearance of control, even if they are not the most beneficial pedagogically. The sociopolitical context of teaching... often necessitates such a dissonant approach." At the same time he notes that "we do not need to create a new methodology" and suggests that teachers, presumably those who are prepared to do one thing one day and a different one another day, can "work within existing political frameworks and methodological approaches to create space for dialogue related to advancing social justice" (ibid.).

Sideways shift / career development

Janeway (in a feminist work with the interesting title *Powers of the Weak*, 1980: 160) considers an early sociological analysis (Emerson, 1962) of power-dependent relations. Noting that "sociologists...tend to labor the obvious," she nevertheless holds up approvingly (as I am about to) "the need for *creativity* in personal life and larger social relations, which...can be described as a capacity to imagine alternatives to accepted roles and behavior." Analyzing a power-dependent relationship in which the weaker individual is under pressure to agree to morally repugnant behavior, one possibility is "to reduce the psychic costs involved in continuing the relationship by redefining [one's] moral values" (Emerson, 1962: 34). But preferable (if possible) is to reduce the advantage of the power-holder by enlarging the space within which this somewhat unsatisfactory relationship holds; in Emerson's example, the weaker individual should develop, and act upon, career-developing strategies so as to be able to withdraw her/his "motivational investment" in the connection. I agree with Janeway – this is not rocket science, and is an appropriate line to take in a work supposed to aid professional development.

Change

While this is not the place (and I do not have the space) for much discussion of educational and language-teaching change at the level of the institution or the field, I should at least allude to the concept and its literature at this point. After all, despite some moderately pessimistic comments in some of the earlier subsections, it is sometimes possible to identify changes as a result of which tensions between teachers' philosophy of language teaching and their actual practice are lessened. And at the very least, developing a thorough understanding of techniques and strategies by which educational change can be fostered should somewhat diminish frustrations. For some time, I have been making allusions to the literature of educational change and innovation in our field, which I have felt has not been utilized to the extent logically desirable (given the emphasis on change that the research community of TESOL at least seems to think important; e.g., De Lano, Riley, & Crookes, 1994). Comparatively recently there are signs that some studies in our area are taking a more systematic perspective on how this can be brought about, with useful collections appearing (Hall & Hewings, 2000; Kennedy, 1999; Kennedy, Doyle, & Goh, 1999; and other recent work, e.g., Lamie, 2004, 2005). There are still tensions in the matter of *who*, or which teachers, can make change. In a hierarchical system, it can hardly be denied that generally those on the top have more influence or control; though even there, this is not always the case: Executives may find their freedom of action much less than it appears. Thus, if a teacher finds they cannot implement their philosophy of teaching, this is a legitimate goad to seeking career advancement, and indeed, power. At the same time, those on the bottom still have the standard techniques that the weak have always used to influence the powerful: agitate, educate, organize, and when necessary, direct action gets the goods (cf. Crookes & Talmy, 2004).

Concluding remark

I still think it is somewhat strange that, although compromise, and to some extent resistance, are part of all our lives, and certainly part of the lives of professionals in bureaucratic institutions, there has been so little discussion of the matter. Personally, I have found Benjamin's discussion, and his longitudinal extension of the matter of compromise over a created life, to be helpful. At the same time, I naturally hope that more of us are in a position to resist oppressive forces within our work as teachers. It should not be forgotten that "professional" is still largely an aspiration, rather than a description, for most TESOL specialists. I sketched a series of conceptual positions, and some possible avenues to take, that respond to or are prompted by the need to resist. This should also lead to change, a topic on which we ought to be seeing considerably more systematic work in our field, beyond what I have referenced here. Perhaps a greater number of teachers with more explicit, optimistic, and aspirational philosophies of teaching is a necessary first step.

Discussion questions

1. In what areas of your work do you have any degree of professional autonomy? Thus far in your life as a language teacher, have you been able to teach the way you want to and/or manifest your values as a teacher, or have you had to compromise? In what respects (if the latter)?

2. How do your career plans connect with your philosophy of teaching? Does the concept of a "career plan" for a language teacher (or for you) make sense – is it realistic? Why/why not? What are the implications of your answer?

3. Are there legitimate reasons for compromise? Is someone with multiple roles and duties more likely to compromise? How do the words "now" and "later" play into accounts of compromise? (Consider the saying, "If not me, then who? If not now, then when?" paraphrased from a remark by Rabbi Hillel.)

4. As a teacher, have you ever resisted administrative directives or curricular constraints, and such like? Under what circumstances is this possible? What professional initiatives aid this?

5. Are you *really* going back to the job you came from?

Notes to Chapter 10

1 And in general, "teaching has relatively high rates of [staff turnover] compared with many other occupations" (Ingersoll, 2003: 237).

2 But see Johnston (1997) on the absence of careers for EFL teachers in at least one developed country.

3 Janeway (1980: 171ff) comments that "solitary dissenters" may engage in "drop-out and cop-out" which are, she says nevertheless "political acts...They are a kind of silent withdrawal of consent which, at the very least, denies the powerful access to the capacities of their fellow creatures." However, they are also "dubious weapons for the weak," preventing the bonding together for action which is the logical more active response.

4 Cf. Gardner (1984) on working-class schools in the UK in the 19th century.

5 "Historically, in the United States the control of elementary and secondary schooling developed in an unusual manner. In contrast to most European nations, public schooling in this country was originally instituted on a highly democratized, localized basis. From the early development of public education, the basic operating principle was that communities should themselves be largely responsible for, and have control over, the schooling of the children that reside in their jurisdiction" (Ingersoll, 2003: 220).

6 With, of course, some regional variation (cf. Skuja-Steele & Silver, 2004).

7 One moderately well-known title in education that might have been thought relevant is Sizer (1984). The author begins the work by imagining the compromises entered into

by a teacher whose working conditions do not allow him to live up to his professional aspirations; but the rest of the work, and the two titles that follow, concern reform efforts rather than the topic of compromise.

[8] Though Johnston (2003: 145–6) does at least list dilemmas potentially involving compromise for our field, and Block (2005) makes use of the term in a study of French as a Foreign Language teachers' responses to the culturally different educational system of the UK. (For a partial response to Benjamin, see Ramsay, H., 1997.)

[9] For a detailed analysis of different levels of resistance in "repressive settings" see Scott (1985: 292ff).

[10] Considering the history of education, teachers living under oppressive regimes sometimes engaged in resistant activity, but this was not always possible. Mann (1939: 46–7) writes of the impossible circumstances of resistant teachers in Nazi Germany: "The small heroisms of daily life exhaust any independence or courage left in [educationists]: a teacher is a hero if he says 'Good morning!' instead of 'Heil Hitler!' to a pupil." Mann's book suggests, however, that this is a historical case in which most teachers who would have been resistant were identified and removed from their positions, and those who remained were subject to intense scrutiny (by pupils as well as others). Only the "smallest" of heroisms were possible, she suggests (cf. Klemperer, 1946/2000). This area is one that deserves further discussion and both historical and contemporary research (cf. O'Leary, 2006).

11 Aims and other components of a teaching philosophy – empirical studies

Introduction

Having come this far, we have reviewed a substantial range of sources, providing a diversity of orientations and matters to be considered in constructing one's philosophy of language teaching – without, however, exhaustively considering the range of possible components of one, and largely without specifying preferred elements. This is because I did not wish to preempt thinking on the part of the reader by prematurely exposing him or her to a particular way of viewing the item under consideration; and because the existing literatures do not in any case offer extensive support for just one way of looking at the matter. It is true that the chapters of this work themselves provide some indication of topics I believe are generally of significance for a philosophy of teaching (as I recognized toward the end of Chapter 1), but so far I have not pinned my colors to the mast concerning any one of them. I have, however, formed the opinion that one broad category within any philosophy of teaching is sufficiently important to deserve priority: aims. And this is not too surprising a point at all. If a philosophy of teaching is in some sense to guide a language teacher's actions or orientation, it should presumably provide support for an answer to the questions, "What is to be done? What are the main targets? – Where are we trying to go, in some overarching sense?" This is one way to understand our professional beliefs; and the matter should be addressed at a level that does some justice to the idea of one's profession as a way of making sense of one's working life, and accordingly contributes or at least points toward high and worthy goals.

In previous writings, I have often commented on the negative aspects of most teachers' working conditions; and I feel those conditions are disproportionately bad for many language teachers around the world, particularly those who often have only part-time employment,[1] or those who work with second rather than foreign language learners, and thus work usually with immigrants, a marginalized sector whose teachers are often equally marginal. I feel that these teachers, and perhaps indeed the majority of teachers, have not been encouraged to see themselves as intellectuals, and indeed have tended to be treated by governments and employers as more like hired hands than professionals. Thus they have not had the chance, or the conditions, under which to articulate the highest aims they might aspire to. Precisely for that reason, this final substantive chapter addresses itself to aims as its principal theme. I begin with the specialist (philosophical, nonempirical) literature I have drawn on all through the material. If a teacher has not had a chance to think about this topic, s/he might like to know what those who have been so favored have had to say.[2] But after that discussion (of aims), to give greater range to what other components might be considered, I turn to empirical literature, which draws on the voices and thoughts of teachers. (Though as we shall see, what little empirical literature there is is not focused on quite the same targets as the philosophical literature; again, in my opinion, a reflection of working conditions among other things.)

Aims as part of the philosophy of education

Educational philosophers of all kinds have often addressed themselves to aims. Obviously individuals such as Plato, Rousseau, and Dewey certainly had things in mind they thought that teachers, teaching, and education, should strive for. However, systematic treatment of the topic, dealing with the nature and range of educational aims across educational systems of thought or domains of educational action, has been only intermittent. Within the literature available in English, analyses focusing on the term "aims" developed particularly in response to the work of a prominent British philosopher of education, R. S. Peters, who actually challenged the utility of the term (Peters, Woods, & Dray, 1965). The topic was then developed by scholars taking issue with this position who analyzed substantive areas in which one might, as a teacher, have aims.[3] Thus it is that White (1982: ix) begins his study of the matter of the aims of education by saying that "It may sound odd, in view of the importance of the issue, but, unless I am mistaken, there just has not been as yet any book-length investigation of priorities among educational aims."[4] The work of White was responded to and extended by Wringe in an attempt also to bring it more up to date (Wringe, 1988), which I will review in some detail. Treatments of the topic remain surprisingly scarce; Noddings's (2003) book is perhaps the most extended recent survey. Noddings covers much of the same ground as Wringe but proceeds, analytically, in the reverse direction, accepting "happiness" as the preordinate aim (a position Wringe dismisses completely), while reviewing some of the same areas (vocational education, or education for societal participation) as contributing to the individual aim of fostering happiness. She is primarily concerned with what curricular elements might assist a student to have a good (or happy) life, and so her work is in the area of curricular critique.[5] In what follows, I use Wringe's taxonomy, bringing in Noddings's comments in some parts. The question of how language teaching can target possible aims has to be deferred until the range of aims in question has been considered.

An initial, definitional distinction can be made between ideals, aims, and goals. Ideals are "the embodiment of perfection in an imperfect world" (Wringe, 1988: 8) and thus "their espousal readily lays one open to the charge of being a fool, a fanatic, or a hypocrite." Aims, by contrast, "are not dreamy visions of a distant state which we may or may not be doing something to bring about. Typically, they may be pointed to as explanations of actual conduct...[They] may be pursued ruthlessly, but they may also be pursued prudently and in a spirit of compromise.... To compromise over an aim does not imply the same moral falling short as compromising over an ideal"(ibid.). Wringe is critical of some philosophers of education who presented educational ideas using the term aims (e.g., Dewey, 1916/1961; Russell, 1926; Whitehead, 1929) when in his opinion they were talking more of ideals.

A more familiar distinction is then drawn between aims and objectives; the latter being "specific pieces of learning which we intend to see achieved" at the conclusion of some segment of instruction (ibid.: 10). But Wringe goes on to assert that aims are not merely objectives "writ large," though

> ordinary language does...sometimes use "aims" in this way, to mean a fairly distant sort of goal that is nevertheless finite and intended to be achieved by a certain date.... For our purposes the essential logical feature of aims is that...they are of an open-ended, on-going kind.
>
> (ibid.: 14)

Within the context of a syllabus or course this is clear:

> [M]any teachers' aims will be closely connected with the point of the subject...they are engaged in teaching...[for example] increase [students'] confidence and range of oral expression, promote responsiveness to literary work [etc.].... The aims of these teachers will no doubt include the fostering of interest in and commitment to the various values and standards implicit in these aims.
>
> (ibid.)

However, Wringe goes on beyond this to comment that:

> In addition to lesson and syllabus objectives and the aims inherent in teaching particular subjects, teachers may also think that

their work is related to such larger purposes as developing the potential of individual pupils, contributing in various ways to the creation of a better world, promoting a commitment to certain intrinsically worthwhile activities, or the pursuit of such things as rationality and truth. Aims of this order are neither objectives nor ideals. They are implicit in much that takes place in schools, and help explain the spirit of seriousness with which education is often undertaken, and the passion with which educational issues are often debated.

(ibid.: 16)

Pursuing this further, Wringe remarks:

Our arguments for particular educational aims must necessarily involve more fundamental value judgements regarding such matters as the nature of the good life for the individual or society, the ways in which individuals ought to relate to each other, what goals it is in general desirable to pursue, and so on.

(ibid.: 17)

I think it is clear that philosophy has always engaged with questions such as these. It is surely axiomatic that professionally oriented language teachers see themselves, and their work, as broadly benefiting either individuals or society (or both), and if they are to rationally direct their efforts, they should consider their aims. Given the breadth of range of possible aims (particularly once "society" is drawn into the discussion), for those of us developing a philosophy of teaching, some rough guide to the categorization of aims would be useful. White (1982) considers "intrinsic aims," "the good of the pupil," "the good of society" and then goes on to review the conditions for the realization of aims. Similarly, Wringe (1988: 20) sets up the following simple taxonomy:

1. Aims that would confer benefits specifically upon the individual and favor his own ends and development;
2. Aims concerned to preserve or bring about a desirable state of society;
3. Aims to bring about such goals as the promotion of truth, rationality, excellence and so on which are sometimes held to be intrinsically desirable or worthwhile.

Aims for the individual

Happiness, growth, needs, and interests

Wringe's first grouping identifies a set of aims that have often been advanced as pertinent to the individual. These concern happiness,

217

growth, autonomy, and employment. We may note that an individual orientation in educational aims is characteristic of the romantic tradition, of Rousseau, in distinction to the societal orientation of Plato, or for that matter Dewey (Noddings, 2003).

On the initial term here, Wringe suggests that merely aiming for individual happiness (for students) is not sufficient nor satisfactory. The main problem he identifies for this as an aim is its derivation from utilitarianism, which is not sufficiently coherent or focused toward educational matters. As a sole goal, it seems implausible, though as associated with others or as a precursor to others perhaps it has something to offer. Wringe's rapid dismissal of happiness as an aim may be premature, and further analysis of what is assumed to be involved in happiness or an analysis of what leads to happiness is necessary.

In the first case, we could note one obvious, indeed perhaps crass understanding of happiness – that it follows from economic success. Certainly a major lay (or policy makers') understanding of education is that its aim is to provide people with the "qualifications" that they need to take various forms of paid employment and thereby make a living or make far more than is needed just to live. The qualifications in question are mainly associated with what Noddings calls traditional college curricula. But she poses various questions about the aim here: "Clearly we [are] trying to prepare many more students for college. . . . [Does] society need more people with a . . . traditional college education? . . . [Must access to economic success] come through successful competition in traditional schooling? . . . It is shortsighted and arrogant to suppose that all people can escape problems [associated with a lack of money] through better education, particularly if that education favors those with specific academic talents or resources" (Noddings, 2003: 85). Noddings passes from this critique of one limited understanding of happiness that has had negative effects on curricula, to a survey of some matters fostering happiness that have unduly been left out of educational curricula.[6] These include an individual-oriented group (homemaking and parenting skills, the development of good character, interpersonal skills), the well-accepted vocational area, and in the social dimension, education for civic participation.

Growth is a widely used metaphoric term associated with educational aims in progressive traditions and "child-centered" or student-centered education (it was the preordinate aim of Dewey, e.g., 1916/1961). In this way of thinking, one aim would be "to foster the natural growth" of the student. As has been discussed much earlier, this is a central metaphor within studies of second language acquisition and also appears repeatedly in functional language-teaching methodologies, such as the natural approach or the direct method. Student-centered curricula also associate growth with concerns for the students' needs and/or interests, as opposed to the line taken in more traditional education in which it is the discipline (or the teacher) who determines what is to be taught.

Given the strength of the metaphor in our field, I think that language teachers will be reluctant to abandon it completely even if problems can be found with it. However, within the SLA field there has been an interesting movement from a primary emphasis on the inevitability of child and adult second language learning as a progression through fixed sequences of development which cannot be affected by instruction, to a recognition of the importance of teacher (or other) form-focused error treatment, or even instruction.

Similarly, although many specialists in curriculum design in our field emphasize needs analyses, as Wringe notes, one needs to ask whose needs and whose interests are being responded to. These things are not objective, and whether a language teacher favors, say, liberal education or, perhaps because of the circumstances of her employment, is constrained toward a narrow vocationalism, will make a difference as to how this aim manifests itself. Given the original work-driven emphasis on needs analysis for language curriculum design, it is salutary to note, as Wringe (1988: 42) does, that "many of the alleged needs of pupils are therefore not really *their* needs at all. It is ultimately the typist's employer who needs her typing skills."

Autonomy

Within modern lines of thought, and in democracies, the ability of the free individual to independently make decisions and choices about his/her life is thought to be crucial. Thus "autonomy," as an educational aim, is widely favored. Two aspects of autonomy can be quickly identified. First, it is fostered or enhanced by the removal of external restrictions on a person; thus, enabling students to make their own choices of aspects of language to be learned is at one level favoring their autonomy. Second, it is supported by developing the learner's mental capacity to make independent judgment, not only about their learning but about their life. The latter is associated with a sense of the individual's rationality and is also enhanced by providing them with the wherewithal to exercise critical judgment. "Being critical," Wringe cautions, "is not simply an attitude of mind. We cannot properly be critical without both factual knowledge and a grasp of the ways in which various claims are to be criticized, the standards of evidence it is appropriate to expect or the canons of rationality that must be met" (Wringe, 1988: 45).

Philosophically, autonomy is an important concept. The term has proved very attractive to the language-teaching field (e.g., Benson &

Voller, 1997; Dam, 2001) and derives most obviously from the work of Kant, which Chapter 8 located in a liberal sociopolitical context. It can also be found in other philosophical traditions. Like most educational philosophers outside of conservative or authoritarian traditions, Wringe favors autonomy, and links it with the existential concept of "authenticity." In this connection, existentialists would say that we are the ones who make decisions about our lives but there will always be an element of indeterminacy about the more difficult ones. In ourselves, making our lives through the (autonomous) choices we make, in choosing to commit to being a particular kind of individual, we live an authentic life.

Vocational aims

I have already alluded to the substantial effect that employment-related concerns have had on curriculum design, and indeed overall outlook, on our field. There are some odd tensions in this area as it manifests in our field. At the time of the beginning of the English for Specific Purposes "movement" (the 1970s, say), there was a shift away from English for General Purposes, whose syllabi were the entire structural content of the language. Instead, a needs-analysis–driven process moved courses toward the functions and notions of English that students "really" needed to perform, usually work-related tasks in the target language. Subsequently, this went along with a trend in developed countries, beginning in the 1980s in the UK and continuing elsewhere, for state education to become more tightly focused to the world of work. This could be considered to reflect a return of the corporate dominance of state education that existed in much earlier times (e.g., in the United States, from the 1890s to the 1920s).

At the same time, many EFL countries continued the use of (usually structurally oriented) English proficiency exam scores as entry requirements for university education. This practice has become consistent with the more recent movement in English-speaking countries to promote "standards" for all curricular areas and among countries in general to promote English in terms of the economic competitiveness of the country and the economic competitiveness of the individual who has high English test scores (cf. Noddings, 2003, *passim*). This has led many English language teachers to constrain their aims to "helping students get a better job" either directly, through the acquisition of job-related English, or indirectly, through helping them enter prestigious (or any) university education.

In trying to find a way that education could be practical, and not divorced from reality, as well as liberal, in the sense of getting beyond mere vocationalism, some 20th-century educational theorists developed practical curricula, which emphasized learning that was pragmatic and problem-solving, for the (progressive) modern world. The problem is to preserve the distinction between learning through work and learning exclusively for work. Similarly, in language teaching, we have probably benefited from the emphasis that needs-analysis–driven curriculum design has placed on our identifying the practical needs of our students with respect to the languages we teach. Where we suffer is if our higher aims are obliterated in the ESP/conversation school world of "just give them the language they need to do the job," or on the other hand, through the corruption of a state education originally intended to be of practical use, toward the chasing of impractical entrance examination scores.

Aims and society

I think that the general trend of developed societies toward increasing individualism, along with the vocational emphases of teaching in our field just referred to, make it hard for many English teachers to see their work as having a social benefit. Nevertheless, at the same time as individualism is on the rise, so is globalism, so perhaps our societies can more easily be seen in an international context, which is of advantage to the foreign language teacher. The adult orientation of much of the field, however, somewhat gets in the way of language teachers seeing that they sometimes have responsibilities that go beyond merely teaching the language. Seeing their work in "civic" terms may help with this point.

Civic duties, and law and order

Societies expect teachers, most obviously in state schools but also even in the private sector, to make a contribution to the development of young people (and this can also apply to adult education) to be good citizens, thereby fostering an orderly society. This could be an appropriate educational aim ("if the society in question is a reasonably just one," notes Wringe, 1988: 73). Since there is a shrinking, in democracies, from indoctrination, such a purpose would probably take the form of moral and civic education. The latter is notably on the rise in recent years, particularly under the slightly modified heading of citizenship education. This means education for active participation in society (e.g., Potter, 2002); in some cases for the civil enculturation of immigrant groups, obviously of relevance to the ESL teacher (cf. Schiffauer et al., 2004); and in certain cases of relevance to the EFL educator, it may even mean education for active participation in international society, as the mobility of many individuals across national boundaries is much greater than before (cf. Hoffman, 2004; Mazzucato, 2004). Wringe comments:

> In a fairly just society, successful moral education ought to result in a degree of law and order.... In so far as injustice remained, [a moral] person would be committed to work for change through resistance and protest, including symbolic acts of non-conformity if necessary.... That teachers, or anyone else, should attempt to improve society may seem to have overtones of arrogance and paternalism. Yet it can scarcely be right to refrain from doing so when the opportunity lies readily to hand.
>
> ... We are not strictly concerned with social reform being pursued by teachers themselves, but by their morally educated ex-pupils. There is no question of the teachers attempting to achieve their own political aims by using their pupils instrumentally to this end. For to educate morally is not to commit individuals to certain kinds of action, but to place them in a position to choose what seems the morally right course of action for themselves.
>
> (1988: 74)

Thus, this form of moral and civic education, within which it would seem that language teaching with a content orientation might have some place, links back again to the concept of autonomy as a possible educational aim.[7]

Equality

If we are working in democracies and considering social aims of language education, then it could be argued that given the importance of equality to democracy, this topic is potentially included in the area.[8] Wringe (1988) takes a social reconstructionist view of this:

> It must be borne in mind that schooling is an important part of the process by which the differentiation between those who are destined to be affluent and influential and those who are not takes place.... Schools, by virtue of the organizational, curricular and other policies may compound and amplify these differences or – if such is their aim – take deliberate steps to avoid doing so.
>
> (1988: 87)

Wringe suggests that there is no conflict between education promoting social equality and education promoting educational excellence. Each should not be pursued exclusively of the other, however; and he recognizes that conflicts could arise if there were resource scarcities (and resources were to be jointly administered). As language teachers, we naturally want very high levels of achievement, but to some extent this is less reflected in resources and more in persistence.

It may be noted that the emphasis here is on the domestic scene, but recognizing the internationalization of society, and the role of English in it, it may be of interest that some theorists of equality (e.g., Walzer, 2004) also suggest that the possibility of movement toward global equality is greater now than before, given the increase in international regulation of some matters (e.g., child labor), along with the greater support of some national governments (who may be still more directly involved in fostering equality) by international agencies. Once again, the implication of the international language of English in such interstate and international communication (as well as global commerce) suggests, at least initially, a role for ELT practices consistent with the aim under review here (cf. McKay, 2002, *inter alia*).

Justice

In considering justice as involved in the aims of a language teacher's philosophy of teaching, both an international and a local school perspective seem to be plausibly implicated. Wringe comments,

> There ought not only to be justice in the provision of education, but the promotion of a just society is a legitimate and necessary educational aim. There is no truth in the gibe that schools should leave justice to the courts and attend to their own business, which is teaching. If schools are organs of public provision they are no more entitled to pursue policies which lead to injustice than the police, [or local government, or state social services]. They are under an obligation to review their policies and practices, including curricular policies and classroom practices, to ensure that they are neither unjust in the present, nor likely to give rise to injustice in the future. Content, teaching styles or the communication of attitudes which make it more likely that some or all of a school's pupils will suffer (or inflict) injustice need to be identified and avoided. Needless to say, this includes all educational processes which predispose some sections of the school population to accept unduly low expectations of themselves or needlessly acquiesce in subordinate roles. It also includes [but militates against] the communication of attitudes of superiority and the expectation of privilege in other pupils.
>
> (1988: 101)

This discussion can be easily cashed out in regard to the practices of ESL teachers in multicultural, pluralistic societies with immigrant groups or other marginalized groups (even including international students) for whom English, and notably standard English, is a language of power to which access is facilitated by language teachers. The way a language curriculum is structured and handled, other aspects of language use and assessment across an educational institution, and support for second and foreign language users in such institutions, are very much matters of a teachers' practice in which issues of justice could come to the fore, or be specifically aimed at by a teacher. And again, with English as the international language of power in a globally hierarchical and often unjust world, for some students (and their teachers), perhaps this aim in the long run might play out internationally.

Aims and intrinsically worthwhile activities

Given the extremely utilitarian orientation of much EF/SL teaching, and similar reasons given for learning a variety of other languages (most often job-related), it is worth considering the older, alternate, indeed prior position: that education in its best aspects is worthwhile in and of itself, because it improves the individual learner regardless of the external world in which s/he must in due course exist.

> Important among the aims, traditionally those of a liberal edu-
> cation ... are commitment to and appreciation of certain artistic
> and cultural pursuits. The central place, however, is occupied by
> the intellectual activities involved in the pursuit of knowledge,
> understanding, truth and rationality.
>
> (Wringe, 1988: 117)

Presumably, then, at some level, some language teachers might have "improving students' minds" as an aim. Taking the fostering of knowledge and understanding as broad aims would seem to be hard to argue against, providing it is not (as it has sometimes been in the past) conflated with the knowledge of a particular sector of society. Education at its best should not be the promulgation of the cultural resources of a privileged elite (and the associated specialized language resources[9]), nor should its acquisition, aided by teachers, merely serve as a stepping-stone toward a position higher up the ladder of a stratified society.

Empirical studies

Marland's line

Since the mid-1980s, educational researcher Marland had been drawing on the "teacher thinking" line of research, one of the areas identified in

Chapter 1 as pertinent to the topic of a philosophy of teaching, (e.g., Marland, 1986, 1997; Marland & Osborne, 1990). More recently, he has joined forces with an established TESOL specialist, Mangubhai, to investigate teacher thinking in the area of Communicative Language Teaching (CLT). Mangubhai and his associates (2004, 2005) studied the understandings of CLT of a number of teachers of Languages Other Than English (LOTE) in Australian high schools and report in detail on the understanding of one teacher of German as a foreign language. Some elements of Marland's work deserve scrutiny to see if they can offer some empirical complement to the philosophical work we have just reviewed.

In his (1997) analysis of the mainstream literature on teacher thinking, Marland was concerned with "teachers' practical theories." Here is his initial list of "concepts which are frequently used to communicate the substance of teachers' practical theories":

- Values and beliefs
- Goals
- Student states
- Cues
- Strategies
- Principles
- Teacher attributes
- Contextual factors
- Metaphors and images
- Pedagogical content knowledge

(1997: 18)

On the face of it, just considering some of the major terms in this list, it would seem that this taxonomy might be useful for us in our concern for developing a philosophy of teaching or understanding the things teachers refer to in their "practical theories." But what specifically is implied by "values and beliefs," and "goals," and other less immediately transparent terms that Marland uses? What else, what other elements not mentioned in this list, should be included? Can we be guided by his analysis? Let us examine some exemplars for each of these from Marland's descriptions.

Set one: Values, beliefs, goals, and aims

Marland is in the mainstream of opinion when he writes (drawing on Dill et al., 1990; Sockett, 1987; and Tom, 1984) that "the values we hold, that is, the ideas in life we attach great value or importance to and try to live by, can have a pervasive and determining influence on the way we teach" (1997: 18). Some teacher values he highlights are "students experiencing security, belongingness and respect"; drawing on one empirical study (Marland, 1994) he mentions "student welfare . . . bound up with notions of student independence, positive self-image and personal integrity." He notes that,

> In teachers' value systems, not all values carry the same weight. Some tend to be more strongly subscribed to than others. In the past, considerable emphasis was placed on neatness, tidiness, conformity and compliance. Now, in many contemporary classrooms, these values are played down and a higher priority is placed on other values such as independence, initiative and creativity.
>
> (1997: 19)

Drawing on another study (Marland & Osborne, 1990), Marland refers to the "value that many educators place on preparation of lessons and resources is usually justified by reference to a set of beliefs" that relate it to "effective use of classroom time [and] the effectiveness of teaching and learning" (1997: 20). He also refers to a teaching dilemma resulting from a conflict between the two values of "coverage of the curriculum content" and "class discussion." Thus, while the term seems an essential one for a philosophy of teaching, it seems that Marland's interpretation of it is as a term whose referents are fairly close to the immediate practice of teaching at a quite concrete level. For comparison, we might consider Johnston's (2003) ELT-specific treatment of values. Johnston is not exactly systematic about how the values he discusses are arrived at, but he highlights a range of values that find manifestation in a number of ELT teachers he has worked with or interviewed over the years, and that he suggests are embodied in "our field" (p. 147) as a whole: "commitment to our students, commitment to ourselves, equity, caring, and dialogue . . . fundamental values underlying our pedagogical beliefs."

Let us turn now to the term "belief." The level at which Marland uses this term is indicated when he writes,

> Perhaps a reasonable approach to the identification of beliefs would be to document the principal beliefs we hold in some of the key areas. Those areas might include planning; the nature of learners and learning process; teaching strategies, including ones for motivating and challenging; management principles, including reward, punishment and discipline; relationships with students; assessment practices and the place of feedback; and ways of providing learners with access to content to be learned.
>
> (1997: 21)

I would not say that Marland is inaccurate in his use of the term "belief" to refer to practices such as how to grade or how to motivate. One of my past students included the following in a piece of reflective writing: "A belief I have about teaching is that the classroom atmosphere should be comfortable, but not too comfortable." In addition, it is at this level that an important and almost contemporary study of language teacher thinking, Woods (1996), operates. As previously mentioned, Woods used the broad term "beliefs, assumptions, knowledge" (BAK) to specify a central concept of his investigation (of eight ESL teachers in Canada). And indeed, the beliefs that they articulated in interviews with him (though not separated from knowledge or assumptions) mostly involve views concerning how a second language is learned, appropriate ways of teaching it in specific classroom contexts, and so on. I still think that other teachers, however, when asked a question like "What are your beliefs as a teacher?" might refer to higher matters, such as beliefs in justice, equity, fairness, and so on, as things they should manifest in their teaching; but this is not what the existing empirical literature appears to indicate.

On the matter of goals, here is Marland again:

> When teachers explain why they teach the way they do, they inevitably make reference to their teaching goals or what they are trying to achieve for or with students. This, not unexpectedly, has been reported in a number of studies of teachers' practical knowledge, most recently by Cooper and McIntyre (1996) who referred to the statement of direction made by teachers in talk about teaching as "aims." Although teachers are probably aware of the broad aims of education as recorded in curriculum documents, those of the subjects they teach and the numerous objectives into which aims are translated, they tend not to cite these when discussing the basis for their approach to teaching (outlined in their practical theories). Instead, they generally refer to a small number of key, broad, long-term goals which help to identify . . . their own perspectives and missions as educators . . .
>
> (1997: 23)

In this case, there is some disagreement about terms. "What [teachers] are trying to achieve for or with students" is, for Marland, a goal, though for Cooper and McIntyre it is an aim; but it is not an aim of the "broad" kind, that appears in curriculum documents; though it is of the "broad, long-term" kind that is in teachers' own "missions as educators."

The possibility of a difference between the aims of education as recorded in curriculum documents and those of teachers' own missions is interesting and in line with the position on "tensions" articulated in the previous chapter. But it at first leaves the reader unclear about what exactly Marland has in mind by the term "goals." Citing one educational ethnography (Janesick, 1977), he refers to a teacher's

227

"dominant or superordinate goal" (p. 23), as "dominated by a commitment to creating and maintaining a cohesive and stable class." Similarly, Marland et al.'s (1994) study of an Australian teacher "indicated that he was working towards establishing team spirit in his classroom and school." Some of the goals that Marland suggests teachers might consider include:

- improve the practical skills of learners;
- teach learners to be skeptical and reflective;
- acquaint learners with knowledge and theory;
- develop capacities for group problem-solving;
- enhance employment opportunities for learners;
- promote deep learning.

By comparison, consider some of the aims mentioned in a recent collection of philosophical studies of "the aims of education" (Marples, 1999). These include liberalism, citizenship, critical thinking, autonomy, national identity, self-determination, well-being, fairness (a fair education), moral seriousness, and social commitment.

Having discussed the first three of the terms in Marland's taxonomy (values, goals, and beliefs) particularly because they sound relatively high-level, or broad, the remainder sound less so, so for this reason (and for reasons of space) I will not discuss them further. I turn now to more language-related work.

A study of a language teacher

This taxonomy just discussed lies behind Mangubhai et al. (2004), which brings Marland's earlier work into a language context. The authors note in passing that the only similar study they had been able to identify is Golombek (1998; mentioned in Chapter 1), but that as the focus of that study was on ESL teachers' "personal practical knowledge" in general, rather than in regard to a specific approach, it was not relevant to their work. That may be indicative, also, for present purposes. In their study, Mangubhai and his colleagues were interested in how language teachers understood a particular methodological orientation that was at the time being advocated and for which training was being provided by the local Australian authorities. Unfortunately, as a result, because Mangubhai et al. were primarily concerned with a teacher's understanding of Communicative Language Teaching, they were comfortable deriving most of their analytic concepts a priori from Joyce and Weil's (1992) "framework... for describing models of teaching" (Mangubhai et al., 2004: 295).[10] This reflects the problem of disagreement in previous literature as to the extensiveness of "teachers' practical theories"; that is indeed somewhat of the issue I am concerned with here.[11] Mangubhai and colleagues' report discusses in detail one of seven FL teachers studied ("Doreen"). In addition to several hours of interviews, the focal teacher was also twice videotaped teaching, and stimulated recall was used to elicit comments on "parts of practical theories related to classroom events" (ibid.: 296).[12]

The study documents Doreen's "goals," but it places them at the level of the lesson or the course: "to have students able to 'converse' in German with Germans: 'At the moment our goal is to learn the language, to make it useful in Germany....'" Somewhat similarly, although potentially a little more abstract, "Doreen's use of a CLT approach is grounded in certain values.... Two of these are 'listening to each other' and 'supporting each other.'... Other values considered important by Doreen are independence, taking responsibility for their own learning and 'giving it a go.'" The latter is a core Australian cultural value, that applies across the culture, not just in school, let alone in language teaching. Similarly, and equally Australian, Doreen also "wants classroom interactions to be tempered with justice: 'I believe in giving everyone a fair go. That's why we've got one of our classroom expectations on the wall, 'please give everybody a go.'" (Mangubhai et al., 2004: 301). Finally, her beliefs, here glossed as "key pedagogical beliefs," include "catering for all," "going from the known to the unknown," making the lesson student-centered, and "showing sensitivity to the backgrounds... of students."

One component of Doreen's "practical theory of CLT" that may be suggestive is what the researchers call her "social system," comprising teacher roles, student roles, teacher–student relationships, and "normal student behaviors." The first of these is varied and extensive: It includes information transmitter ("chalk and talk") but also facilitator, mediator, and "friend," and even "mother." Student roles include more conventional learner and listener, but also "group worker," "sharer," and "initiator." Normal student behaviors are related to the "classroom atmosphere Doreen seeks to establish in her CLT lessons... one that is positive, nonthreatening... features a cooperative relationship between herself and students and among students, and... is relaxed and informal.... Cooperative behaviour, particularly helping and supporting peers, is one that she appears to stress" (ibid.: 303). This clearly would not be unusual in CLT classrooms and seems very much in the mainstream of the progressive tradition.

For reasons of space, I have not fully summarized the study. The authors comment that "Doreen's practical theory of CLT is an amalgam of many of the features of CLT approaches... and many features of general teaching" (and there are some features regarded by the authors as part of CLT approaches that were missing). For our purposes, it and the earlier work of Marland might be regarded as suggestive, perhaps stimulating, though perhaps a little frustrating. Mangubhai and associates set out to study a teacher's understanding of CLT, not her overall philosophy of teaching, so their work does not fully target the question I am approaching this chapter with: What should be, or are, major components of a language teacher's philosophy of teaching? Although I am a pedagogy specialist, because of the importance I attach to one's values as a teacher, I would like to think that they come first and the choice of "Method" or methodology would be subsidiary. Another problem for the use of this study for present purposes is that Mangubhai et al. are driven by an orientation which is more toward "knowledge" or "teacher theory," and is concerned with the uptake (or lack of it) of a theoretical approach articulated within applied linguistics, rather than the articulation of a teacher's own philosophy of teaching (whether or not influenced by any of the history or philosophy we have reviewed). However, goals, values, and beliefs, with possibly some other lower-level key concepts, still bid fair to be important elements of a philosophy of teaching. In the study under consideration here, one might wish to see a slightly greater sense of where they come from, and less sense that the beliefs have simply floated in along with some ideas from CLT.

Breen's work

Breen's early (1991) study broke ground in this area for our field; but only later, when involved with government-funded evaluation of language teacher development programs, was he able to do more extensive work on the topic. With his research team, he developed a fairly extensive, step-by-step process of observing teachers, interviewing them about what they had done and had been observed to do in their classes (using video recordings to prompt recall and analysis), and then subjecting this material to an abstracting process to derive principles related to (and manifesting in) practice. "A purpose here was to uncover experienced teachers' constructions of their work in direct relationship to observed classroom behavior" (Breen et al., 2001: 472). Breen and colleagues confine their main investigative terms to "beliefs" and "pedagogic principles." Referring to the (1991) study initiating their set of reports, they say "the diverse reasons the teachers gave for particular techniques that they adopted during language lessons revealed a finite set of guiding principles that appeared . . . to derive from underlying beliefs or personal theories the teachers held regarding the nature of the broader educational process, the nature of language, how it is learned, and how it may be best taught" (ibid.). Here I note the equating of "personal theories" and "beliefs"; somewhat similar to Marland and colleagues' use of "personal practical theory."

Breen's team worked with 18 teachers. The principles of several of them were highlighted for exemplification. For one teacher, they included:

- Students need to use the language which they have learned.
- Everything we do in class must have a purpose / be useful in the students' daily lives.
- It is important to be alert to the emotional states and self-esteem of these particular students.
- Students' ideas on their own learning are valid because they are taking responsibility for their own learning.
- Because there is so much to learn, the language needs to be broken down and categorized for ease of mental processing.

(Breen et al., 2001: 481)

For another, some sample principles were:

- Breaking down the information makes it easier to understand and produce later.
- It is important for students to hear input more than once and hearing each other speak helps them to remember by hearing things in different ways.
- The teacher needs to take account of the differences between students and how they learn.
- Students need to know the correct forms and uses of language in our society.

(ibid.: 486)

After review and analysis of a large amount of data, the teachers' principles were summarized by the research team under the following headings:

a concern with how the learner undertakes the learning process, a concern with particular attributes of the learner, a concern with how to use the classroom and its human and material resources to optimize learning, a concern with the subject matter of learning, and a concern with the specific contributions that [teachers] can make in their role as teacher.

(Breen et al., 2001: 484)

Breen's team was interested in both the connection between principles and practices and also whether there were commonalities in these areas. They found 12 principles that were held in common by their teachers; looking at just one of them ("taking account of individual differences between students and/or the specific characteristics of individual students") they found this principle had a set of "over 30 distinct classroom practices" as exemplars (e.g., "shows interest in students' personal lives," "assesses students individually," and so on).

It seems that in this investigation, one of the most recent in the general area of language teacher beliefs, the focus is fairly close to practice level. The authors note the diversity of views across the group of teachers; for our purposes it is notable that the general thrust of research on teacher beliefs and thinking, with its laudable connection to practice, as yet tends to result in a viewpoint indeed close to the nitty gritty of individual lessons, rather than the broad perspectives that might appear in the initial statements of one's philosophy of teaching. Let me turn now, finally, to another somewhat recent study that has, by contrast, more of a philosophical inheritance, but (regrettably) no particular connection with language teaching.

Goodman on "a practical philosophy of teaching"

Goodman (1988) developed a line of work originating from the same pool of concepts and research agendas as Marland, but selected one that was, however, less cognitive and "Method"-oriented, and, from its beginnings, ethnographic and somewhat philosophical. For him, the thinking of teachers is encapsulated in their "practical philosophies" of teaching: "a 'practical' philosophy emerges from an individual's personal experience and is used as a guide for one's actions" (Goodman, 1988: 121). Within it, or as a broad characteristic of such an entity, some researchers identified an element they call a "teaching perspective." The concept of a teaching perspective derives from studies of occupational socialization (e.g., Becker et al., 1961, 1969), and probably was then taken up by a diverse group of educational researchers (Hammersley, 1977; cf. Adler, 1984; Gibson, 1976; Tabachnick & Zeichner, 1984). Hammersley (1977: 4) refers to teacher perspectives as "the knowledge on which teachers operate, how they define teaching and categorize situations, and their routine plans for ordering and coping with the world." These are closely connected with "the assumptions about society, knowledge, children, ability, etc., which underlie teacher actions" (ibid.). Hammersley notes that there has been an unfortunate tendency to typologize teacher perspectives merely as dichotomies.[13] In addition, the basis for selecting dimensions underlying typologies has not been made clear. Typologies existing at the time of his study had "usually been directly tied to the promotion of a particular version of teaching or have resulted from a concern with those factors expected to influence 'pupil achievement' as presently defined by the education system" (p. 18). Hammersley went on to develop a typology of teacher perspectives that reflected his concern with "selection and socialization" and also "with what 'being taught' involves, what 'achievement' and 'ability' mean, how pupils are selected . . . "; it required five dimensions:

teacher role, pupil action, conceptions of knowledge and learning, and preferred techniques.

In developing the concept of teaching perspective a decade later, Goodman was positive about this as a way of conceptualizing one's own philosophy of teaching, because (like Hammersley) he was dissatisfied with earlier ways, which he refers to as "static dichotomies such as traditional versus progressive, conservative versus liberal, or custodial versus humanistic." Not only are such categories static, he notes, they emerge from academic philosophers of education, rather than reflecting the words and actions of teachers themselves. His study looked at student teachers (because of prior evidence that suggested that it is very early in a professional's development that his/her views are determined) and emphasized "the linguistic framework" of his student teachers, that is, how they expressed their philosophies of teaching, and central "perspectives," in their own words.[14]

Goodman studied an elementary education program that was unusual in that it had a well-defined theoretical perspective that "evolved from humanistic principles of education" and in which "having students develop a 'teaching philosophy'" was an important programmatic goal. As stated in the student handbook of the program he investigated, "one of the primary purposes of the program was 'to help each student discover his own personal meanings through exploration of self as well as ideas and experiences he has been exposed to'" (Goodman, 1988: 122).

Goodman's study takes our exploration of the structure or components of a philosophy of teaching only so far, because he approaches the topic via the theoretical concept of "teaching perspective." He finds that his participants "organized their philosophy of teaching around two broad perspectives: (1) Teaching as a Problem of Control, and (2) Teaching as the Facilitation of Children's Growth" (ibid.: 123–4). His other analytic unit lies between the participants' "key phrases" and their teaching perspectives: It is the "guiding image" (a concept that he derives from Clandinin & Connelly, 1984: 5; see also Connelly & Clandinin, 1985), something that "reaches into the past gathering up experiential threads meaningfully connected to the present. And it reaches into the future and creates new meaningfully connected threads as situations are experienced.... Image carries intentionality." Emphasizing the nonpropositional aspects of teachers' knowledge, Goodman remarks that:

> Although [teachers'] practical philosophy of teaching was expressed in verbal terms, the roots of their perspectives were *visual*. Based on their past experiences as pupils, their present experiences in their teacher preparation program, and their future expectations of themselves as regular teachers, [teachers]

233

> created various images about teaching and then verbalized those
> images into a given perspective.
>
> (ibid.: 124)

The guiding images underlying "Teaching as a Problem of Control" were cooperation, authority, and autonomy. Though shared by subgroups of student teachers, such images could be interpreted differently. Thus, in the case of "authority," most of Goodman's participants tried to manifest institutional authority, whereas just a couple "expressed a desire to have children, rather than schools as institutions, give them [the student teachers] power" (ibid.: 125). And with regard to autonomy, most wanted it for their pupils, but several thought it crucial for teachers themselves. The images underlying "Teaching as the Facilitation of Children's Growth" were "individualization" and "self-concept." To take just the latter as illustrative, Goodman found both mainstream and more critical interpretations. For some teachers, helping their students succeed was important for the children's self-concept (important in itself), but others observed that, for example, "'traditional schooling' often gave children a bad self-concept" in the first place, covertly teaching them that what they know is not important.

Incidentally, Goodman has some interesting, nuanced things to say about the development of these student teachers' personal practical philosophies of teaching. "Early childhood and school experiences had a significant impact"; professional preparation did not necessarily. "No matter how logical or sound an idea seemed, if it directly contradicted a student [teacher]'s intuitive screen, it was usually rejected." On the other hand, "it was not that student [teacher]s neglected to use their intelligence ... some individuals thought long and hard about what they were doing ... most ... seemed willing to seriously consider alternative points of view. A number of the informants spent considerable effort intellectually analyzing a variety of ideas as they read books and articles" (ibid.: 131); "[Their] ideas were in a state of flux (p. 132)"; and "their notions had not been organized into a well defended theory of teaching." "Openness was tempered by a need for security. . . . Few, as yet, had had the opportunity or inclination to seriously question their previous cultural background or notions of reality" (p. 132).

Concluding remark

This chapter is perhaps more obviously tentative than most others in this collection of material. That reflects both my own thinking and, I believe, the state of play in the professional literature I have been drawing upon. Increasingly, teachers are drawing up somewhat formal philosophy of teaching statements. But somewhat relevant empirical lines of work are not extensive in this area and as yet do not seem to have come in contact with the full range of what might be possible. I think it is potentially useful to compare what empirical inquiry might have to offer in this area with what rational inquiry suggests, but much more needs to be done. Clearly, I have my own suspicions about why we do not see much research-based discussion of the more high-flown aims that language educators might espouse, and these mainly focus on working conditions and self-image. In any case, on the other hand, neither domain can do more than indicate potential suggestions to the individual who is engaged in developing a philosophy of S/FL teaching; in the final analysis, the work has to be done by that person's own, individual and collaborative, reflection.

Discussion questions

1. Have you ever been asked to consider the kind of broad aims that are reviewed in the first part of this chapter as something that is within your own sphere of action? If so, when? If not, why not? Is it "realistic" to do so? If it is not, is it in any way nevertheless useful?

2. Compare Wringe's lines on compromise with Benjamin's position from the previous chapter.

3. Is having the aim of making your students happy a good aim? How about making them "better-off," or even wealthy, then? (Give details.)

4. Can language teaching be seen in terms of fostering civic duty? (Explain.)

5. Can you encapsulate part (or all) of your philosophy of language teaching as a "teaching perspective" like those identified by Goodman in his student teachers? If so, how would you phrase yours ("Teaching as a. . . . ")?

6. What aims would you specify in your philosophy of language teaching?

7. Besides aims, what other elements or headings would you include in your philosophy of language teaching?

8. What is your philosophy of teaching?

Notes to Chapter 11

[1] A common case for ESL teachers, as the TESOL organization has noted. See also Crookes & Arakaki (1999) on working conditions.

2   Most philosophers of education are and have been teachers. A crucial distinction between them and more ordinary classroom teachers is their conditions of work: highly favorable, with a *requirement* to reflect, rather than attempting to reflect in just a few minutes in an otherwise extremely pressured day. So although the voice of philosophers of education tends to be couched somewhat abstractly, and perhaps indicates their conditions of privilege, nevertheless these people are teachers, too.

3   This line of work also benefits from the highly systematizing German tradition in philosophy of education (Brezinka, 1997).

4   He alludes to the well-known book by the philosopher Whitehead (1929), but points out that this is a set of essays, only one of which treats educational aims. The same could be said of a work that White did not mention, Hollins (1964). And even later, introducing a related work, Marples (1999: x) comments that "there is surprisingly little in book form specifically concerned with the aims of education."

5   It thus goes broader than we, as language teachers, need to go. And if readers might be wondering how there could be such a difference of opinion on this point, I think it stems from Noddings's view of happiness as (a) related to the good life rather than a momentary state; and (b) informed by recent psychological research; whereas Wringe is thinking of it rather narrowly and in an older philosophical perspective, that of the utilitarians, as mentioned.

6   A much earlier and less sophisticated iteration of this perspective was the "life adjustment" curriculum of the 1950s in the United States (e.g., Kliebard, 2004).

7   Though we should be warned that "conspicuously successful moral educators have sometimes ended up drinking hemlock, or swinging from a cross" (Wringe, 1988: 80).

8   "Democracy is . . . the ultimate dispersal of political power: each citizen, as Rousseau argued, has a 1/n share of 'sovereign authority,' where n is the total number of citizens [and this suggests] . . . the equality of citizens" (Walzer, 2004: 22).

9   Ancient Greek and Latin here come to mind.

10   They note that this choice reflected a "compromise solution" intended to "allow an interviewer to promote, in non-leading ways, teacher talk on as many constructs and links among constructs as would ensure full disclosure of a practical theory. . . . These questions usually took the form: 'Do . . . (e.g., strategies, teacher-student relationships, teacher skills, etc.) feature in your use of a CLT approach?'" (pp. 295–6). They addressed "fifteen foci": "aims, assumptions (beliefs, values, principles), strategies, teacher role, student role, teacher–student relationship, student behaviour norms, teaching skills, teacher attributes, special resources, principles of teacher reaction, instructional effects, nurturant effects, metaphors and images" (p. 297).

11   That is to say, I would like them to include "aims"; but by and large we do not have the empirical evidence to tell us directly if they do or not. The work reviewed here may provide some indications, though if it indicates that teachers do not state aims when asked about their personal practical knowledge, this does not eliminate the possibility that language teachers do have such aims. Or, it may very well be that they do in fact not articulate their work in those terms when asked questions about what appear to them to be different matters. If they do not articulate their work in those terms, this does not mean they could not, if given some encouragement and resources by which to so conceptualize it.

12   Nevertheless, the authors regard the study as a pilot study and recognize various limitations.

13 "Even when diversity in teaching is explicitly recognized the most common response is to formulate it in terms of a contrast between two types" (Hammersley, 1977: 15).

14 The term is unfortunately broad. Many studies, which concern themselves with the views of teachers on a variety of topics, also use the term (e.g., Kilgore, Ross, & Zbikowski, 1990) in a related manner without adumbrating philosophies of teaching.

12　A concluding comment

In a previous shorter discussion (Crookes, 2003: 45–64) of the main topic of this book, I closed by drawing on the words of a famous specialist in adult education, Brookfield:

> [A teaching] philosophy [cannot] be exemplified to its fullest degree in every educational encounter.... Such an insistence would be so intimidating to practitioners as to prevent *any* attempt to implement a philosophy. We should regard this rationale as a variable that can be realized to a greater or lesser extent at different times, in different settings, with different groups.
>
> (1986: 288)

I naturally agreed with his view that "a clear rationale" for one's teaching was necessary (and I still do), and with his description of that entity as one's philosophy of teaching. I also thought then, and still do, that we are sensible not to be too hard on ourselves if we cannot implement our principles all the time. Brookfield continues:

> Nonetheless, it is vital that a clear rationale be articulated so that practitioners may have a benchmark for judging the extent to which their activities exemplify fundamental purposes, principles, and practice. Without a clear rationale (even if full implementation is not always possible), practice will be condemned to an adaptive, reactive mode.
>
> (ibid.)

I recently encountered the work of another philosopher of education, Covaleskie, who is less sanguine than Brookfield. His pessimistic, or should we say realistic, view is in line with my continuing concern that the working conditions of language teachers, and the kind of self-concept they are encouraged to have in too many institutions, do not allow for them to manifest the highest degree of educational practice and action that might be possible. It is not always the case, he says,

> that teachers teach according to their beliefs. Far too often, teachers' practice is shaped by *other people's* beliefs about the world, humanity, value, and knowledge. These beliefs are embodied

in curriculum design and/or textbook content given to teachers. Teaching is an activity-oriented profession, where the ability to deal with problems of practice swiftly is highly valued; "too philosophical" is a condemnation. . . . This often leads to an instruction that is based in technique rather than in philosophy, technique that is . . . the reflection of someone else's philosophy, not the teacher's.

(Covaleskie, 2004: 327)

So by all means, let us reflect, and articulate a rationale. Though let us carefully scrutinize the initial sets of ideas we call our philosophy of teaching for what is missing, and above all for what we have accepted, perhaps unconsciously, without asking where it came from and what baggage it brings along with it. That done, let us identify our aims and set course. Let us also recognize when it is time to compromise, if necessary; to keep our heads down, if we must. But at the same time, let us keep our powder dry, and our teaching philosophy developed. Can we really know what we should be doing without one?

References

AAUW (American Association of University Women). 1995. *How schools short-change girls*. New York: Marlowe.

Adams, J. N. 2003. *Bilingualism and the Latin language*. Cambridge: Cambridge University Press.

Adler, S. 1984. A field study of selected student teacher perspectives toward social studies. *Theory and Research in Social Education*, 12, 13–30.

Agger, B. 1989. *Fast capitalism*. Urbana, IL: University of Illinois Press.

Alexander, R. 2000. *Culture and pedagogy: International comparisons in primary education*. London: Blackwell.

Alexander, R. J., Broadfoot, P., and Phillips, D. (eds.). 1999. *Learning from comparing: New directions in comparative educational research*. Oxford: Symposium Books.

Alitto, G. S. 1986. *The last Confucian: Liang Shu-ming and the Chinese dilemma of modernity* (2nd ed.). Berkeley, CA: University of California Press.

Anderson, B. C. 2003. The antipolitical philosophy of John Rawls. *Public Interest*, 151, 39–51.

Anderson, C. 2006. *The long tail*. New York: Hyperion.

Anderson-Levitt, K. 2002. *Teaching cultures: Knowledge for teaching first grade in France and the United States*. Cresskill, NJ: Hampton Press.

Anon. 1969. The first universities: Takshashila and Nalanda. *Convergence [UNESCO]*, 2(3), 80–83.

Anthony, E. M. 1963. Approach, method and technique. *English Language Teaching*, 17, 63–7.

Appleton, M. 2000. *A free range childhood: Self regulation at Summerhill School*. Brandon, VT: Foundation for Educational Renewal.

Ashton-Warner, S. 1963. *Teacher*. New York: Simon and Schuster.

Auerbach, E. R. and Wallerstein, N. 1987. *ESL for action: Problem-posing at work* (Students' book and Teachers' book). Reading, MA: Addison-Wesley.

Avrich, P. 1980. *The Modern School movement*. Princeton, NJ: Princeton University Press.

Ayers, W. 1988. Fact or fancy: The knowledge base quest in teacher education. *Journal of Teacher Education*, 39(5), 24–29.

BAAL. 1994. *Recommendations on good practice in Applied Linguistics*. Lancaster: British Association for Applied Linguistics. (Retrieved August 13, 2003, from www.baal.org.uk/goodprac.htm)

Bacon, F. 1625/1985. *The essayes or counsels, civill and morall* (ed. M. Kiernan). Cambridge, MA: Harvard University Press.

Baker, K. 1976. *Condorcet: Selected writings*. Indianapolis: Bobbs-Merrill.

References

Bakhtin, M. M. 1935/1981. Discourse in the novel. In M. Holquist (ed.), *The dialogic imagination* (pp. 259–422). Austin, TX: University of Texas Press.

Barnes, G. A. 1989. Why Norwegians speak English – well. *TESOL Newsletter*, 23(1), 7–9.

Basedow, J. B. (1770–72/1909). *Das Elementarwerk* (ed. T. Frizsch). Dessau: Weigand.

Basile, C. G. 2004. *A good little school*. Albany, NY: State University of New York Press.

Battistoni, R. M. 1985. *Public schooling and the education of democratic citizens*. Jackson, MO: University Press of Missouri.

Baumeister, R. F. 1991. *Meanings of life*. New York: Guilford Press.

Becher, T. 1989. *Academic tribes and territories: Intellectual enquiry and the cultures of disciplines*. Milton Keynes: Open University Press.

Beck, L. G. and Murphy, J. 1994. *Ethics in educational leadership programs: An expanding role*. Thousand Oaks, CA: Sage/Corwin Press.

Beck, R. N. 1979. *Handbook in social philosophy*. New York: Macmillan.

Becker, H. S., Geer, B., Hughes, E. C., and Strauss, A. 1961. *Boys in white: Student culture in medical school*. Chicago, IL: University of Chicago Press.

Becker, H. S., Geer, B., Hughes, E. C., and Strauss, A. 1969. *Making the grade*. London: John Wiley.

Beijaard, D., Verloop, N., and Vermunt, J. D. 2000. Teachers' perceptions of professional identity: An exploratory study from a personal knowledge perspective. *Teaching and Teacher Education*, 16, 749–64.

Benjamin, M. 1990. *Splitting the difference: Compromise and integrity in ethics and politics*. Lawrence, KS: University Press of Kansas.

Bennett, W. and Hokenstad, M. C. 1973. Full-time people workers and conceptions of the professional. In P. Halmos (ed.), *Professionalisation and social change* (pp. 21–45). Keele, UK: University of Keele Press.

Benson, P. and Voller, P. (eds.). 1997. *Autonomy and independence in language learning*. New York: Longman.

Bentham, J. 1789/1961. *An introduction to the principles of morals and legislation*. Garden City, NJ: Doubleday.

Biesta, G. 2001. How can philosophy of education be critical? In F. Heyting, D. Lenzen, and J. White (eds.), *Methods in philosophy of education* (pp. 125–43). London: Routledge.

Biggs, J. B. 1996. Learning, schooling, and socialization: A Chinese solution to a Western problem. In L. Sing (ed.), *Growing up the Chinese way: Chinese child and adolescent development* (pp. 147–67). Hong Kong: Chinese University of Hong Kong.

Black, S. 1993. From whole to part. *The Executive Educator*, 15(10), 35–8.

Block, D. 2005. Convergence and resistance in the construction of personal and professional identities: Four French modern language teachers in London. In A. S. Canagarajah (ed.), *Reclaiming the local in language policy and practice* (pp. 167–96). Mahwah, NJ: Erlbaum.

Block, D. and Cameron, D. (eds.). 2002. *Globalization and language teaching*. London: Routledge.

Blum, L. 1980. *Friendship, altruism and morality*. Boston, MA: Routledge.

Blum, L. 1991. Moral perception and ethicality. *Ethics*, 101, 701–25.

Blum, L. 1994. *Moral perception and particularity*. Cambridge: Cambridge University Press.

Board of Education [England]. 1931. *Report of the Consultative Committee on the Primary School*. London: His Majesty's Stationery Office [HMSO].

Borg, S. 2003. Teacher cognition in language teaching: A review of research on what language teachers think, know, believe, and do. *Language Teaching*, 36, 81–109.

Borko, H., Cone, R., Russo, N. A., and Shavelson, R. J. 1979. In P. L. Peterson and H. J. Walberg (eds.), *Research on teaching* (pp. 136–60). Berkeley, CA: McCutchan.

Bowen, J. 1972. *A history of Western education* (vols. 1 & 2). London: Methuen.

Bowen, J. 1981. *A history of Western education* (vol. 3). London: Methuen.

Bowles, S. and Gintis, H. 1976. *Schooling in capitalist America*. New York: Basic Books.

Breen, M. P. 1991. Understanding the language teacher. In R. Phillipson, E. Kellerman, L. Selinker, M. Sharwood Smith, and M. Swain (eds.), *Foreign/Second Language Pedagogy Research* (pp. 213–33). Clevedon, UK: Multilingual Matters.

Breen, M. P., Hird, B., Oliver, R., and Thwaite, A. 2001. Making sense of language teaching: Teachers' principles and classroom practices. *Applied Linguistics*, 22, 470–501.

Brezinka, W. 1997. *Educational aims, educational means, educational success: Contributions to a science of education* (trans. J. S. Brice). Aldershot, UK: Avebury.

Broadfoot, P., Osborn, M., Planel, C., and Sharpe, K. 2000. *Promoting quality in education: Does England have the answer?* London: Cassell.

Brookfield, S. 1986. *Understanding and facilitating adult learning: A comprehensive analysis of principles and effective practices*. San Francisco, CA: Jossey-Bass.

Brown, R. W. 1973. *A first language: The early stages*. Cambridge, MA: Harvard University Press.

Brumfit, C. J. 1982. Some humanistic doubts about humanistic language teaching. In P. Early (ed.), *Humanistic approaches: An empirical view* (ELT Documents, 113, pp. 11–19). London: British Council.

Brumfit, C. 2001. *Individual freedom in language teaching*. Oxford: Oxford University Press.

Bull, B. L., Fruehling, R. T., and Chattergy, V. 1992. *The ethics of multicultural and bilingual education*. New York: Teachers College Press.

Bullough, R. V. and Knowles, J. G. 1991. Becoming a teacher: Struggles of a second-career beginning teacher. *Qualitative Studies in Education*, 3(2), 101–12.

Bullough, R. V., Knowles, J. G., and Crow, N. A. 1992. *Emerging as a teacher*. London: Routledge.

Burbules, N. C. and Densmore, K. 1991. The limits of making teaching a profession. *Educational Policy*, 5, 44–63.

Burns, A. 1996. Starting all over again. In D. Freeman and J. C. Richards (eds.), *Teacher learning in language teaching* (pp. 11–29). Cambridge: Cambridge University Press.

Burt, M., Dulay, H., and Krashen, S. 1982. *Language two*. New York: Oxford University Press.

References

Bushnell, M. 2003. Teachers in the schoolhouse panopticon: Complicity and resistance. *Education and Urban Society*, 35(3), 251–72.

Butler, Y. G. 2005. Comparative perspectives towards communicative activities among elementary school teachers in Korea, Japan and Taiwan. *Language Teaching Research*, 9(4), 423–47.

Buzzelli, C. A. and Johnston, B. 2002. *The moral dimensions of teaching: Language, power, and culture in classroom interaction*. London: RoutledgeFalmer.

Calderhead, J. 1988. The development of knowledge structures in learning to teach. In J. Calderhead (ed.), *Teachers' professional learning* (pp. 51–64). London: Falmer Press.

Calderhead, J. and Robson, M. 1991. Images of teaching: Student teachers' early conceptions of classroom practice. *Teaching and Teacher Education*, 7(1), 1–8.

Callan, E. 2000. Discrimination and religious schooling. In W. Kymlicka and W. Norman (eds.), *Citizenship in diverse societies*. Oxford: Oxford University Press.

Callan, E. and White, J. 1998. Liberalism and communitarianism. In N. Blake et al. (eds.), *The Blackwell guide to philosophy of education* (pp. 95–109). Oxford, UK: Blackwell.

Callan, E. and White, J. 2003. Liberalism and communitarianism. In N. Blake et al. (eds.), *The Blackwell guide to the philosophy of education*, Oxford: Blackwell.

Canagarajah, A. S. 2002. *A geopolitics of academic writing*. Pittsburgh, PA: University of Pittsburgh Press.

Candlin, C. N. 1984. Syllabus design as a critical process. In C. J. Brumfit (ed.), *General English syllabus design* (ELT Documents 118; pp. 29–46). Oxford: Pergamon and the British Council.

Canguilhem, G. 1988. *Ideology and rationality in the history of the life sciences*. Cambridge, MA: MIT Press.

Carr, D. 2000. *Professionalism and ethics in teaching*. London: Routledge.

Carr-Saunders, A. M. 1928. *Professions: Their organization and place in society*. Oxford: Clarendon Press.

Carson, C. J. 1993. Attacking a legacy of sexist grammar in the French class: A modest beginning. *Feminist Teacher*, 7(2), 34–6.

Carter, K. 1990. Teachers' knowledge and learning to teach. In W. R. Houston (ed.), *Handbook of research on teacher education* (pp. 291–310). New York: Macmillan.

Carter, K. and Doyle, W. 1987. Teachers' knowledge structures and comprehension processes. In J. Calderhead (ed.), *Exploring teachers' thinking* (pp. 147–60). London: Cassell.

Chadwick, R. F. (ed.). 1994. *Ethics and the professions*. Aldershot, UK: Avebury.

Cherryholmes, C. H. 1999. *Reading pragmatism*. New York: Teachers College Press.

Clandinin, D. J. 1986. *Classroom practice: Teacher images in action*. London: Falmer Press.

Clandinin, D. J. and Connelly, F. M. 1984. *Teachers' personal practical knowledge: Image and narrative unity*. Working paper. Toronto: OISE.

Clark, C. M. and Peterson, P. L. 1986. Teachers' thought processes. In M. C. Wittrock (ed.), *Handbook of research on teaching* (3rd ed.; pp. 255–96). New York: Macmillan.

Clark, J. L. 1987. *Curriculum renewal in school foreign language learning.* Oxford: Oxford University Press.

Clarke, P. 2003. Culture and classroom reform: The case of the District Primary Education Project, India. *Comparative Education,* 39(1), 27–44.

Cleverley, J. 1985. *The schooling of China: Tradition and modernity in Chinese education.* Boston: Allen & Unwin.

Cleverley, J. 1991. *The schooling of China* (2nd ed.). Sydney: Allen & Unwin.

Cochran-Smith, M. and Lytle, S. L. 1999. Relationships of knowledge and practice: Teacher learning in communities. In A. Iran-Nejad and P. D. Pearson (eds.), *Review of Research in Education,* 24, 249–305. Washington, DC: American Educational Research Assocn.

Comenius, J. A. 1657. *Didactica magna.* In M. W. Keatinge (trans., ed.), 1907–1910. *The great didactic of John Amos Comenius* (vols. 1 & 2). London: Adam & Chas. Black.

Condorcet, J.-A.-N. de C. 1791/1993. *Cinq memoires de l'instruction publique.* Paris: Flammarion.

Connelly, F. M. and Clandinin, D. J. 1984. Personal practical knowledge at Bay Street School: Ritual, personal philosophy and image. In R. Halkes and J. K. Olson (eds.), *Teacher thinking: A new perspective on persisting problems in education* (pp. 134–48). Lisse: Swets and Zeitlinger.

Connelly, F. M. and Clandinin, D. J. 1985. Personal practical knowledge and the modes of knowing. In E. Eisner (ed.), *Learning and teaching the ways of knowing* (part II, pp. 174–98). Chicago, IL: University of Chicago Press.

Cooper, P. and McIntyre, D. 1996. *Effective teaching and learning: Teachers' and students' perspectives.* Buckingham, UK: Open University Press.

Counts, G. S. 1932. *Dare the school build a new social order?* New York: The John Day Company.

Courtenay, W. J. 1987. *Schools and scholars in fourteenth-century England.* Princeton, NJ: Princeton University Press.

Covaleskie, J. F. 2004. Philosophical instruction. In J. L. Kincheloe and D. Weil (eds.), *Critical thinking and learning: An encyclopedia for parents and teachers* (pp. 325–8). Westport, CT: Greenwood Press.

Crawford, L. M. 1978. *Paulo Freire's philosophy: Derivation of curricular principles and their application to second language curriculum design.* PhD dissertation, University of Minnesota.

Crawford-Lange, L. M. 1981. Redirecting foreign language curricula: Paulo Freire's contribution. *Foreign Language Annals,* 14, 257–73.

Crawford-Lange, L. M. 1982. Curricular alternatives for second language learning. In T. V. Higgs (ed.), *Curriculum, competence, and the foreign language teacher* (pp. 81–113). Skokie, IL: National Textbook Co. Reprinted in J. C. Richards and M. H. Long (eds.), *Readings in TESOL* (pp. 120–44). Rowley, MA: Newbury House.

Crittenden, B. 1984. The moral context of decision-making in education. In P. A. Sola (ed.), *Ethics, values, and administrative decisions* (pp. 15–38). New York: Peter Lang.

Crookes, G. 1997. SLA and teachers: A socio-educational perspective. *Studies in Second Language Acquisition,* 19, 93–116.

Crookes, G. 1998. On the relationship between S/FL teachers and S/FL research. *TESOL Journal,* 7(3), 6–10.

Crookes, G. 2003. *A practicum in TESOL.* Cambridge: Cambridge University Press.

Crookes, G. and Arakaki, L. 1999. Teaching idea sources and work conditions in an ESL program. *TESOL Journal,* 8(1), 15–19.

Crookes, G. and Talmy, S. 2004. Second/Foreign Language program preservation and advancement: Literatures and lessons for teachers and teacher education. *Critical Inquiry in Language Studies,* 1(4), 219–36.

Curran, C. A. 1961. Counseling skills adapted to the learning of foreign languages. *Bulletin of the Menninger Clinic,* 25(2), 78–93.

Curtis, A. and Romney, M. (eds.). 2006. *Color, race, and English Language Teaching.* Mahwah, NJ: Lawrence Erlbaum.

Dam, L. 1995. *Learner autonomy 3: From theory to classroom practice.* Dublin: Authentik Language Learning Resources.

Dam, L. (ed.). 2001. Learner Autonomy: New Insights. *AILA Review,* 15.

Davies, A. 1999. *An introduction to applied linguistics.* Edinburgh: Edinburgh University Press.

De Bary, W. T. and Chaffee, J. W. (eds.). 1989. *Neo-Confucian education: The formative stage.* Berkeley, CA: University of California Press.

De Lano, L., Riley, L., and Crookes, G. 1994. The meaning of innovation for ESL teachers. *System,* (22)4, 487–96.

de los Reyes, E. and Gozemba, P. 2002. *Pockets of hope.* Westport, CT: Bergin & Garvey.

de Staël, A. L. G. 1801. *De la littérature considérée dans ses rapports avec les institutions sociales* (2nd ed.). Paris: Maradan.

Deacon, R. A. 2003. *Fabricating Foucault: Rationalising the management of individuals.* Milwaukee, IN: Marquette University Press.

DeCarvalho, R. J. 1991. *The founders of humanistic psychology.* New York: Praeger.

Delacroix, H. 1925. *La langue et la pensée.* Paris. Félix Alcan.

Demiashkevich, M. J. 1935. *An introduction to the philosophy of education.* New York: American Book Company.

Dempster, N., Carter, L., Freakley, M., and Parry, L. 2004. Contextual influences on school leaders in Australia: Some data from a recent study of principals' ethical decision-making. *School Leadership and Management,* 24(2), 163–74.

Depaepe, M. 1998. *De pedagogisering achterna.* Leuven/Amersfoort: Acco.

Descartes, R. 1640/1998. *Meditations and other metaphysical writings* (trans. D. M. Clarke). London: Penguin.

Dewey, J. 1910. *How we think.* Boston, MA: D. C. Heath.

Dewey, J. 1916/1961. *Democracy and education.* New York: Macmillan.

Dewey, J. and Dewey, E. 1915. *Schools of to-morrow.* New York: E. P. Dutton & Company.

Dharampal. 1983. *The beautiful tree.* New Delhi: Biblia Impex Private Ltd.

Digiovanni, L. W. and Liston, D. D. 2005. Feminist pedagogy in the elementary classroom: An agenda for practice. *Feminist Teacher,* 15(2), 123–31.

Dill, D. D. and assocs. 1990. *What teachers need to know.* San Francisco, CA: Jossey-Bass.

Donmoyer, R. 1996. The concept of a knowledge base. In F. B. Murray (ed.), *The teacher educator's handbook* (pp. 92–119). San Francisco, CA: Jossey-Bass.

Donnelly, J. 1998. *International human rights* (2nd ed.). Boulder, CO: Westview Press.

Dove, L. 1986. *Teachers and teacher education in developing countries*. London: Croom Helm.

Dubray, C. A. 1909. Epistemology. In C. G. Herbermann et al. (eds.), *Catholic Encyclopedia* (pp. 506–509). New York: The Encyclopedia Press.

Duff, P. A. and Polio, C. G. 1990. How much foreign language is there in the foreign language classroom? *Modern Language Journal*, 74(2), 154–66.

Duncan, K. and Stasio, M. 2005. Surveying feminist pedagogy: A measurement, an evaluation, and an affirmation. *Feminist Teacher*, 13(3), 225–38.

Dupuis, A. M. 1966. *Philosophy of education in historical perspective*. Chicago, IL: Rand McNally.

Durant, W. 1944. *Caesar and Christ*. New York: Simon & Schuster.

Edelsky, C. 2005. Relatively speaking: McCarthyism and teacher resisters. In L. Poynor and P. M. Wolfe (eds.). *Marketing fear in America's public schools: The real war on literacy* (pp. 11–28). Mahwah, NJ: L. Erlbaum Associates.

Edelsky, C. and Johnson, K. 2004. Critical whole language in time and place. *Critical Inquiry in Language Studies*, 1(3), 121–41.

Edge, J. 1996. Cross-cultural paradoxes in a profession of values. *TESOL Quarterly*, 30(1), 9–30.

Ehrenspeck, Y. and Lenzen, D. 2001. On the structuralist philosophy of education. In F. Heyting, D. Lenzen, and J. White (eds.), *Methods in philosophy of education* (pp. 88–107). London: Routledge.

Eklof, B. 1986. *Russian peasant schools*. Berkeley, CA: University of California Press.

Elbaz, F. 1983. *Teacher thinking: A study of practical knowledge*. London: Croom Helm.

Ellsworth, E. 1989. Why doesn't this feel empowering? Working through the repressive myths of feminist pedagogy. *Harvard Educational Review*, 59(3), 297–324. Reprinted in L. Stone (ed.), 1994. *The Education Feminism Reader* (pp. 300–328). New York: Routledge.

Emerson, R. 1962. Power-dependent relations. *American Sociological Review*, 27, 31–41.

Eraut, M. 1994. Knowledge creation and knowledge use in professional contexts. *Studies in Higher Education*, 10, 117–32.

Etzioni, A. (ed.). 1969. *The semi-professionals and their organization: Teachers, nurses, and social workers*. New York: Free Press.

Fagan, A. 2005. Human rights. In *The Internet encyclopedia of philosophy*. (Retrieved May 27, 2007, from www.iep.utm.edu/h/hum-rts.htm)

Feinberg, W. 1995. The discourse of philosophy of education. In W. Kohl (ed.), *Critical conversations in philosophy of education* (pp. 24–33). London: Routledge.

Fenstermacher, G. D. 1994. The knower and the known: The nature of knowledge in research on teaching. *Review of Research in Education*, 20, 3–56.

Fenstermacher, G. D. and Richardson, V. 1993. The elicitation and construction of practical arguments in teaching. *Journal of Curriculum Studies*, 25, 101–114.

References

Fernandes, L. 1985. Basic ecclesiastic communities in Brazil. *Harvard Educational Review,* 55(1), 76–85.

Ferrer, F. 1913. *The origins and ideas of the Modern School.* London: Watts.

Ferrier, J. F. 1854. *Institutes of metaphysics: The theory of knowing and being.* London: Blackwood.

Fichte, J. 1808/1979. *Addresses to the German Nation* (trans. R. F. Jones and G. H. Turnbull). Westport, CT: Greenwood Press.

Fink, H. 1981. *Social philosophy.* London: Methuen.

Fitzpatrick, E. A. (ed.). 1933. *St. Ignatius and the Ratio Studiorum.* New York: McGraw-Hill.

Flathman, R. E. 1973. *Concepts in social and political philosophy.* New York: Macmillan.

Flew, A. 1984. *A dictionary of philosophy.* London: Macmillan.

Flexner, A. 1915. Is social work a profession? In *Proceedings of the National Conference of Charities and Correction* (pp. 576–90). Chicago, IL: Hildman Publishing.

Ford, M. P. 2002. *Beyond the modern university.* Westport, CN: Praeger.

Formigart, L. 2004. *A history of language philosophy.* Amsterdam: John Benjamins.

Foucault, M. 1970/1993. The order of discourse/*Die Ordnung des Diskurses* (2nd ed.) Fischer: Frankfurt.

Foucault, M. 1978. *The history of sexuality* (vol. 1). New York: Pantheon Books.

Foucault, M. 1979. *Discipline and punish: The birth of the prison* (trans. A. Sheridan). New York: Vintage Books.

Foucault, M. 1980. *Power/knowledge: Selected interviews and other writings, 1972–1977.* New York: Pantheon.

Foucault, M. 1987. The ethic of care for the self as a practice of freedom – An interview with Michel Foucault. *Philosophy and Social Criticism,* 12(2/3), 112–31.

Foucault, M. 1988. Technologies of the self. In L. H. Martin, H. Gutman, and P. H. Hutton (eds.), *A seminar with Michel Foucault* (pp. 16–49). London: Tavistock Press/Amherst, MA: University of Massachusetts Press.

Freeman, D. and Johnson, K. E. 1998. Reconceptualizing the knowledge-based of language teacher education. *TESOL Quarterly,* 32(3), 397–416.

Freeman, S. J. and Francis, P. C. 2006. Casuistry: A complement to principle ethics and a foundation for ethical decisions. *Counseling and Values,* 50, 142–53.

Freidson, E. 1970. *The profession of medicine.* New York: Harper & Row.

Freidson, E. 2001. *Professionalism: The third logic.* Chicago: University of Chicago Press.

Freire, P. 1967/1974. Education: The practice of freedom. Originally published in 1967 as *Educação ecomo práctica de liberdade.* Rio de Janeiro: Paz e Terra. Published in English in 1974 as part of *Education for critical consciousness* (pp. 3–77). London: Sheed & Ward.

Freire, P. 1971. A few notions about the word conscientization. *Hard Cheese,* 1, 23–28.

Fuller, B., Snyder, C. W., Chapman, D., and Hua, H. 1994. Explaining variation in teaching practices: Effects of state policy, teacher background and curricula in southern Africa. *Teaching and Teacher Education,* 10(2), 141–56.

Gadamer, H.-G. 1960/1975. *Truth and Method*. New York: Crossroad.

Gallego, M. A., Cole, M., and the Laboratory of Human Cognition. 2001. Classroom cultures and culture in the classroom. In V. Richardson (ed.), *Handbook of research on teaching* (4th ed., pp. 951–77). Washington, DC: American Educational Research Association.

Galluzzo, G. R. 1999. Consensus and the knowledge base for teaching and teacher education. In J. D. Raths and A. C. McAninch (eds.), *What counts as knowledge in teacher education?* (pp. 69–84). Stamford, CT: Ablex.

Galyean, B. 1976a. *Human teaching and human learning in the language class: A confluent approach*. Santa Barbara, CA: CEDARC. ERIC Document ED 131729.

Galyean, B. 1976b. *Language from within: A handbook of teaching strategies for personal growth and self-reflection in the language class*. Santa Barbara, CA: CEDARC. ERIC Document ED 131730.

Galyean, B. 1977. A confluent design for language teaching. *TESOL Quarterly*, 11(2), 143–56.

Galyean, B. 1979. A confluent approach to curriculum design. *Foreign Language Annals*, 12(2), 121–7.

Gardner, P. 1984. *The lost elementary schools of Victorian England*. London: Croom Helm.

Genishi, C., Ryan, S., Ochsner, M., and Yarnall, M. M. 2001. Teaching in early childhood education. In V. Richardson (ed.), *Handbook of research on teaching* (4th ed., pp. 1175–1210). Washington, DC: American Educational Research Association.

Gewirth, A. 1994. The moral basis of liberal education. *Studies in Philosophy and Education*, 13, 111–24.

Gibson, R. 1976. The effects of school practice: The development of student perspectives. *British Journal of Teacher Education, 2*, 241–50.

Gilroy, P. 1999. The aims of education and the philosophy of education: The pathology of an argument. In R. Marples (ed.), *The aims of education* (pp. 23–34). London: Routledge.

Gimmler, A. 2004. Pragmatic aspects of Hegel's thought. In W. Egginton and M. Sandbothe (eds.), *The pragmatic turn in philosophy* (pp. 47–66). Albany, NY: SUNY Press.

Ginsburg, M. B. 1988. Ideologically informed conceptions of professionalism. Chapter 5 of M. B. Ginsburg, *Contradictions in teacher education and society* (pp. 129–64). New York: Falmer Press.

Giroux, H. A. 1983. *Theory and resistance in education*. South Hadley, MA: Bergin and Garvey.

Giroux, H. A. 2001. *Theory and resistance in education* (2nd ed.). Westport, CT: Bergin and Garvey.

Glassner, J.-J. 2003. *The invention of cuneiform: Writing in Sumer*. Baltimore, MD: Johns Hopkins Press.

Glendenning, S. 1999. Introduction. In S. Glendenning (ed.), *Edinburgh Encyclopedia of Continental Philosophy*. Edinburgh: Edinburgh University Press.

Godwin, W. 1793a/1976. *Enquiry concerning political justice, and its influence on modern morals and happiness* (3rd ed.). Harmondsworth, UK: Penguin.

Godwin, W. 1793b/1966. *Four early pamphlets*. Gainesville, FL: Scholars Reproduction Press.

References

Godwin, W. 1797/1964. *The enquirer: Reflections on education, manners and literature in a series of essays* (facsimile edition). New York: Augustus M. Kelley.

Golombek, P. R. 1998. A study of language teachers' personal practical knowledge. *TESOL Quarterly*, 32(3), 447–64.

Gomez, M. L., Walker, A. B., and Page, M. L. 2000. Personal experience as a guide to teaching. *Teaching and Teacher Education*, 16, 731–47.

Goodman, J. 1988. Constructing a practical philosophy of teaching: A study of preservice teachers' professional perspectives. *Teaching & Teacher Education*, 4(2), 121–37.

Goodman, K. 1967. Reading: A psycholinguistic guessing game. *Journal of the Reading Specialist*, 6(1), 126–35.

Goodman, P. 1956. *Growing up absurd*. New York: Vintage.

Goodman, P. 1962. *Compulsory miseducation and the community of scholars*. New York: Vintage.

Goodman, P. 1968. Mini-schools: A prescription for the reading problem. *New York Review of Books* (January 4). Reprinted in I. Lister (ed.), 1974. Deschooling: A reader (pp. 34–6). Cambridge University Press.

Gordon, P. and White, J. 1979. *Philosophers as educational reformers: The influence of idealism on British educational thought and practice*. London: Routledge and Kegan Paul.

Gore, J. 1998. On the limits to empowerment through critical and feminist pedagogies. In D. Carlson and M. Apple (eds.), *Power/Knowledge/Pedagogy* (pp. 271–88). Boulder, CO: Westview Press.

Gorlin, R. A. (ed.). 1994. *Codes of professional responsibility* (3rd ed.) Washington, DC: Bureau of National Affairs.

Gorsuch, G. 1998. *Yakudoku* EFL instruction in two Japanese high school classrooms: An exploratory study. *JALT Journal*, 20(1), 6–32.

Green, A. 1990. *Education and state formation*. London: Macmillan.

Green, A. 1997. *Education, globalization, and the nation state*. New York: St. Martin's Press.

Green, T. F. 1971. *The activities of teaching*. New York: McGraw-Hill.

Green, T. H. 1885/1967. *Lectures on the principles of political obligation*. Ann Arbor, MI: University of Michigan Press.

Greene, M. 1973. *Teacher as stranger: Educational philosophy for the modern age*. Belmont, CA: Wadsworth.

Greene, M. 1995. What counts as philosophy of education? In W. Kohl (ed.). *Critical conversations in philosophy of education* (pp. 3–21). New York: Routledge.

Griffin, J. 2002. Do children have rights? In D. Archard and C. M. MacLeod (eds.), *The moral and political status of children* (pp. 19–30). Oxford: Oxford University Press.

Grimmett, P. P. and MacKinnon, A. M. 1992. Craft knowledge and the education of teachers. *Review of Research in Education*, 18, 385–456.

Grotjahn, R. 1991. The research programme subjective theories. *Studies in Second Language Acquisition*, 13, 187–214.

Hafernik, J. J., Messerschmitt, D. S., and Vandrick, S. 2002. *Ethical issues for ESL faculty: Social justice in practice*. Mahwah, NJ: Lawrence Erlbaum.

Halkes, R. 1986. Teacher thinking: A promising perspective into educational processes (Report of the 1983 and 1985 Conferences of the International

Study Association on Teacher Thinking). *Journal of Curriculum Studies,* 18(2), 211–14.

Hall, D. R. and Hewings, A. 2000. *Innovation in English language teaching: A reader.* London: Routledge.

Halliday, M. A. K. 2002. Michael Halliday. In K. Brown and V. Law (eds.). *Linguistics in Britain: Personal histories* (pp. 116–26). Oxford, UK: Blackwell.

Hammersley, M. 1977. *Teachers' perspectives.* Milton Keynes, UK: Open University Press.

Harpham, G. G. 2002. *Language alone.* New York: Routledge.

Harré, R. 1985. *The philosophies of science.* Oxford: Oxford University Press.

Harrington, H. 1994. Teaching and knowing. *Journal of Teacher Education,* 45, 190–98.

Harris, W. V. 1989. *Ancient literacy.* Cambridge, MA: Harvard University Press.

Hart, H. L. A. 1955. Are there any natural rights? *Philosophical Review,* 64, 175–91.

Harvey, D. 1990. *The condition of postmodernity.* Cambridge, MA: Blackwell.

Hawkesworth, M. 1992. The science of politics and the politics of science. In M. Hawkesworth and M. Kogan (eds.), *Encyclopedia of government and politics* (pp. 5–39). London: Routledge.

Hawkins, E. 1984. *Awareness of language.* Cambridge: Cambridge University Press.

He, Z., Bu, J., Tang, T, and Sun, K. 1991. *An intellectual history of China* (trans. He, Z.). Beijing: Foreign Languages Press.

Heiberger, M. M. and Vick, J. M. 1996. *The academic job search handbook* (2nd ed.). Philadelphia, PA: University of Pennsylvania Press.

Henderson, J. 1988. A curricular response to the knowledge base reform movement. *Journal of Teacher Education,* 39(5), 13–17.

Henderson, S. 1947. *Introduction to philosophy of education.* Chicago: University of Chicago Press.

Herbart, J. F. 1835/1901. *Outlines of educational doctrine* (trans. A. F. Lange). London: Macmillan.

Herrera, L. and Torres, C. A. 2006. *Cultures of Arab schooling: Critical ethnographies from Egypt.* Albany, NY: SUNY Press.

Heslep, R. D. 1997. *Philosophical thinking in educational practice.* Westport, CT: Praeger.

Hildebrand, D. L. 2003. *Beyond realism and antirealism: John Dewey and the neopragmatists.* Nashville, TN: Vanderbilt University Press.

Hino, T. 1988. *Yakudoku*: Japan's dominant tradition in foreign language learning. *JALT Journal,* 10(1 & 2), 45–55.

Hird, B., Thwaite, A., Breen, M., Milton, M., and Oliver, R. 2000. Teaching English as a second language to children and adults: Variations in practices. *Language Teaching Research,* 4(1) 3–32.

Hirst, P. 1974. *Knowledge and the curriculum.* London: Routledge & Kegan Paul.

Hodgkinson, C. 1991. *Educational leadership: The moral art.* Albany, NY: SUNY Press.

Hoffman, J. 2004. *Citizenship beyond the state.* London: Sage.

Hoffman, L. M. 1989. *The politics of knowledge: Activist movements in medicine and planning.* Albany, NY: SUNY Press.

251

References

Holcombe, C. 2001. *The genesis of East Asia, 221 B.C.-A.D. 907*. Honolulu: Association for Asian Studies and University of Hawai'i Press.

Holliday, A. 1994a. *Appropriate methodology and social context*. Cambridge University Press.

Holliday, A. 1994b. Student culture and English language education: An international perspective. *Language, Culture and Curriculum*, 7(2), 125–43.

Holliday, A. 2005. *The struggle to teach English as an international language*. Oxford: Oxford University Press.

Hollins, T. H. B. 1964. *Aims in education: The philosophic approach*. Manchester, UK: Manchester University Press.

Holt, J. 1976. *Instead of education*. New York: Dutton.

Holt-Reynolds, D. 1992. Personal history-based beliefs as relevant prior knowledge in course work. *American Educational Research Journal*, 29(2), 225–49.

Holzner, B. 1968. *Reality construction in society*. Cambridge, MA: Schenkman Pub. Co.

hooks, b. 1989. *Talking back, thinking feminism, thinking black*. Boston, MA: South End Press.

hooks, b. 2000. *Feminism is for everybody*. Cambridge, MA: South End Press.

Howatt, A. P. R. 1984. *A history of English language teaching*. London: Oxford University Press.

Howatt, A. P. R. and Widdowson, H. G. 2004. *A history of English language teaching* (2nd ed.). London: Oxford University Press.

Hughes, E. C. 1958. *Men and their work*. Glencoe: Free Press.

Hume, D. 1739/2000. *A treatise of human nature*. Oxford: Oxford University Press.

Hume, D. 1748/1999. *An enquiry concerning human understanding*. Oxford: Oxford University Press.

Hung, E. 2005. Cultural borderlands in China's translation history. In E. Hung (ed.), *Translation and cultural change* (pp. 43–64). Amsterdam: John Benjamins.

Hutcheon, P. D. 1995. Popper and Kuhn on the evolution of science. *Brock Review*, 4(1/2), 28–37.

Huxley, A. 1946. *Ends and means*. London: Chatto & Windus.

Hyson, M. C. and Lee, K. 1996. Assessing early childhood teachers' beliefs about emotions. *Early Education and Development*, 7(1), 59–67.

Illych, I. 1970. *Deschooling society*. New York: Harper & Row.

Ingersoll, R. M. 2003. *Who controls teachers' work? Power and accountability in America's schools*. Cambridge, MA: Harvard University Press.

Italy's "little Senegal." 2004. BBC report. (Retrieved May 24, 2007, from http://news.bbc.co.uk/1/hi/world/africa/3622953.stm)

Jacotot, J. J. 1830. *Enseignement universel, langue etrangère*. Reprinted in A. P. R. Howatt and R. C. Smith (eds.), 1999, *Foundations of foreign language teaching: Nineteenth-century innovators* (vol. 1). London: Routledge.

Janesick, V. 1977. An ethnographic study of a teacher's classroom perspective. Unpublished PhD diss. Michigan State University.

Janeway, E. 1980. *Powers of the weak*. New York: Knopf.

Jaspers, K. 1953. *The origin and goal of history*. New Haven, CT: Yale University Press.

Jenlink, P. M. 2001. Beyond the knowledge-base controversy: Advancing the ideal of scholar-practitioner leadership. In T. J. Kowalski (ed.), *21st century challenges for school administrators* (pp. 65–88). Lanham, MD: Scarecrow Press.

Jespersen, O. 1904. *How to teach a foreign language.* London: George Allen & Unwin.

Jespersen, O. 1924. *The philosophy of grammar.* London: Allen & Unwin.

Johnson, K. 1998. *Language teaching and skill learning.* London: Blackwell.

Johnston, B. 1997. Do EFL teachers have careers? *TESOL Quarterly,* 31(4), 681–712.

Johnston, B. 1999. The expatriate teacher as postmodern paladin. *Research in the Teaching of English,* 34, 255–280.

Johnston, B. 2003. *Values in English language teaching.* Mahwah, NJ: Lawrence Erlbaum Associates.

Johnston, B. and Varghese, M. M. 2006. Neo-imperialism, evangelism, and ELT: Modernist missions and a postmodern profession. In J. Edge (ed.), *(Re)locating TESOL in an age of empire.* London: Palgrave Macmillan.

Johnston, B., Juhász, A., Marken, J., and Ruiz, B. R. 1998. The ESL teacher as moral agent. *Research in the Teaching of English,* 32, 161–81.

Jones, D. M. 2003. "Women's lib", gender theory, and the politics of home: How I became a black male feminist. *Feminist Teacher,* 13(3), 213–224.

Joyce, B. and Weil, M. 1992. *Models of teaching* (4th ed.). Boston, MA: Allyn & Bacon.

Kagan , D. M. 1992. Professional growth among preservice and beginning teachers. *Review of Educational Research,* 62(2), 129–69.

Kant, I. 1781/1990. *Critique of pure reason* (trans. J. M. D. Meiklejohn). Buffalo, NY: Prometheus Books.

Kant, I. 1788/2002. *Critique of practical reason* (trans. W. S. Pluhar). Cambridge: Hackett Pub. Co.

Kasten, B. J., Wright, J. L., and Kasten, J. A. 1996. Helping preservice teachers construct their own philosophies of teaching through reflection. Paper presented at the Annual Meeting of the National Association of Early Childhood Teacher Educators (Dallas, TX, November 20). ED402072.

Kelly, L. G. 1969. *25 centuries of language teaching: An inquiry into the science, art, and development of language teaching methodology.* Rowley, MA: Newbury House.

Kennedy, C. 1999. *Innovation and best practice.* Longman/British Council.

Kennedy, C., Doyle, P., and Goh, C. 1999. *Exploring change in English language teaching.* Oxford: Macmillan Heinemann.

Kenny, B. and Savage, W. (eds.). 1997. *Language and development: Teachers in a changing world.* New York: Longman.

Kern, R. 2000. *Literacy and language teaching.* Oxford: Oxford University Press.

Kettle, B. and Sellars, N. 1996. The development of student teachers' practical theory of teaching. *Teaching and Teacher Education,* 12(1), 1–24.

Kilgore, K., Ross, D., and Zbikowski, J. 1990. Understanding the teaching perspectives of first-year teachers. *Journal of Teacher Education,* 41(1), 28–38.

Klemperer, V. 1946/2000. *The language of the Third Reich : LTI – Lingua Tertii Imperii: A philologist's notebook* (trans. M. Brady). London: Athlone Press.

References

Kliebard, H. M. 2004. *The struggle for the American curriculum, 1893–1958* (3rd ed.). New York: RoutledgeFalmer.

Kliebard, H. M. 1999. *Schooled to work: Vocationalism and the American curriculum, 1876–1946*. New York: Teachers College Press.

Klinker, J. F. and Hackman, D. G. 2003. An analysis of principals' ethical decision making using Rest's four component model of moral behavior. Paper presented at the Annual Meeting of the American Educational Research Assocn. (April, Chicago, IL). ERIC Document 478255.

Kneller, G. F. 1958. *Existentialism and education*. New York: Philosophical Library.

Knight, G. R. 1982. *Issues and alternatives in educational philosophy*. Berrien Springs, MI: Andrews University Press.

Kobayashi, V. N. 1964. *John Dewey in Japanese educational thought*. Ann Arbor, MI: University of Michigan, School of Education.

Koops, W. 2003. Imaging childhood. In W. Koops and M. Zuckerman (eds.), *Beyond the century of the child* (pp. 1–20). Philadelphia, PA: University of Pennsylvania Press.

Krashen, S. D. and Terrell, T. 1983. *The natural approach*. Pergamon.

Kroeh, C. F. 1887. Methods of teaching modern languages. *Transactions and proceedings of the Modern Language Association of America* 3, 169–85.

Kroksmark, T. 1995. Teaching and teachers' "didaktik". *Studies in Philosophy and Education,* 14, 365–82.

Kropotkin, P. 1899/1974 (ed. C. Ward). *Fields, factories and workshops tomorrow*. London: Allen & Unwin.

Kropotkin, P. 1910. Anarchism. *Encyclopedia Britannica*, 11th ed., vol. 1.

Kubota, R. 1999. Japanese culture constructed by discourses. *TESOL Quarterly,* 33(1), 9–35.

Kubota, R. and Lin, A. (eds.). 2006. *Race and TESOL*. Special issue of *TESOL Quarterly,* 40(3).

Kuhn, T. S. 1962. *The structure of scientific revolutions*. Chicago, IL: University of Chicago Press.

Kumaravadivelu, B. 1994. The postmethod condition: (E)merging strategies for second/foreign language teaching. *TESOL Quarterly,* 28(1), 27–48.

Kumaravadivelu, B. 2003. Critical language pedagogy: A postmethod perspective on English language teaching. *World Englishes,* 22(4), 539–50.

Kymlicka, W. 1989. *Liberalism, community and culture*. Oxford: Oxford University Press.

Kymlicka, W. 2004. Dworkin on freedom and culture. In J. Burley (ed.), *Dworkin and his critics* (pp. 113–33). Oxford: Blackwell.

Laird, S. 1995. Who cares about girls? Rethinking the meaning of teaching. *Peabody Journal of Education,* 70(2), 82–103.

Lamie, J. M. 2004. Presenting a model of change. *Language Teaching Research,* 8(2), 115–42.

Lamie, J. M. 2005. *Evaluating change in English Language Teaching*. London: Palgrave Macmillan.

Lampe, J. R. 1994. Teacher education students' moral development and ethical reasoning processes. Paper presented at the annual meeting of the American Educational Research Association (New Orleans, LA, April 4–8). ED375129.

Lancaster, J. 1803. *Improvements in education as it respects the industrious classes*. London: Darton and Harvey.

Larsen-Freeman, D. 1986. *Techniques and principles in language teaching*. New York: Oxford University Press.

Lasswell, H. 1936. *Politics: Who gets what, when, how*. New York: McGraw Hill.

Lather, P. 1987. The absent presence: Patriarchy, capitalism, and the nature of teacher work. *Teacher Education Quarterly*, 14(2), 25–38; reprinted in L. Stone (ed.), *The Education Feminism Reader* (pp. 242–51). New York: Routledge.

Lave, J. 1988. *Cognition in practice*. Cambridge: Cambridge University Press.

Lawton, D. and Gordon, P. 2002. *A history of Western educational ideas*. London: Woburn Press.

Leach, M. 1991. Mothers of in(ter)vention: Women's writings in philosophy of education. *Educational Theory*, 41(3), 287–300.

Lee, D. 1992. *Competing discourses: Perspective and ideology in language*. London: Longman.

Leinhardt, G. 1988. Situated knowledge and expertise in teaching. In J. Calderhead (ed.), *Teachers' professional learning* (pp. 146–68). London: Falmer Press.

Leinhardt, G. and Greeno, J. G. 1986. The cognitive skill of teaching. *Journal of Educational Psychology*, 78(2), 75–95.

Leinhardt, G., Young, K. M., and Merriman, J. 1995. Integrating professional knowledge: The theory of practice and the practice of theory. *Learning and Instruction*, 5, 401–408.

Levi-Strauss, M. 1963. *Structural anthropology*. New York: Basic Books.

Lewis, M. G. 1998. Foreword. In B. Ropers-Huilman (ed.), *Feminist teaching in theory and practice* (pp. ix–xxi). New York: Teachers College Press.

Lin, A. and Luk, J. 2002. Beyond progressive liberalism and cultural relativism: Towards critical postmodernist, sociohistorically situated perspectives in classroom studies. *Canadian Modern Language Review*, 59(1), 97–124.

Lin, A., Grant, R., Kubota, R., Motha, S., Sachs, G. T., Vandrick, S., and Wong, S. 2004. Women faculty of color in TESOL: Theorizing our lived experiences. *TESOL Quarterly*, 38(3), 487–503.

Lindley, R. 1986. *Autonomy*. London: Macmillan.

Locke, J. 1689–1690/1960. *Two treatises of government*, (ed. P. Laslett). Cambridge: Cambridge University Press.

Locke, J. 1690/1975. *An essay concerning human understanding* (ed. P. H. Nidditch). Oxford: Clarendon Press.

Loughran, J. and Russell, T. 1997. Meeting student teachers on their own terms: Experience precedes understanding. In V. Richardson (ed.), *Constructivist teacher education* (pp. 164–81). London: Falmer Press.

Lovejoy, A. O. 1908. The thirteen pragmatisms. *Journal of Philosophy, Psychology, and Scientific Method*, 5, 5–12, 29–39.

Loyola, I. 1547/1959. *Letters of St. Ignatius of Loyola* (trans., ed., W. J. Young). Chicago, IL: Loyola University Press.

Lucas, C. J. 1972. *Our Western educational heritage*. New York: Macmillan.

Lurie, Y. 2006. *Tracking the meaning of life: A philosophical journey*. Columbia, MO: University of Missouri Press.

References

Lyotard, J.-F. 1979/1984. *The postmodern condition: A report on knowledge* (trans. G. Bennington and B, Massumi). Minneapolis, MN: University of Minnesota Press.

MacDonald, M. G. 1997. Using portfolios as a capstone assessment in TESL programs. Paper presented at the 31st TESOL Convention (Orlando, FL, March 11–15; ERIC Document (RIE) 411677).

Macedo, S. 1990. *Liberal virtue.* Oxford: Clarendon Press.

Macedo, S. (ed.). 1999. *Deliberative politics.* Oxford: Oxford University Press.

MacIntyre, A. 1981. *After virtue.* Notre Dame, IN: University of Notre Dame Press.

Mackey, W. F. 1965. *Language teaching analysis.* London: Longman.

Maher, F. and Tetrault, M. K. 2001. *The feminist classroom* (2nd ed.). New York: Rowman & Littlefield.

Makdisi, G. 1981. *The rise of colleges in Islam and the West.* Edinburgh: Edinburgh University Press.

Makdisi, G. 1995. Baghdad, Bologna, and scholasticism. In J. W. Drijvers and A. A. MacDonald (eds.), *Centres of learning: Learning and location in pre-modern Europe and the Near East* (pp. 141–57). Leiden: E. J. Brill.

Mangubhai, F., Marland, P., Dashwood, A., and Son, J.-B. 2004. Teaching a foreign language: One teacher's practical theory. *Teaching and Teacher Education,* 20, 291–311.

Mangubhai, F., Marland, P., Dashwood, A., and Son, J.-B. 2005. Similarities and differences in teachers' and researchers' conceptions of communicative language teaching: Does the use of an educational model cast a better light? *Language Teaching Research,* 9(1), 31–66.

Mann, E. 1939. *School for barbarians.* London: Lindsay Drummond.

Marks, R. B. 2002. *The origins of the modern world: A global and ecological narrative.* Lanham, MD: Rowman & Littlefield.

Marland, P. 1986. Models of teachers' interactive thinking. *Elementary School Journal,* 87(2), 209–26.

Marland, P. 1994. Secondary teachers' practical knowledge and conceptions of effective teaching in mathematics and science classrooms. Paper presented to the annual conference of the Australian Assocation for Research in Education (Newcastle, New South Wales).

Marland, P. 1995. Implicit theories of teaching. In L. W. Anderson (ed.), *International encyclopedia of teaching* (2nd ed., pp. 131–6). Oxford: Pergamon.

Marland, P. 1997. Teachers' practical theories: Substance and structure. (Chapter 2 of *Towards more effective open and distance learning,* pp. 15–49). London: Kogan Page.

Marland, P. W., Gibson, I., Gibson, K., Lester, N., and Young, P. 1994. Effective multigrade teaching: An exploratory study. In P. W. Marland and K. Smith (eds.), *Knowledge and competence for beginning teaching: Report of a policy initiative* (pp. 167–201). Brisbane, Australia: Board of Teacher Registration (Queensland).

Marland, P. and Osborne, A. 1990. Classroom theory, thinking and action. *Teaching and Teacher Education,* 6(1), 93–109.

Marler, C. D. 1975. *Philosophy and schooling.* Boston, MA: Allyn and Bacon.

Marples, R. 1999. *The aims of education.* London: Routledge.

Marshall, J. 1995. Michel Foucault: Governmentality and liberal education. *Studies in Philosophy and Education,* 14, 23–34.

Martin, J. 2002. *The education of John Dewey.* New York: Columbia University Press.

Martin, J. R. 1981. Sophie and Emile: A case study of sex bias in the history of educational thought. *Harvard Educational Review,* 51(3), 357–72.

Martin, J. R. 1982. Excluding women from the educational realm. *Harvard Educational Review,* 52(2), 133–48.

Martin, J. R. 1985. *Reclaiming a conversation: The ideal of the educated woman.* New Haven, CT: Yale University Press.

Martin, J. R. 1992. *The schoolhome: Rethinking schools for changing families.* Cambridge, MA: Harvard University Press.

Martin, J. R. 1994. *Changing the educational landscape.* New York: Routledge.

Martin, J. R. 1998. Education. In A. M. Jaggar and I. M. Young (eds.), *A companion to feminist philosophy* (pp. 441–7). Oxford: Blackwell.

Matthews, M. R. 1993. A problem with constructivist epistemology. In H. A. Alexander (ed.), *Philosophy of education 1992.* Champaign, IL: University of Illinois Press.

Mattison, M. 2000. Ethical decision making: The person in the process. *Social Work,* 45(3), 201–212.

May, T. 1994. *The political philosophy of poststructuralist anarchism.* University Park, PA: Pennsylvania State University Press.

May, T. 2001. *Our practices, our selves.* University Park, PA: Pennsylvania State University Press.

Maynes, M. J. 1985. *Schooling for the people.* New York: Holmes & Meier.

Mayo, E. 1832. *Lessons on objects.* London: Seelye & Burnside.

Mazzucato, V. 2004. Transcending the nation: Explorations of transnationalism as a concept and phenomenon. In D. Kalb, W. Pansters, and H. Siebers (eds.), *Globalization and development: Themes and concepts in current research.* Dordrecht: Kluwer.

McBride, W. L. 1994. *Political and social philosophy.* New York: Paragon House.

McCollough, H. B. 1994. *Political ideologies and political philosophies* (2nd ed.). Toronto: Thompson Educational Publishing, Inc.

McDonough, S. H. 1981. *Psychology in foreign language teaching.* London: Allen & Unwin.

McHoul, A. 1996. Kant's pragmatics. *Journal of Pragmatics,* 25(4), 587–92.

McHoul, A. and Luke, A. 1989. Discourse as language and politics: An introduction to the philology of political culture in Australia. *Journal of Pragmatics,* 13, 323–32.

McKay, S. 1992. *Teaching English overseas.* Oxford: Oxford University Press.

McKay, S. 2002. *Teaching English as an international language: Rethinking goals and approaches.* Oxford: Oxford University Press.

McLaren, P. 1994. *Life in schools: An introduction to critical pedagogy in the foundations of education* (2nd ed.). New York: Longman.

McMahill, C. 1997. Communities of resistance: A case study of two feminist English classes in Japan. *TESOL Quarterly,* 31(3), 612–21.

McMurray, C. A. 1903. *The elements of general method based on the principles of Herbart.* New York: John Wiley and Sons.

McMurrin, S. M. 1968. On the meaning of the philosophy of education. *The Monist,* 52, 60–69.

McNamara, T. (ed.). 2001. Special issue of *Language Testing,* 18(4).

McNamara, T. 2003. Language testing and social policy: The message of the Shibboleth. *Measurement*, 1(4). (Retrieved June 13, 2005, from http://bearcenter.berkeley.edu/measurement/pubs/)

Meijer, W. A. J. 2001. Rights of children and future adults: A cultural educational perspective. In F. Heyting, D. Lenzen, and J. White (eds.), *Methods in philosophy of education* (pp. 160–75). London: Routledge.

Middlehurst, R. and Kennie, T. 1997. Leading professionals: Towards new concepts of professionalism. In J. Broadbent, M. Dietrich, and J. Roberts (eds.), *The end of the professions?* (pp. 50–68). London: Routledge.

Mill, J. S. 1859/1975. *On liberty.* New York: Norton.

Mill, J. S. 1861/1998. *Utilitarianism.* Oxford: Oxford University Press.

Millar, F. 2006. *A Greek Roman empire.* Berkeley, CA: University of California Press.

Miller, D. 2003. *Political philosophy: A very short introduction.* Oxford: Oxford University Press.

Miller, R. 2002. *Free schools, free people.* Albany, NY: SUNY Press.

Mitch, D. 1992. The rise of popular literacy in Europe. In B. Fuller and R. Robinson (eds.), *The political construction of education: The state, school expansion, and economic change* (pp. 31–46). New York: Praeger.

Mitchell, R. and Hooper, J. 1991. Teachers' views of language knowledge. In C. James and P. Garrett (eds.), *Language awareness in the classroom* (pp. 40–50). London: Longman.

Mitchell, R. and Myles, F. 2004. *Second language learning theories* (2nd ed.). London: Edward Arnold.

Moffatt, L. and Norton, B. 2005. Popular culture and the reading teacher: A case for feminist pedagogy. *Critical Inquiry in Language Studies,* 2(1), 1–12.

Montaigne, M. de. 1575/1991. On educating children. In *The essays of Michel de Montaigne* (#26, pp. 163–99). London: Allen Lane The Penguin Press.

Moore, W. E. 1970. *The professional: Rules and roles.* New York: Russell Sage Foundation.

Moran, P. M. 1996. "I'm not typical." In D. Freeman and J. C. Richards (eds.), *Teacher learning in language teaching* (pp. 125–53). Cambridge: Cambridge University Press.

Morgan, T. 1998. *Literate education in the Hellenistic and Roman worlds.* Cambridge: Cambridge University Press.

Moriarty, P. and Wallerstein, N. 1979. Student/teacher/learner, a Freire approach to ABE/ESL. *Adult Literacy and Basic Education,* 3(3), 193–200.

Moriarty, P. and Wallerstein, N. 1980. By teaching we can learn, a Freire process for teachers. *California Journal of Teacher Education,* 7(1), 39–46.

Morris, V. C. 1961. *Philosophy and the American school.* Boston, MA: Houghton Mifflin.

Morris, V. C. 1966. *Existentialism in education.* New York: Harper & Row.

Moskowitz, G. 1978. *Caring and sharing in the foreign language class: A sourcebook of humanistic techniques.* Rowley, MA: Newbury House.

Moulton, J. F. 1924. Law and manners. *The Atlantic Monthly,* 134: 1–5.

Munby, H. 1986. Metaphor in the thinking of teachers. *Journal of Curriculum Studies,* 18, 197–209.

Munby, H., Russell, T., and Martin, A. K. 2001. Teachers' knowledge and how it develops. In V. Richardson (ed.), *Handbook of research on teaching* (4th ed., pp. 877–904). Washington, DC: American Educational Research Association.

Murphy, J. J. 2001. Introduction. In J. J. Murphy (ed.), *A short history of writing instruction from ancient Greece to modern America* (pp. 1–8). Mahwah, NJ: Erlbaum.

Murray, S. E., Evans, W. N., and Schwab, R. M. 1998. Education-finance reform and the distribution of education resources. *American Economic Review,* 88(4), 789–812.

Musumeci, D. 1997. *Breaking tradition: An exploration of the historical relationship between theory and practice in second language teaching.* New York: McGraw-Hill.

Myers, C. B. and Simpson, D. J. 1998. *Re-creating schools.* Thousand Oaks, CA: Corwin Press.

Nagl-Docekal, H. 2004. *Feminist philosophy.* Boulder, CO: Westview Press.

Nakosteen, M. 1964. *History of Islamic origins of Western education.* Boulder, CO: University of Colorado Press.

Narveson, J. 1995. Social philosophy. In R. Audi (ed.), *The Cambridge dictionary of philosophy* (2nd ed.; p. 747). Cambridge: Cambridge University Press.

Nash, M. A. 2005. *Women's education in the United States, 1780–1840.* New York: PalgraveMacmillan.

National Education Association [NEA]. 1977. Code of ethics of the education progression. In National Education Association, *NEA Handbook 1977–78.* Washington DC: National Education Association.

Neill, A. S. 1960/1993. *Summerhill School: A new view of childhood.* New York: St. Martin's Press.

Neumann, R. 2003. *Sixties legacy: A history of the public alternative schools movement, 1967–2001.* New York: Peter Lang.

Newman, F. M. and Oliver, D. W. 1967. Education and community. *Harvard Education Review,* 37(1), 61–106.

Newmark, M. 1948. *Twentieth century modern language teaching: Sources and readings.* New York: Philosophical Library.

Noddings, N. 1984. *Caring, a feminine approach to ethics and moral education.* Berkeley, CA: University of California Press.

Noddings, N. 1992. *The challenge to care in schools.* New York: Teachers College Press.

Noddings, N. 1995. *Philosophy of education.* Boulder, CO: Westview Press.

Noddings, N. 2003. *Happiness and education.* Cambridge: Cambridge University Press.

Nussbaum, M. 1997. *Cultivating humanity: A classical defense of reform in liberal education.* Cambridge, MA: Harvard University Press.

Nussbaum, M. 2002. Education for citizenship in an era of global connection. *Studies in Philosophy and Education,* 21, 289–303.

Nylan, M. 2003. Childhood, formal education, and ideology in China. In W. Koops and M. Zuckerman (eds.), *Beyond the century of the child: Cultural history and developmental psychology* (pp. 136–55). Philadelphia, PA: University of Pennsylvania Press.

References

Ohara, Y., Saft, S., and Crookes, G. 2001. Toward a feminist critical pedagogy in a beginning Japanese as a foreign language class. *Japanese Language and Literature: Journal of the Association of Teachers of Japanese*, 35(2), 105–33.

Okin, S. M. 1989. *Justice, gender and the family*. New York: Basic Books.

O'Leary, R. 2006. *The ethics of dissent: Managing guerrilla government*. Washington, DC: CQ Press.

Orlikowski, W. J. 2002. Knowing in practice: Enacting a collective capability in distributed organizing. *Organizational Science*, 13(3), 249–73.

Osborn, T. 2006. *Teaching world languages for social justice*. Mahwah, NJ: Lawrence Erlbaum.

Osborne, C. 2004. *Presocratic philosophy: A very short introduction*. Oxford University Press.

Ozmon, H. A. and Craver, S. M. 1999. *Philosophical foundations in education* (6th ed.). Columbus, OH: Merrill/Prentice Hall.

Palmer, H. 1927. *Everyday sentences in spoken English*. W. Heffer & Sons.

Palmer, R. R. 1985. *The improvement of humanity: Education and the French revolution*. Princeton, NJ: Princeton University Press.

Parsons, T. 1937. *The structure of social action*. New York: McGraw-Hill.

Pedersen, O. 1997. *The first universities: Studium generale and the origins of university education in Europe* (trans. R. North). Cambridge: Cambridge University Press.

Peirce, C. S. 1878. How to make our ideas clear. *Popular Science Monthly*, 12, 286–302.

Pendlebury, S. 1998. Feminism, epistemology and education. In D. Carr (ed.), *Education, knowledge and truth* (pp. 174–88). London: Routledge.

Pennington, M. C. 1990. A professional development focus for the language teaching practicum. In J. C. Richards and D. Nunan (eds.), *Second language teacher education* (pp. 132–53). Cambridge University Press.

Pennington, M. C. 1992. Second class or economy? The status of the English language teaching profession in tertiary education. *Prospect,* 7(3), 8–19.

Pennycook, A. 1989. The concept of method, interested knowledge, and the politics of language teaching. *TESOL Quarterly*, 23(4), 589–618.

Pennycook, A. 1994. Incommensurable discourses? *Applied Linguistics*, 15(2), 115–38.

Pennycook, A. 2000. History: After 1945. In M. Byram (ed.), *Routledge encyclopedia of language teaching and learning* (pp. 275–82).

Pennycook, A. 2001. *Critical applied linguistics: A critical introduction*. Mahwah, N.J.; and London: L. Erlbaum.

Pennycook, A. 2004. Critical moments in a TESOL praxicum. In B. Norton and K. Toohey (eds.), *Critical pedagogies and language learning* (pp. 327–45). Cambridge: Cambridge University Press.

Pennycook, A. and Coutand-Marin, S. 2004. Teaching English as a missionary language (TEML). *Discourse: Studies in the Cultural Politics of Education*, 24, 338–53.

Pestalozzi, J. H. 1781/1910. *Leonard and Gertrude* (abr., trans. E. Channing). Boston, MA: D. C. Heath.

Peteet, J. 2000. Refugees, resistance, and identity. In J. A. Guidry, M. D. Kennedy, and M. N. Zald (eds.), *Globalizations and social movements* (pp. 183–209). Ann Arbor, MI: University of Michigan Press.

260

Peters, R. S., Woods, J., and Dray, W. H. 1965. Aims of education – a conceptual inquiry. In B. Crittenden (ed.), *Philosophy of education* (pp. 1–32); reprinted in R. S. Peters (ed.), 1973. *The philosophy of education* (pp. 11–29). Oxford: Oxford University Press.

Peyton, J. 1995. *Philosophies and approaches in adult ESL literacy instruction* (ERIC Digest, ED386960). Washington, DC: Center for Applied Linguistics.

Phillipson, R. 1992. *Linguistic imperialism*. Oxford: Oxford University Press.

Pike, B., Bradley, F., and Mansfield, J. 1997. Philosophy of teaching: Developing a statement that thrives in the classroom. *The Clearing House,* 70(3), 125–9.

Plant, R. 1998. Nature of political philosophy. In E. Craig (ed.), *Routledge encyclopedia of philosophy* (pp. 525–8). London: Routledge.

Polanyi, M. 1964. *Personal knowledge: Towards a post-critical philosophy.* New York: Harper and Row.

Pollis, A. 1992. Human rights in liberal, socialist, and third world perspectives. In R. P. Claude and B. H. Weston (eds.), *Human rights in the world community.* Philadelphia, PA: University of Pennsylvania Press.

Pollis, A. and Schwab, P. (eds). 1980. *Human rights: Cultural and ideological perspectives.* New York: Praeger.

Popkewitz, T. S. 1994. Professionalization in teaching and teacher education: Some notes on its history, ideology, and potential. *Teaching and Teacher Education,* 10, 1–14.

Popper, K. 1963. *Conjectures and refutations: The growth of scientific knowledge.* London: Harper & Row.

Potter, J. 2002. *Active citizenship in schools: A good-practice guide to developing a whole-school policy.* London: Kogan Page.

Power, E. J. 1982. *Philosophy of education: Studies in philosophies, schooling, and educational policies.* Englewood Cliffs, NJ: Prentice-Hall.

Poynor, L. and Wolfe, P. M. (eds.). 2005. *Marketing fear in America's public schools: The real war on literacy.* Mahwah, NJ: L. Erlbaum Associates.

Prabhu, N. S. 1990. There is no best Method. Why? *TESOL Quarterly,* 24(2), 161–76.

Pugh, A. K. 1996. A history of English language teaching. In N. Mercer and J. Swan (eds.), *Learning English: Development and diversity* (pp. 159–204). London: Routledge.

Purcell-Gates, V. and Waterman, R. 2000. *Now we read, we see, we speak: Portrait of literacy development in an adult Freirean-based class.* Mahwah, NJ: Lawrence Erlbaum.

Quinton, A. 1995. Popular philosophy. In T. Honderich (ed.), *The Oxford companion to philosophy* (pp. 703–4). Oxford: Oxford University Press.

Ramsay, H. 1997. *Beyond virtue: Integrity and morality.* New York: St. Martin's Press.

Ramsay, M. 1997. *What's wrong with liberalism? A radical critique of liberal political philosophy.* London: Leicester University Press.

Rardin, J. 1982. A humanistic philosophy of education. In [British Council], *Humanistic approaches: An empirical view* (*ELT Documents 113,* pp. 59–67). London: British Council.

Rawls, J. 1971. *A theory of justice.* Cambridge, MA: Harvard University Press.

Rawls, J. 1993. *Political liberalism.* New York: Columbia University Press.

Rawls, J. 1999. *The law of peoples.* Cambridge, MA: Harvard University Press.

261

References

Rawls, J. 2001. *Justice as fairness: A restatement* (ed. E. Kelly). Cambridge, MA: Harvard University Press.

Rawski, E. S. 1979. *Education and popular literacy in Ch'ing China*. Ann Arbor, MI: University of Michigan Press.

Reagan, T. G. 1996. *Non-western educational traditions*. Mahwah, NJ: Erlbaum.

Reagan, T. G. and Osborn, T. A. 2002. *The foreign language educator in society*. Mahwah, NJ: Lawrence Erlbaum.

Reath, A. 1998. Ethical autonomy. In E. Craig (ed.), *Routledge encyclopedia of philosophy* (pp. 586–92). London: Routledge.

Reynolds, D. and Farrell, S. 1996. *Worlds apart? A review of international surveys of educational achievement involving England*. London: Her Majesty's Stationery Office.

Reynolds, M. C. 1989. Preface. In M. C. Reynolds (ed.), *Knowledge base for the beginning teacher* (pp. ix–xii). Oxford: Pergamon.

Rich, J. M. 1984. *Professional ethics in education*. Springfield, IL: C. C. Thomas.

Richards, J. C. 1984. The secret life of Methods. *TESOL Quarterly*, 18(1), 7–24.

Richards, J. C. 1996. Teachers' maxims in language teaching. *TESOL Quarterly*, 30(2), 281–96.

Richards, J. C. and Rodgers, T. S. 1982. Method: Approach, design, and procedure. *TESOL Quarterly*, 16(2), 153–68.

Richards, J. C. and Rodgers, T. S. 1986. *Approaches and methods in language teaching*. Cambridge University Press.

Richardson, V. and Placier, P. 2001. Teacher change. In V. Richardson (ed.), *Handbook of research on teaching* (4th ed., pp. 905–50). Washington, DC: American Educational Research Association.

Richert, A. E. 1992. The content of student teachers' reflections within different structures for facilitating the reflective process. In T. Russell and H. Munby (eds.), *Teachers and teaching: From classroom to reflection* (pp. 171–91). London: Falmer Press.

Ritchie, J. S. and Wilson, D. E. 2000. *Teacher narrative as critical inquiry*. New York: Teachers College Press.

Rofes, E. and Stulberg, L. M. (eds.). 2005. *The emancipatory promise of charter schools: Toward a progressive politics of school choice*. Albany, NY: SUNY Press.

Rogers, B. 1999. Portrait: John Rawls. *Prospect*, 42, 50–55.

Rogers, C. R. 1969. *Freedom to learn: A view of what education might become*. Columbus, OH: C. E. Merrill.

Rohrer, P. 1994. At what price individualism? The education of Isabel Archer. *Philosophy of Education 1993* (pp. 315–24). Champaign, IL: Philosophy of Education Society.

Rojas, E. D. and Reagan, T. 2003. Linguistic human rights: A new perspective on bilingual education. *Educational Foundations*, 17(1), 5–19.

Ross, S. D. 1994. *The limits of language*. New York: Fordham University Press.

Rothschild, E. 1998. Condorcet and Adam Smith on education and instruction. In E. O. Rorty (ed.), *Philosophers on education* (pp. 209–26). London: Routledge.

Rousseau, J.-J. 1762/1963. *Emile*. New York: Dutton.

Rubinstein, R. E. 2003. *Aristotle's children: How Christians, Muslims, and Jews rediscovered ancient wisdom and illuminated the Dark Ages.* New York: Harcourt.

Runes, D. D. (ed.). 1983. *Dictionary of philosophy.* New York: Philosophical Library.

Russell, B. 1926. *On education.* London: Allen & Unwin.

Ryder, J. 2003. Reconciling pragmatism and naturalism. In J. R. Schook (ed.), *Pragmatic naturalism and realism.* (pp. 55–76). Amherst, NY: Prometheus Books.

Ryle, G. 1949. *The concept of mind.* London: Hutchinson.

Sadler, J. E. 1966. *J. A. Comenius and the concept of universal education.* London: George Allen & Unwin.

Said, E. W. 1978. *Orientalism.* New York: Pantheon.

Sandel, M. 1982. *Liberalism and the limits of justice.* Cambridge: Cambridge University Press.

Sandel, M. 1996. *Democracy's discontent.* Cambridge, MA: Harvard University Press.

Sankowski, E. T. 1995. Political philosophy, history of. In T. Honderich (ed.), *The Oxford companion to philosophy* (pp. 693–7). Oxford: Oxford University Press.

Santayana, G. 1905. *The life of reason: Or, the phases of progress* (vol. 1). New York: Scribner.

Sartre, J.-P. 1956. *Being and nothingness: A phenomenological essay on ontology* (trans. H. E. Barnes). New York: Pocket Books.

Sartre, J.-P. 1957. *Existentialism and human emotions.* New York: Philosophical Library.

Sattler, C. L. 1997. *Talking about a revolution: The politics and practice of feminist teaching.* Cresskill, NJ: Hampton Press.

Saussure, F. de. 1916/1959. *Cours de linguistique générale.* (ed. C. Bally and A. Sechehaye, coll. A. Riedlinger). Paris: Payot. W. Baskin (trans.), *Course in General Linguistics.* New York: Philosophical Library.

Savignon, S. 1972. *Communicative competence: An experiment in foreign language teaching.* Philadelphia, PA: Center for Curriculum Development.

Schacht, S. P. 2000. Using a feminist pedagogy as a male teacher: The possibilities of a partial and situated perspective. *Radical Pedagogy,* 2(2). (Retrieved May 27, 2007, from http://radicalpedagogy.icaap.org/currentissue.html)

Schatzki, T. R. 1996. *Social practices.* Cambridge: Cambridge University Press.

Scheffler, I. 1978. *Conditions of knowledge: An introduction to epistemology and education.* Chicago, IL: University of Chicago Press.

Schiffauer, W., Bauman, G., Kastoryano, R., and Vertovec, S. (eds.). 2004. *Civil enculturation: Nation-state, schools and ethnic difference in four European countries.* New York: Berghahn Books.

Schniedewind, N. 1993. Teaching feminist process in the 1990s. *Women's Studies Quarterly,* 21(3 & 4), 17–30.

Schön, D. A. 1983. *The reflective practitioner: How professionals think in action.* New York: Basic Books.

Schrier, L. L. 1993. Prospects for the professionalization of foreign language teaching. In G. Guntermann (ed.), *Developing language teachers for a changing world* (pp. 105–23). Lincolnwood, IL: National Textbook Co.

Schubert, W. H. 1991. Teacher lore: A basis for understanding praxis. In C. Witherell and N. Noddings (eds.), *Stories lives tell* (pp. 207–31). New York: Teachers College Press.

Schubert, W. H. and Ayers, W. (eds.). 1992. *Teacher lore: Learning from our own experience*. White Plains, NY: Longman.

Scott, J. C. 1985. *Weapons of the weak: Everyday forms of peasant resistance*. New Haven, CT: Yale University Press.

Scott, S. 2000. Developing a research agenda for TESOL. *TESOL Matters*, 10(3), 1 & 4.

Scribner, S. 1986. Thinking in action: Some characteristics of practical thought. In R. J. Sternberg and R. K. Wagner (eds.), *Practical intelligence: Nature and origins of competence in the everyday world* (pp. 13–30). New York: Cambridge University Press.

Senge, P. M. 1995. On schools as learning organizations: A conversation with Peter Senge. *Educational Leadership*, 52, 20–23.

Senge, P. M., Cambron-McCabe, N., Lucas, T., Smith, B., Dutton, J., and Kleiner, A. 2000. *Schools that learn: A fifth discipline fieldbook for educators, parents, and everyone who cares about education*. New York: Doubleday.

Sergiovanni, T. J. 1980. A social humanities view of educational policy and administration. *Educational Administration Quarterly*, 16(1), 1–19.

Sextus Empiricus. 1961. *Sextus Empiricus* (trans. R. G. Bury; vol. 1). London: Heinemann.

Shannon, P. 2001. Turn, turn, turn: Language education, politics, and freedom at the turn of three centuries. In C. Dudley-Marling and C. Edelsky (eds.), *The fate of progressive language policies and practices* (pp. 3–30). Urbana, IL: National Council of Teachers of English.

Shapin, S. 1994. *A social history of truth: Civility and science in seventeenth-century England*. Chicago, IL: University of Chicago Press.

Sharpes, D. K. 2002. *Advanced educational foundations for teachers: The history, philosophy, and culture of schooling*. New York: RoutledgeFalmer.

Shin, H. and Crookes, G. 2005a. Indigenous critical traditions for TEFL? – A historical and comparative perspective in the case of Korea. *Critical Inquiry in Language Studies*, 2(2), 95–112.

Shin, H. and Crookes, G. 2005b. Exploring the possibilities for EFL critical pedagogy in Korea – A two-part case study. *Critical Inquiry in Language Studies*, (2)2, 112–38.

Shor, I. 1992. *Empowering education: Critical teaching for social change*. Chicago, IL: University of Chicago Press.

Shor, I. and Freire, P. 1987. *A pedagogy for liberation: Dialogues on transforming education*. South Hadley, MA: Bergin & Garvey.

Shotton, J. 1992. Libertarian education and state schooling in England, 1918–90. *Educational Review*, 44(1), 81–91.

Shotton, J. 1993. *No master high or low*. Bristol, UK: Libertarian Education.

Shrewsbury, C. 1993. What is feminist pedagogy? *Women's Studies Quarterly*, 21, 8–16.

Shulman, L. S. 1987. Knowledge and teaching: Foundations of the new reform. *Harvard Educational Review*, 57(1), 1–22.

Siegfried, C. H. 1995. Pragmatism. In R. Audi (ed.), *The Cambridge dictionary of philosophy* (2nd ed., pp. 730–31). Cambridge: Cambridge University Press.

Simon, R. L. 2002. Social and political philosophy – Sorting out the issues. In R. L. Simon (ed.), *The Blackwell guide to social and political philosophy* (pp. 1–13). London: Blackwell.

Simpson, D. J. 1990/1995. The philosophical context. In C. B. Myers and L. K. Myers (eds.), *An introduction to teaching and schools*. New York: Holt, Rinehart, and Winston. Revised 1995. In C. B. Myers and L. K. Myers (eds.), *The professional educator: A new introduction to teaching and schools* (pp. 368–407). Belmont, CA: Wadsworth.

Sizer, T. R. 1984. *Horace's compromise*. Boston, MA: Houghton Mifflin.

Skuja-Steele, R. and Silver, R. 2004. Pedagogical practices in English language education. In N. F. McGinn (ed.), *Learning through collaborative research: The Six Nation Educational Research Project* (pp. 53–90). New York: RoutledgeFalmer.

Small, R. 2005. *Marx and education*. Aldershot, UK: Ashgate.

Smith, A. 1776/1966. *An inquiry into the nature and causes of the wealth of nations* (Book Five, Chapter I, Part 3, Article II: Of the Expense of the Institutions for the Education of Youth). New York: A. M. Kelly.

Smith, M. P. 1983. *The libertarians and education*. London: George Allen & Unwin.

Smith, S. B. 1989. *Hegel's critique of liberalism: Rights in context*. Chicago, IL: University of Chicago Press.

Smith, W. A. 1955. *Ancient education*. New York: Philosophical Library.

Sockett, H. 1987. Has Shulman got the strategy right? *Harvard Educational Review, 57*(2), 208–19.

Sockett, H. 1990. Accountability, trust, and ethical codes of practice. In J. I. Goodlad, R. Soder, and K. A. Sirotnik (eds.), *The moral dimensions of teaching* (pp. 224–50). San Francisco, CA: Jossey-Bass.

Sola, P. A. 1973. Plutocrats, pedagogues and plebes: Business influences on vocational education and extracurricular activities in the Chicago high schools, 1899–1925. PhD dissertation, University of Illinois at Urbana-Champaign.

Sola, P. A. 1974. The Chicago Association of Commerce and the organization of extra-curricular Activities in the Chicago high school, 1914–1925. ERIC Document ED 115756.

Sontag, M. 1968. Attitudes toward education and perception of teacher behaviors. *American Educational Research Journal, 5*, 385–402.

Spada, N. and Massey, M. 1992. The role of prior pedagogical knowledge in determining the practice of novice ESL teachers. In J. Flowerdew, M. Brock, and S. Hsia (eds.), *Perspectives on second language teacher education* (pp. 23–37). Hong Kong: City Polytechnic of Hong Kong.

Spring, J. 1975. *A primer of libertarian education*. New York: Free Life Editions.

Spring, J. 1994. *Wheels in the head: Educational philosophies of authority, freedom, and culture from Socrates to Paulo Freire*. New York: McGraw-Hill.

Spring, J. 2000. *The universal right to education*. Mahwah, NJ: Lawrence Erlbaum.

References

Spring, J. 2006. *Pedagogies of globalization: The rise of the educational security state*. Mahwah, NJ: Lawrence Erlbaum.

Stabiner, K. 2003. *All girls: Single-sex education and why it matters*. New York: Riverhead Books.

Staczek, J. J. 1987. Professionalism and the M.A. in TEFL. *TESOL Newsletter*, 21(1), 13.

Staczek, J. J. 1991. Professional development and program administration. *TESOL Journal*, 1(1), 21–22, 27–28.

Stamm, J. and Wactler, C. 1997. *Philosophy of education workbook: Writing a statement of beliefs and practices*. New York: McGraw/Hill.

Stanton, C. M. 1990. *Higher learning in Islam*. Savage, MD: Rowman & Littlefield.

Stenhouse, L. 1975. *An introduction to curriculum research and development*. London: Heinemann.

Stevenson, H. W. and Stigler, J. W. 1992. *The learning gap: Why our schools are failing and what we can learn from Japanese and Chinese education*. New York: Simon & Schuster.

Stevick, E. W. 1980. *Teaching language: A way and ways*. Rowley, MA: Newbury House.

Stevick, E. W. 1990. *Humanism in language teaching*. Oxford: Oxford University Press.

Stone, L. 1994. Introducing education feminism. In L. Stone (ed.), *The Education Feminism Reader* (pp. 1–13). New York: Routledge.

Stoutland, F. 2002. Putnam on truth. In M. Gustafsson and L. Hertzberg (eds.), *The practice of language* (pp. 147–76). Dordrecht: Kluwer.

Stoynoff, S. 1993. Ethics and intensive English programs. *TESOL Journal*, 3(1), 4–6.

Strain, J. P. 1971. *Modern philosophies of education*. New York: Random House.

Strasser, S. and Monshouwer, A. 1967. *Herbart als opvoedkundig denker*. 's-Hertogenbosch: Malmberg.

Strike, K. A. 1989. *Liberal justice and the Marxist critique of education*. New York: Routledge.

Strike, K. A. 1996. Liberalism. In J. J. Chamblis (ed.), *Philosophy of education: An encyclopedia* (pp. 355–60). New York: Garland.

Strike, K. A. and Soltis, J. 1992. *The ethics of teaching* (2nd ed.). New York: Teachers College Press.

Tabachnick, B. E. and Zeichner, K. M. 1984. The impact of the student teaching experience on the development of teacher perspectives. *Journal of Teacher Education*, 35, 28–36.

Taylor, C. 1975. *Hegel*. Cambridge: Cambridge University Press.

Taylor, G. 1981. Integrity. *Aristotelian Society*, 55, 143–59.

Taylor, P. V. 1993. *The texts of Paulo Freire*. Buckingham, UK: Open University Press.

Terrell, T. 1982. The natural approach to language teaching: An update. *Modern Language Journal*, 66, 121–32.

Tetrault, M. K. 2004. Classrooms for diversity: Rethinking curriculum and pedagogy. In J. A. Banks and C. A. McGee Banks (eds.), *Multicultural education: Issues and perspectives* (5th ed.). New York: John Wiley/Jossey-Bass.

Thøgersen, S. 2002. *A country of culture: Twentieth-century China seen from the village schools of Zouping, Shandong*. Ann Arbor, MI: University of Michigan Press.

Thomas, M. 1998. Programmatic ahistoricity in second language acquisition theory. *Studies in Second Language Acquisition*, 20, 387–405.

Thomas, M. 2004. *Universal grammar in second language acquisition: A history*. New York: Routledge.

Thorne, S. L. 2004. Cultural historical activity theory and the object of innovation. In K. van Esch and O. St. John (eds.), *New insights into foreign language learning and teaching* (pp. 51–70). Berlin: Peter Lang.

Thorne, S. L. 2005. Epistemology, politics, and ethics in sociocultural theory. *Modern Language Journal*, 89(3), 393–409.

Titone, C. and Maloney, K. E. 1999. *Women's philosophies of education*. Upper Saddle River, NJ: Prentice-Hall.

Titone, R. 1968. *Teaching foreign languages: An historical sketch*. Washington, DC: Georgetown University Press.

Titone, R. 2000. History: The nineteenth century. In M. Byram (ed.), *Routledge encyclopedia of language teaching and learning* (pp. 265–70). London: Routledge.

Tobin, J. J., Wu, D. Y., and Davidson, D. H. 1989. *Preschool in three cultures: Japan, China and the United States*. New Haven, CT: Yale University Press.

Tollefson, J. W. 1989. *Alien winds: The reeducation of America's Indochinese refugees*. New York: Praeger

Tolstoy, L. (trans. L. Wiener). 1967. *Tolstoy on education*. Chicago: University of Chicago Press.

Tom, A. R. 1984. *Teaching as a moral craft*. New York: Longman.

Toulmin, S. E. 1990. *Cosmopolis: The hidden agenda of modernity*. New York: Free Press.

Tsang, W. K. 2004. Teachers' personal practical knowledge and interactive decisions. *Language Teaching Research*, 8(2), 163–98.

Tyler, R. 1949. *Basic principles of curriculum and instruction*. New York: Harcourt Brace.

Ulichny, P. 1996. What's in a methodology? In D. Freeman and J. C. Richards (eds.), *Teacher learning in language teaching* (pp. 178–96). Cambridge: Cambridge University Press.

van Ek, J. and Alexander, L. 1975. *Threshold Level English*. Oxford: Pergamon Press.

van Essen, A. 2000. History: From the Reform Movement to 1945. In M. Byram (ed.), *Routledge encyclopedia of language teaching and learning* (pp. 270–75).

Van Norden, B. W. 2004. What is living and what is dead in the Confucianism of Zhu Xi? In R. Wang (ed.), *Chinese philosophy in an era of globalization* (pp. 99–120). Albany, NY: SUNY Press.

Van Scotter, R. D., Haas, J. D., Kraft, R. J., and Scott, J. C. (eds.). 1979/1991. *Social foundations of education* (3rd ed.). Boston, MA: Allyn & Bacon.

Vandenberg, D. 1971. *Being and education: An essay in existential phenomenology*. New York: Prentice Hall.

Vandrick, S. 1994. Feminist pedagogy and ESL. *College English* 4(2), 69–92.

References

Vandrick, S. 1998. Promoting gender equity in the postsecondary ESL class. In T. Smoke (ed.), *Adult ESL: Politics, pedagogy, and participation in classroom and community programs* (pp. 73–88). Mahwah, NJ: Lawrence Erlbaum.

Vandrick, S. 2003. Examining the new backlash: Pitting male disadvantage against female disadvantage in educational settings. Paper presented at TESOL International Convention, March 2003, Baltimore, MD. (Retrieved June 2005 from www.tokyoprogressive.org.uk/gale/articles/vandrick.html)

Varghese, M. 2001. "La lengua es el espiritu del alma": Bilingual teachers as language planners. Paper presented at AAAL Conference, Feb., St. Louis, MO.

Wakabayashi, J. 2005. Translation from Chinese in 18th-century Japan. In E. Hung (ed.), *Translation and cultural change* (pp. 119–45). Amsterdam: John Benjamins.

Walker, D. F. and Soltis, J. F. 1992. *Curriculum and aims* (2nd ed.). New York: Teachers College Press.

Wallace, C. 2003. *Critical reading in language education*. London: Palgrave Macmillan.

Wallerstein, I. 1974. *The modern world-system* (vol. 1). New York: Academic Press.

Wallerstein, N. 1983a. *Language and culture in conflict: Problem-posing in the ESL classroom*. Reading, MA: Addison-Wesley.

Wallerstein, N. 1983b. Problem posing can help students learn: From refugee camps to resettlement country classrooms. *TESOL Newsletter,* 17(5), 1–2, 5.

Wallerstein, N. 1983c. Teaching approach of Paulo Freire. In J. Oller and R. Amato (eds.), *Methods That Work* (pp. 190–206). Rowley, MA: Newbury Press.

Walton, L. 1999. *Academies and society in Southern Sung China*. Honolulu, HI: University of Hawai'i Press.

Walzer, M. 2004. *Politics and passion: Toward a more egalitarian liberalism*. New Haven: Yale University.

Weiler, K. 1991. Freire and a feminist pedagogy of difference. *Harvard Educational Review*, 61(4), 499–74. Reprinted in J. Holland, M. Blair, with S. Sheldon (eds.), 1995. *Debates and issues in feminist research and pedagogy* (pp. 23–44). Clevedon, UK: Multilingual Matters/Open University.

Weiler, K., Weiner, G., and Yates, L. 1999. Series editors' preface. In B. Lingard and P. Douglas, *Men engaging feminism* (pp. ix–x). Philadelphia, PA: Open University Press.

Weisner, J. 2005. Awakening teacher voice and student voice: The development of a feminist pedagogy. *Feminist Teacher*, 15(1), 34–47.

Welker, R. 1992. *The teacher as expert: A theoretical and historical examination*. Albany, NY: SUNY Press.

Wenden, A. L. 1995. Critical language education. In C. Schäffner and A. L. Wenden (eds.), *Language and peace* (pp. 211–27). Aldershot, UK: Dartmouth.

What are Pakistanis doing in Japan? 2001. *News International* [Pakistan] report. (Retrieved May 27, 2007, from http://pakavenue.com/overseas/news_updates/news_updates_007.htm)

White, B. 2003. Caring and the teaching of English. *Research in the Teaching of English*, 37, 295–328.

White, C. 1998. *The philosophy of human learning*. London: Routledge.

White, J. 1982. *The aims of education restated*. London: Routledge & Kegan Paul.

White, J. 2006. *Intelligence, destiny and education: the ideological roots of intelligence testing*. London: Routledge.

White, J. and White, P. 2001. An analytic perspective on education and children's rights. In F. Heyting, D. Lenzen, and J. White (eds.), *Methods in philosophy of education* (pp. 13–29). London: Routledge.

Whitehead, A. N. 1929. *The aims of education, and other essays*. New York: Macmillan.

Whitty, G. 1975. Sociology and the problem of radical educational change: Notes towards a reconceptualization of the 'new' sociology of education. In M.Young and G. Whitty (eds.), *Society, state and schooling* (pp. 26–55). Lewes, UK: Falmer Press.

Wilensky, H. L. 1964. The professionalization of everyone? *American Journal of Sociology*, 70, 137–58.

Williams, B. 1973. A critique of utilitarianism. In J. J. C. Smart and B. Williams (eds.), *Utilitarianism: For and against* (pp. 77–150). Cambridge: Cambridge University Press.

Wilson, R. A. and Mitchell, J. P. 2003. Introduction: The social life of rights. In R. A. Wilson and J. P. Mitchell (eds.), *Human rights in global perspective: Anthropological studies of rights, claims, and entitlements* (pp. 1–15). London: Routledge.

Winch, C. 1998. *The philosophy of human learning*. London: Routledge.

Wink, J. 1997. *Critical pedagogy: Notes from the real world*. New York: Longman.

Wiseman, D. L., Cooner, D. D., and Knight, S. L. 1999. *Becoming a teacher in a field-based setting: An introduction to education and classrooms*. Belmont, CA: Wadsworth.

Wittgenstein, L. 1933. *The blue and brown books*. Oxford: Blackwell.

Wodak, R. 1996. *Disorders of discourse*. London: Longman.

Wollstonecraft, M. 1792/2004. *A vindication of the rights of woman* (ed. M. Brody). London: Penguin.

Woods, D. 1996. *Teacher cognition in language teaching*. Cambridge: Cambridge University Press.

Woodside, A. 1992. Real and imagined continuities in the Chinese struggle for literacy. In R. Hayhoe (ed.), *Education and modernization: The Chinese experience* (pp. 23–45). Oxford: Pergamon Press.

Woodside, A. 1994. The divorce between the political center and educational creativity in late imperial China. In B. E. Elman and A. Woodside (eds.), *Education and society in late imperial China* (pp. 458–82). Berkeley, CA: University of California Press.

Wright, S. 1988. TESOL: Our evolving profession. *TESOL Newsletter*, 22(5), 23, 29.

Wringe, C. 1988. *Understanding educational aims*. London: Unwin Hyman.

Xu, H. 1993. My personal philosophy in teaching English as a Second Language: Some methods I used in teaching English to Chinese freshmen in Xi'an language university. ERIC Document ED 366179.

References

Young, M. and Whitty, G. 1977. *Society, state and schooling.* Lewes, UK: Falmer Press.

Young, W. J. (ed.). 1959. *Letters of St. Ignatius of Loyola.* Chicago, IL: Loyola University Press.

Yu, T. 2004. *In the name of morality: Character education and political control.* New York: Peter Lang.

Zack, N. 2005. *Inclusive feminism: A third wave theory of women's commonality.* New York: Rowman & Littlefield.

Zheng, Y. 1994. Local government schools in Sung China: A reassessment. *History of Education Quarterly,* 34(2), 193–213.

Zhu, C. 1936. Zouping di shi-yi xiangxue daoyouzhi gongxuetuan de shiyan. (An experiment with the friend-guide system and study groups in Zouping's 11th township school.) *Xiangcun jianshe,* 5(1).

Zinn, L. M. 1990. Identifying your philosophical orientation. In M. W. Galbraith (ed.), *Adult learning methods* (pp. 39–76). Malabar, FA: Krieger.

Index

activity,
    and Dewey/progressive movement, 62
    and pragmatism, 86
    basis for communicative approaches, 8,
        65, 69–71, 176
    in European classrooms curriculum, 67
    language as, 122
activity theory, 119, 123
aesthetics, 78
agency,
    aided by philosophy of teaching, 25
    and rights, 161
    in continental philosophy, 106, 110
        (fn. 18)
    learner's, 71
    teachers', 22
aims,
    of schools, 13, 155
    of teachers 25, 126, 214–37
    vocational, 215, 218, 220–21
alternative
    approaches, 6–7, 96, 99
        precursors to, 55, 62–4
        sectors of education hospitable to, 182,
            201
    beliefs or values in curriculum, 154
    schools, 181
    teaching traditions, by culture and
        geography, 51, 177
    theories of society, 176–8
    vision of education, 196
analytic philosophy, 15
anarchist education, 179–180
    and Freirean ideas, 197 (fn. 11)
approach (general educational),
    Freirean, 181–6
    in Revolutionary France, 52
    libertarian, 176–181
    monitorial, 60, 73 (fn. 12)
    of Rousseau, 53
    of teachers, 228–31 passim
    progressive, in China, 63–5
    radical, 175ff.
approach (language teaching), 3–8
    audiolingual, 6
    formal and functional, in history, 48
    natural (or direct), 57–8, 61, 69, 218

communicative, 62, 68–9
    grammar-translation, 89
    humanistic, 6, 86, 100
    metaphor of growth in, 9, 218
approach (philosophical methods), 15–16,
    96, 101, 105, 122, 138, 158
Arabic, 34, 36, 40
Asian,
    countries, progressive pedagogy in, 63–5
    philosophical traditions, 79–80
    values, 161
Augustine, 32, 40
autonomy, 6, 138, 152–5
    aim, 219, 232
    and epistemology, 189
    and human rights, 161–163, 166, 173
        (fn. 17)
    in civic education, 222
    in feminist pedagogy, 193
    in teachers' philosophies, 234
    of teachers and professionals, 125, 200,
        209
axiology, 75, 78–79, 136

Bakhtin, 103
BANA, 29, 68
Basedow, 53
behaviorism, 7
beliefs, teachers', 1, 15, 17, 19, 225–32
    about ethics, 141
    about knowledge, 112
    category in Methods analysis, 4
    compromising, 204, 207
    cultural differences in, 13–14
    feminist, 194
    research area, 9, 10, 20, 26 (fn. 9)
    see maxims
Bentham, J., 139, 152, 161
Berlitz, 57–58, 73 (fn. 11)
bilingual education, 48
Buddhism, 31, 33, 40, 80

career, 2, 58, 170, 199, 200, 210, 211, 212
    (fn. 2)
caring, 143, 226
categorical imperative, 138
child-centered, 53, 60, 62, 85, 155, 176, 218

271

Index

children,
  autonomy of, in classrooms, 99, 155, 234
  critical thinking of, 154
  employees or citizens, 88, 202
  in feminist education, 190
  natural learning of, 180
  of the poor, 55
  rights of, 162–4
  teachers' beliefs about, 13, 19, 232
  whole child theory, 50
China,
  ancient education in, 30, 35–8, 175, 177
  progressive educators in, 63–5, 179
Christianity, 34, 39, 43, 45 (fn. 15), 93, 138
Chu Hsi, 35
Cicero, 32, 45 (fn. 5)
civic (duties/education), 39, 51, 85, 218, 221–2
class,
  and ethics, 139
  and theory of justice, 168
  basis of social critique, 176
  social, and knowledge, 129
classical languages (in education), 38, 47, 53, 88–9
cognitive psychology, 6
Comenius, J., 48–9, 66, 73 (fn. 4)
communicative approaches, 7–8, 69–70
Communicative Language Teaching, 7, 49, 69, 225, 228
communitarian philosophy, 161, 165–6, 174 (fn. 18)
community,
  classroom, 193
  Freiean needs analysis in, 184
  management of schools, 168
  model for, 55, 114
  morality, 138, 152
  schools (early), 52
compromise, 203–205, 216
conceptual analysis, 15, 134 (fn. 1)
Condorcet, 45 (fn. 7), 51
Confluent Education, 7, 100
Confucius, 33, 38, 39, 80, 175
consciousness, 82, 94, 96–7, 102, 105, 109 (fn. 4)
  of teachers, 10, 15, 17, 132
  produced by discourses, critical, 184, 192, 193, 194
constructivism, 118–19
continental philosophy, 92–108
control,
  by teachers, 125–6, 128, 178, 186, 210, 233
  of teachers, 38, 201, 207, 212 (fn. 5)
  teachers not controlling students, 99
conversation schools, 20, 55–7, 68, 71, 72

Council of Europe, 87
critical pedagogy, 87, 143, 181–5, 192, 195, 206
critical thinking/judgment, 155, 184, 219, 228
culture, 5
  alternative, 7, 101, 154
    integrated into mainstream, 102
  and ethics, 139, 144, 145
  and language, 122
  high, language of, 38
  historical context for education, 28
  in Freirean tradition, 185–7, 196
  mainstream, 165
  values of, transmitted by teachers and schools, 39, 88, 229
curricular nullification, 207, 208
curriculum,
  activities-based, 54, 65, 70, 86, 176
  and ethics, 146
  and justice, 224
  and needs analysis, 53, 184, 200, 219
  Buddhist, 34
  classical/essentialist, 88
  constructivism in, 119
  coverage, 226
  early business, 41
  early elementary, 31
  early university, 51
  expert, teacher as, 66, 186, 200, 207
  feminist, 187, 190, 193
  holistic, 55, 64
  humanist, 47
  natural approaches and, 56
  philosophy, 84, 153, 227
  reconstructionist, in language teaching, 87, 176
  vocational, 141, 220, 236 (fn. 6)

democracies,
  education for, 84
  individual autonomy in, 219–22
  inequitable education in, 167
  sociopolitical concepts in, 150–54
Descartes, R., 6, 43, 79, 94, 106, 110, 115, 122
Dewey, J., 43, 61–2
  and communitarian philosophy, 165
  and epistemology, 117
  and ethics, 139
  and growth, 218
  and pragmatism, 81–83
  and progressive education, 86
  and UK elementary education, 70
  in China, 63
Direct Method, 61
discourse, *see* language
duty, 24, 51, 138, 148 (fn. 7), 169, 204

Index

Index